WAR T!ME

Praise for the book

Bold, courageous, thought-provoking and absorbing.

—Yashwant Sinha
Former Minister of External Affairs and Finance

After a noted career in diplomacy, Rajiv Dogra developed a literary life. His earlier books, especially *Durand's Curse,* have been very educative. Now with the world as his canvas, he identifies different areas of potential conflagration, giving us his sharp assessments of how major countries are likely to conduct themselves. His perceptive analyses command even greater relevance in the wake of the conflict in and over Ukraine.

—Jairam Ramesh
Member of Parliament, former Union Minister and author

Ambassador Rajiv Dogra's analysis of the emergent global situation, as geopolitical fault lines widen and deepen, and as an age of pervasive uncertainty beckons, is definitive, masterful and incisive. His is a practitioner's eye, acutely observant and detailed, and his conclusions are both meaningful and undeniably relevant to a well-informed understanding of the post-pandemic world we live in.

—Nirupama Rao
Former Foreign Secretary and Ambassador of
India to China and the United States

WAR
THE WORLD IN DANGER
T!ME

RAJIV DOGRA

RUPA

First published by
Rupa Publications India Pvt. Ltd 2022
7/16, Ansari Road, Daryaganj
New Delhi 110002

Sales Centres:

Allahabad Bengaluru Chennai
Hyderabad Jaipur Kathmandu
Kolkata Mumbai

ISBN: 978-93-5520-356-4

First impression 2022

10 9 8 7 6 5 4 3 2 1

Printed in India

For
Dr Arun Ummat

CONTENTS

1

HEALING WELLS

Sing in me, Muse, and through me tell the story...

—Homer

In seventeenth-century Naples, a nobleman fought 20 duels to prove Dante a greater poet than Ariosto. At last, on his confession, he admitted that he had read the works of neither. Like that nobleman from Naples, the world was catastrophically unprepared when Covid-19 caught us clueless about the disease. Yet, we have learned little from this experience, and the pattern may repeat itself. To make matters worse, the world is now even more divided. When the really big catastrophe strikes and the end of history is about to happen, it will be equally sudden but far greater in impact and total in destruction.

The world has already had a warning of such an apocalypse. As he saw the 'Trinity' nuclear test on 16 July 1945, J. Robert Oppenheimer, the creator of that bomb, recalled what Krishna, the maker of world, reveals in the Bhagavad Gita: 'Now I am become Death, the destroyer of worlds.'

But the god and his admirer were not the only ones to imagine the end of the world.

Many others have thought about the possibility, fully or partially. It will not be wise to dismiss these as fanciful flights of imagination or as a fascination with the macabre. Such belief as theirs is an essential warning as we ponder the state of the world after Covid-19. It gives meaning and a sense of drama to history. It also provides order and shape to the human experience because if we need beginnings, we also need endings. Following this logic, Georg Wilhelm Friedrich Hegel, Max Weber and Alexandre Kojève considered their moment as the 'end of history'.

Let us also join this illustrious list and add to the speculation about the 'end of the world'. The apocalypse, were it to happen by 2035, will not be caused by Covid-19 or climate change. That final eradication of us, and everything around us, will be brought about by war and the use of nuclear bombs. Even a few nuclear bombs will cause massive devastation to the cities they are dropped on. But they will not wipe out the entire human race. For that to happen, the nuclear powers will have to use a large number of bombs.

Are we approaching such an end of the world?

For an answer, let us turn to the wise men of the past. How did they visualize the end? Will people get some sort of notice or will the world just fold over to eternity without protest or without a groan? Søren Kierkegaard, for instance, thought there will be general merriment among the disbelieving wits, 'I think the world will come to an end amid the general applause from all the wits who believe that it is a joke.'

T.S. Eliot took a more serious look at the possibility and felt that there will be some sign of a protest before people resign themselves to the inevitable, 'This is the way the world ends/ Not with a bang but a whimper.'

If this is the overwhelming opinion of the wise, is the 'apocalypse' finally upon us?

Annus Horribilis

The Greek root from which the word 'apocalypse' is derived means 'an unveiling' or 'a revelation'. Later, the biblical interpretation given in the *Book of Revelation* depicts 'apocalypse' as the complete and final destruction of the world. Hindus term it the more nuanced 'pralay', meaning 'the process of dissolution and destruction of the universe that takes place at the end of each age (kalpa) and precedes a new creation'. Flexibly, for Hindus, parlay is malleable. It provides hope even after apocalypse, leaving open the scope for redemption and reincarnation.

Despite that faint hope, the common theme running through these ancient beliefs is the acknowledgement of the finite. But it is not only the ancients who were concerned about the world's fragility. This has bothered the modern mind as well. As the writer James Baldwin noted, 'A society must assume that it is stable, but the artist must know, and he must let us know, that there is nothing stable under heaven.'[1]

As if in proof, there have already been five mass extinctions, the last being 65 million years ago. What we are witnessing now are the early signs of a sixth. If that is so, dear reader, you may ask: what is different this time? If the world has risen from the ashes of the previous five extinctions, it will do so a sixth time. Actually, this time, with all our scientific and technical advances, we should be better prepared to ride over the worst.

This is how it should be.

Alas, it is not so. In some respects, we seem as unprepared and as helpless as we were before. For instance, from the Middle Ages, Italian folklore has maintained that 'influenza' occurs due to the influence of stars. Centuries later, the cause of this flu remains mysterious. Whether avian or swine, the virus seems to arrive each winter, stealing an estimated half a million lives worldwide, only to retreat in spring.

Meanwhile, in our inability to tackle it well, we flail about ineffectively. We do not aim to defeat the disease once and for all. Our response has been preventive—to erect a wall around us so the disease cannot access us.

Unfortunately, this approach has not varied over the centuries.

As the Florentine poet Petrarch wrote, 'The year of 1348 has left us alone and helpless. Where are our dear friends now? Where are the beloved faces? Where are the affectionate words, the relaxed and enjoyable conversations?'

Doesn't it sound painfully familiar? Almost eight centuries later, Petrarch's lament remains just as valid. Our scientific advances along the way could not help us cope better with Covid-19. The World Health Organization (WHO) should have taken the lead in stirring up the world. But it kept watching from the sidelines as each nation tackled it in the manner it deemed fit. When, at last, the WHO emerged out of its seance, it pronounced Cassandra-like that the effect of the pandemic will last for decades.

Economists were quick to add to the gloom by predicting another Great Depression the world over. Strategists moaned that a world war is around the corner; just the date of it eluded them. Accordingly, a terrible future awaits us.

Even if the world somehow avoids the apocalypse, there is no doubt that it is speeding downhill. This slide could have been prevented with good leadership. Instead, the failure of leadership was almost universal in scale. Consequently, the Covid-19-induced shutdowns of 2020 and 2021 were the most unnecessary interruptions to ordinary life in modern history.

Its apologists have spoken about them as a war. But unlike a war, these shutdowns involved demobilization, not mobilization. While the hospitals were on full alert, the majority of us were confined to quarters. With a near-complete shutdown of all industrial and commercial activity, the world succeeded in inducing a severe recession. Sadly, there is no indication if and when the world will be able to claw itself out of the hole it has dug itself in. Such a feeling of gloom was once echoed by Leon Trotsky: 'Anyone desiring a quiet life has done badly to be born in the twentieth century.'[2]

This dark message was conveyed in the background of the

two world wars and a pandemic that had wiped out millions. Compared to it, 2020 or 2021 were not the worst years ever, but they were certainly the worst years of our lifetime. A sense of doom and a paralysis of fear overwhelmed us throughout 2020 and also through most of 2021.

Creeping Authoritarianism

When the pandemic struck in the beginning of 2020, the world kept watching helplessly while, in a single season, civilization was brought low by a microscopic parasite virus 10,000 times smaller than a grain of salt. Had the leaders of the world been more agile, the pandemic may have been contained as was successfully done in the case of Ebola. But this was not to be.

Sadly, we are no longer led by men like John F. Kennedy, who dreamed big, or leaders who had faith in the world as an idyllic space—where there was scope for ideas, ideals and idealism. They, too, made mistakes; but their's were errors of judgment, not the abandonment of principles.

A lot else has changed since then. The world had just about sighed in relief after the disastrous four years of a self-centred Donald Trump, when the United States (US) surprised it again by electing a hesitating and hesitant Joe Biden as its president. It did not take long for Biden to show that his ideals belong to another time. Instead of rising up for a free world, he has introduced his version of 'the survival of the fittest'. When Ukraine faced an imminent threat of war by Russia, Biden declared that 'minor incursions' were not a matter of concern.[3]

Since then, strategists have been busy interpreting its larger import. Does it mean that the powerful like Vladimir Putin and Xi Jinping can nibble small amounts of other countries' territory? And what if 'minor incursions' expand by nibbles—at first a little infringement in one part and then a bit more in another area? The world has seen this script loop earlier too, and it led to the

Second World War. Now, in our uncertain times, the world stands poised at a more dangerous brink.

This near-global failure of effective leadership is making people introspect. Already, questions are being asked if Covid-19 has introduced a sharp fork in international politics, where a wrong turn could lead to disastrous consequences. They add darkly that in the event of a major war, the devastation might be total. Some also talk in the long term of nations within a fortress, a series of walled states led by authoritarian leaders.

If this becomes a pattern, it may well be a reminder of what Karl Marx wrote in 1843, 'The glorious robes of liberalism have fallen away, and the most repulsive despotism stands revealed for all the world to see.'[4]

Luckily, each time the world has recovered. It dusted off its despotic spell to bounce back, and the final stages of the twentieth century saw a near-complete global embrace of democracy. From then on, liberalism seemed to have prevailed over Marx in large parts of the world.

But this glimmer had a short shelf life. Lately, the discerning have begun to fear that liberalism may not be the final religion of the world, and in its place, there will be a universal rise of the authoritarian leader. Every country, or almost every country, may eventually have a leader whose word becomes the final arbiter within the national boundaries and sometimes beyond it. In that event, the human project will be devoted to the aggrandizement of the Trump-type leader, and the world will then be worshipping multiple gods—one for each country.

In this authoritarian space, no one is entirely free and noble.

However, declining democracy is not the only woe the world is faced with. In the previous crises of epic proportions, intellectuals had, at least, the illusion that they knew which direction the world was going. In the case of the pandemic, even that temporary assurance is missing. To that extent, it has been a unique transformative event, where no one knows the end result or even the direction in which to proceed.

One major cause of it is the fear that has gripped the world. This fear of disease is made more complex by an uncharacteristic hesitation to accuse the country that is the cause of global misery. The criticism of China, the world's largest dictatorship, has become almost sacrilegious, making people wonder if the gap between the sacred and the profane was ever as wide.

Historically speaking, this friction with China has been long in the making. A century back, in 1917, the then US President Woodrow Wilson baldly stated his intention 'to keep the white race strong against the yellow' and to preserve 'white civilisation and its domination of the planet'.[5]

Apprehending such a divide, Samuel P. Huntington warned of the consequences it could lead the world to: 'The dangerous clashes of the future are likely to arise from the interaction of Western arrogance, Islamic intolerance and Sinic assertiveness.'[6]

Since the time Huntington wrote about it, Sinic assertiveness has become a deeply worrying fact of global life. The battle between these two worlds—one liberal and tolerant, the other, Xi's hyper-nationalist and dictatorial China—is almost apocalyptic. Xi seems determined to destroy the 'idea of post-war world' as a sanctuary of liberalism and diversity.

Coupled with this struggle and the suspicion of China as the cause of Covid-19, our mutual mistrust is increasing. The great ideological struggles that defined East–West rivalries are a steadily receding memory. Instead, the big debate now is about China's intentions and global survival.

Imposed Isolation

Meanwhile, during the pandemic, societies have become fragmented and some business firms, in an impulsive flourish, have declared their employees can 'work from home' for their entire work life. But we have yet to ask if this state of eternal bliss is for the ultimate good and whether it is practical in the long term.

The lockdown has brought in some other behavioural changes. People are opting for online purchases as against the traditional delight of dressing up, going out and shopping. The pleasure of a leisurely promenade or just window shopping has given way to tapping your preference on a laptop or mobile phone.

This trend has also permeated religious practices. Temples and churches are no longer communal spaces like they were once. The rituals of religion, the celebratory joy of festivals are no longer a shared experience. All this has increasingly become a private affair, devoid of the strength, colour and variety that a shared belief and its performance can bring.

Even after the Covid-19 restrictions are lifted, we may be at risk of not being spontaneously 'social' any longer. The fear of infection may remain a latent hesitation. Thus separated and confined to their cocoons, people risk losing the sense of interaction, cooperation and competition—the basic ingredients for a society's progress and essential to the unleashing of a country's animal spirits.

It isn't just people who might undergo lifestyle changes; there could be profound changes at the governmental level too. Already, monarchy and communism have both become relics of the past. The follow-up questions now being asked are: will democracy and capitalism be next? Will the post-Second World War global institutions survive? Unfortunately, the signs are not propitious because Covid-19 has become a global political stress test.

Despite this, people do not consider it polite to forecast decline. Doing so is to risk the charge of *wanting* decline, and of keeping bad company. But the fact is that nothing is forever, not even the Pax Americana. And no great power in history has been exempt from that familiar dilemma that domination is finite. The Roman, Ottoman, Mughal, Spanish, Napoleonic and Victorian empires were all great once. So was our world till Covid-19 struck.

But the post-pandemic world need not be one of only decline and gloom. After the destruction and despair of the Second World War, it was hardly thought that Western Europe would be free, united and prosperous. Yet, this is what it became.

Therefore, even in our despair, some hope persists that fluidity of memory and a capacity to forget may ward off the brink. It may allow us to come to terms with any degree of social, moral or environmental degradation. A new world may yet rise from the ashes of Covid-19's devastation, as it had done in the past after each of the previous five extinctions.

After all, if the Great Depression produced fascism, it also reinvigorated liberal democracy. It is, therefore, possible that the pandemic may eventually infuse new energy in people.

As the Irish poet Seamus Heaney wrote,

Believe that a farther shore
Is reachable from here.
Believe in miracles
And cures and healing wells.

2

ALL UNDER HEAVEN

Stars will move a different way.
We'll both end. We'll both begin.

—William Stafford

Faith in healing wells and a promising turn isn't just a poet's fancy. Historical experience, too, provides some comfort. During and immediately after every major catastrophe, people predict the world will never be the same again. Yet, time is witness to the sameness of the world. It is true that periodically there are some changes in lifestyle—a new fashion or passion and some technological advances to make life more comfortable. But otherwise, the world spins back to the same loop as before, and the predictions of big change lie buried with the remains of the catastrophe.

Occasionally, as a new tragedy begins to unfold, those with long memories recall for the world the horror it had experienced before and its vow not to let it happen again. Yet, it happens again because it is fated that humans will not learn from their mistakes. Even as the world retreads its familiar path, there are bound to be some changes. This is the way of the world.

Some of this mix of repetitive mistakes, the decline and the change is already being seen at the individual, national and even global level. The old order that held the post-World War world together is slowly withering away. A new order will get defined, and illiberal forces are already raring to fashion it in their manner.

This possibility of the rise of illiberalism should be of worry because, unlike democracy with its many demands, populists make just one. They insist that people be loyal, and in their dictionary, loyalty means surrender to the nationalist vision. The distinction between fact and fiction, and the distance between true and false must cease to exist for people. What State dictates must be the only truth.

In trying times like the one the world is going through now, the promise of a firm hand at the helm appeals to people. This is also the case at the international level. There, too, power is expansionist. Therefore, international order will remain as hierarchical as it was in 1945. The central issue of global politics will be who wields how much power.

This invariably translates to a periodic churn in the affairs of the world. It is equally certain that it leads to selection, even pruning, among countries. The fit and the strong thrive, the weak and the meek miss the bus. Some get pushed up the global ladder in this new arrangement, others find themselves reduced.

To paraphrase V.S. Naipaul, the world being what it is, countries that are insignificant, which do not pull their weight, have no place in the making of global affairs.

Contrarily, there are wayward countries like North Korea that punch well above their weight; they somehow manage to make a place for themselves in the world. In direct contrast, there are countries like Bhutan that seek the world within; they would rather chase Gross National Happiness. But Bhutan is an exception. For most other countries, it is not practical to be an island content within their boundaries; they must reach out to carve their place in the world.

Each of these is valid as a proposition. But in the trauma of the present, the shock of Covid-19 has made people wonder whether the world is entering an entirely new age, where the rules of governance, people's behaviour and their place in the world will be determined by an altogether different standard. A standard that is even more severe and constricting than the one George Orwell imagined in *Ninteen Eighty-Four*, where 'the eyes follow you about when you move, where the big brother watches you'.

This flight of Orwell's imagination has, ever since, terrified the succeeding generations with the possibility that one day it may actually happen. But people were content with the thought that it wouldn't happen during their lifetime. That comfort is no longer available.

The 'eyes' that Orwell anticipated have arrived.

It is now taken as a given that Big Government is watching people as never before. So far, surveillance was associated with foreign powers and their prying agencies. The big difference, as we enter an overwhelmingly intrusive age, is that the surveillance now is of our own making, by our own people, and already upon us. It is all-embracing. The State, for instance, might want to know how many of us are watching the authoritarian leader when he decides to address the nation via TV. How normally, or abnormally, our pulse beats when we are watching the leader speak? How many showed disrespect to the leader by not switching on the TV to watch him? The art and science of watching people assumes a frighteningly new dimension, leaving the totalitarianism of a Hitler, Stalin or Ceauşescu far behind.

It is no longer a question of if and when this will happen. This intrusive age is already upon us. In this new age, is there still a place for democracy that many in the world had taken for granted? Is there scope for free movement of people and goods at a time when nationalism is busy putting up protective and protectionist walls?

A Place in the World

These questions will be debated by the world in the months and years ahead. Let us, for now, reflect on the proposition that in the hierarchical reshuffle after Covid-19, countries will squiggle to find their new place in the world. The fundamental point that we must start from is: when did this quest for a place in the world begin? Is it a new pursuit—a modern-day chase in a connected world?

It is true that people are more aware now of the inter se ranking of countries, and there are periodic surveys to rank countries on any and everything. While people may have become more conscious than ever before of a country's latest status, the desire to conquer the world or be its best part has existed from the earliest times. The king and the philosopher, each for his own reason, adopted a Universalist view.

If one goes by the ancient Indian scripture *Maha Upanishad*, India has had the world in its view from the earliest times. '*Vasudhaiva Kutumbakam*' (The world is a family) may have been an ambitious coinage in those unconnected times. Or it may just have been the aspirational wish of a liberal society, reflecting the then upwardly mobile country's attitude towards the world. Whatever it was, the emphasis certainly was on reaching out.

As mobility increased, this concept got translated into practice. People started seeking new lands for trade, employment, out of curiosity or in a population shift due to disease or war at home.

There were other reasons as well for migration. The curiosity about the other took the significant shape of a Silk Route about two millennia ago. Its trade reach was phenomenal, and the route it followed led through high mountains, deserts and swamps, over thousands of miles. It wasn't just lucre that drove men to take the risk of this long journey, they were also fired by the spirit of adventure and a desire to discover the wider world.

The military variation of this broad theme triggered

Alexander's desire to conquer the world. He almost succeeded in this mission by creating one of the largest empires of the ancient world that stretched from Greece to northwestern India. After him, the early Roman Caesars were not as ambitious; still their empire covered a broad swath of Europe and parts of Asia and Africa. A thousand years later, in the early thirteenth century, rapacious Genghis Khan, the founder of the Mongol Empire, ruled almost all of Eurasia.

While these early conquerors may have been driven by ego and ambition, the British Empire, between the late sixteenth and early twentieth centuries, combined its lust for trade with a desire for empire-building. At its peak, this empire covered more than 20 per cent of the world's surface, giving validity to the claim that 'the sun never sets on the British Empire'. Later, in the second half of the twentieth century, the US could have claimed that its influence covered much of the world. But its' was an influence with a difference. Unlike the previous overlords of history, America's was not a conquest of territory but a control over the policy mechanism of other countries.

However, conquest alone did not drive men to leave their homes. Wanderlust and curiosity set them off too. In the late fifteenth century, the Portuguese explorer Vasco da Gama became the first European to reach India (the real India) by sea. Around the same time, his rival, the Genovese explorer Christopher Columbus, also set sail for India but ended up discovering America.

It wasn't just the men of action and explorers who were restless, writers and philosophers, too, were driven by the spirit that the world could be their oyster. From Homer's *Odyssey* to Jules Verne's *Around the World in 80 Days*, the thinker's mind has floated free. This desire to embrace the world was idea-driven and idealistic.

Alas, all this was possible in a different age. Today's world is one of multiple restrictions; of Covid-19-imposed isolation;

of economic decline; of obsessive surveillance; and of mistrust at the individual, societal, national and international level. The age of innocence is behind us. The world seems to be entering a frightful new period of conflict, even multiple wars, with China as the raging bull.

Xi often terms this era as one of 'changes unseen in a 100 years.'[1] By this, he seems to convey that the US, the world's top superpower, is in decline and it is China's moment to rise. This bold assertion is worrying because Xi is sometimes called a 'mafia boss'. Within China, he is also derided as the 'accelerator in chief', meaning that his aggressive approach is leading to domestic and international conflict.

It is not China alone that wishes to order the world in its fashion. Others, too, are furrowing for a larger place in this new world. Therefore, in the coming times of frequent contention between states and multiple wars, the enquiring mind will wonder whether Russia will continue to menacingly lurk in the shadows, fixing an election here, nibbling a bit of some neighbour's territory there and manipulating regimes elsewhere. Will Pakistan still terrorize all except China? Israel, too, is restless; it worries incessantly about Iran going nuclear. A war between the two is just one impulsive trigger away. And, what about America? Will it still have the energy to police the world?

Setting Sights

Before speculating about the next big war, let us consider the present state of the world and the goals it had set for itself in 2020. For some reason, rather than any other, 2020 became the favourite goal-setting year for the United Nations (UN) and many countries of the world. It may have been a coincidence, but even ophthalmology regards 20/20 as a sign of perfection.

Like an ophthalmologist, the world had set great store by 2020. It was called a 'make-or-break year', targeted to end extreme poverty, conquer inequality and fix the climate crisis. At the end of 2019, the world's extreme poverty rate had indeed fallen below 8 per cent, the lowest recorded level in human history. In India, former President A.P.J. Abdul Kalam claimed proudly, 'My 2020 Vision for India is to transform it into a developed nation.' President Xi of neighbouring China promised his people the 'China Dream' by 2021—the hundredth year of the founding of the Chinese Communist Party (CCP). By this 'China Dream', the Chinese people would have doubled their incomes. It also assured the 'rejuvenation of the great Chinese nation,' which includes the 'recovery of sovereignty over Chinese territories lost through the imposition of unequal treaties by Imperialist foreign powers.'[2]

Even as the rest of the world spent 2020 forgetting its ambition and salving its wounds, China was quickly off its feet. It has now set a new marker for itself and its new goal is the year 2035.

Others in the world are still in a state of shock, struggling with lockdowns and calculating losses. Therefore, setting new targets for 2035 is not a part of their immediate agenda. In any case, the world cannot be expected to dream big when it is busy counting the dead and is uncertain about the remains of each passing day.

But nothing prevents us from looking into a crystal ball. Such speculative peeps have forever fascinated people, and not just astrologically. In modern times, people have also put machines to this task.

A computer program developed at Massachusetts Institute of Technology (MIT), in 1973, was about global sustainability. However, instead of coming up with predictions that please, it maintained darkly that our civilization will end by 2050: 'Around 2040 to 2050, civilized life as we know it on this planet will cease to exist.'[3]

Another US-based organization, Stratfor, had also used the crystal ball and looked at the world as it might be in 2025. Some of its predictions were drastic, laced perhaps by a bit of wishful thinking. For instance, this about Russia: 'Moscow's power may loosen to the point that Russia will effectively become a string of semi-autonomous regions that might not even get along with one another…It is unlikely that the Russian Federation will survive in its current form.'[4]

Since Stratfor's predictions were slated for 2025, there is still time for the worst to happen to Russia. But on some other issues, Stratfor seems to have hit closer to the bullseye. It may not have predicted Brexit or the way Spain, Portugal, Italy and Greece have suffered in recent years, but its prediction about Europe has come remarkably close to what is happening to it: 'Some states might maintain a residual membership in a highly modified European Union, but this will not define Europe.'[5]

Whether this happens remains to be seen, but the cracks in the European Union (EU) are already beginning to show. Germany, France and the Scandinavian countries are gasping at the constant effort to shore up the laggards of the south and the wayward of Eastern Europe.

Stratfor does not convey good tidings for China either: 'China may have a rough decade ahead as economic growth slows, leading to widespread discontent towards the ruling Communist Party.'[6]

There is no doubt that China is in an aggressive mode, but it is doing so on the strength of an engine that is short of ballast. As shadows begin to darken on its overextended economy and internal tensions rise, it could opt for a diversion—raise the nationalistic tempo domestically by military engagement(s) abroad.

Some of what has been forecast is already underway, while many others remain words in the wind. But a few of these long-term predictions are worrying. For instance, many scientists maintain that if we do not make major strides in combating global warming, we could see out-of-control rises in sea levels, enormous crop shortfalls and wars over increasingly scarce freshwater resources.

Then, there are predictions about the coming times that are easy to make because the trend we see today could shape tomorrow's world. Thus, it is possible that large migrations from countries in Africa and West Asia may disrupt western governments and affect the social fabric of countries like Italy, France, Germany and Spain, which are already stretched considerably. Some governments in Europe, especially those in France, Belgium and the Netherlands, are increasingly concerned about radicalism and its demands among their Muslim populations.

It is also being said with some confidence that by 2035, the world is likely to be more complicated, divided between a broad American sphere of influence in Europe, parts of West Asia, Japan, Australia and India, and a Chinese sphere in Russia, Pakistan, Iran, Southeast Asia and Africa.

However, there is need to regard all this with caution because, generally speaking, making predictions is an 'iffy' undertaking, a matter of 'chance'. Even the acknowledged masters of the craft can falter.

John Maynard Keynes was venturing into such an 'iffy' territory when he predicted that by 2030, capital accumulation, improvements in productivity and technological advances would have solved the 'economic problem' and ushered in an age in which no one besides a few 'purposeful money-makers' worked more than 15 hours a week.[7]

The American baseball legend Yogi Berra may not have had Keynes in view when in one of his many hilarious quips he said, 'It's tough to make predictions, especially about the future.'

A Plan for 2035?

Still, the result may be sound if we base our forecast on the empirical facts of today and on reasonable assumptions about tomorrow. For instance, there could be a change in the global balance of power in the coming years because historical evidence suggests that power is fickle and so are loyalties; states ally readily with the rising and discard the declining.

In China, for over 2,000 years, its people saw 'all under Heaven' as the tributary system of the Chinese emperor. Separately, and for many centuries, Islamic states expanded power over regions populated by the non-believers. Later, following the Peace of Westphalia in 1648 and the subsequent calm, Europeans used that balance to dominate the world. Nearer our times, in the last century, America viewed itself as a beacon whose values had universal validity. Therefore, for almost two millennia, these four greats—the Chinese, Islamic, European and American—have dominated the world.

India did not figure in this list except as a passing reference—a jewel in someone's crown. Is India now in a better position internally and, therefore, externally? Many global assessments predict that by 2035, India could be the third-largest economy, not too far behind US but still far from a galloping China.

It was the shape of the world in future that engaged the attention of former Indian Prime Minister (PM) Dr Manmohan Singh when he was visiting Moscow in 2005. We were a small group of six who had gathered around him at an after-meeting dinner, where he said that the race for natural resources would define the global competition in the coming decades. The country that controlled the critical natural resources, he added, would have easy passage to great power.

Dr Singh is too gentle to be a neocon, but he was reflecting the temper of the time when many in America endorsed the ambition of George Bush and his neocon advisors to control the energy resources of the world.

Since then, the world looks distracted, and its priorities have changed. But this may just be a temporary phase, and once the world settles down to its familiar ways, the race for resources may be renewed one more time. One way or the other, we could then be heading towards a future where both the then American president's ambition and the former Indian PM's thoughts may see a revival. Such a battle for resources and power is what the Chinese Belt and Road Initiative (BRI) project is essentially about.

As others try to muscle in, or resist this Chinese advance, misunderstandings and frictions will multiply. Some aggression and even conflict could be the result of the pushing and shoving that will follow in foreign waters and territories. The next decade will, therefore, be one of uncertainties in international life.

Against this background, was Trump right in choosing to retreat, in making America withdraw from greater engagement abroad? He may not have said that globalization is dead, but his 'America First' policy conveyed that impression. Now that Trump is bad memory, is the US still going to hunker down in its American shell and shut its eyes to the world?

The history of the world is proof that hegemony and benevolence are terms in contradiction. Practical evidence, too, suggests that politics involve power. So whether the US likes it or not, it will remain engaged with the world, it will still have to take up arms for one reason or the other, and it will keep manoeuvring to retain its position as the sole superpower of the world. In pursuing that course, it will have to provide leadership. Either that or China will slip in to take the pole position.

There are other changes that could take place in the coming years because the world is rapidly being recast in a new fashion. The rules-based global order may be reshaped and disputes between countries may no longer concern the adjustment of differences in the so-far-accepted framework. The tinkering that will follow may test the validity of the framework itself, including that of the UN.

Moreover, unlike in the traditional world of diplomacy, new technological innovations, like artificial intelligence (AI), might bring in choices that are both complex and difficult to predict. Will fake news and cyber intrusions be the new instruments of proxy war? Do China and Russia have the means to critically wound countries without going to war?

All these are untested and complex new challenges that could fundamentally affect us and alter our world. But do men know the antidote to the dire? A century and a half before Naipaul, Italian poet Giacomo Leopardi wrote in his diary in 1832: 'Two truths that most men will never believe, one that they know nothing, the other that they are nothing …'

Leopardi's truths are not comforting. But just for that reason there has to be a plan to anticipate and counter the ill effects of tomorrow. For instance, how will countries, especially the rising powers, respond and position themselves in this new world? Are they prepared for 2035, when China hopes to replace America as Capo dei Capi?

If they are ready with a plan, what might be the contours of it? To narrow down our focus, we could ask if the democratic world, still led by America, has a plan. Perhaps there is such a plan. But on a note of caution, let's also keep in view the boxer Mike Tyson's words, 'Everyone has a plan till they get punched in the mouth.'

Alas, when the world was punched in the mouth by Covid-19, it found itself leaderless and without a plan.

3

CHINA: THE CHALLENGER

Give me thy mind and give me thy heart, give me thy offerings and thy adoration; and thus with thy soul in harmony, and making me thy goal supreme, thou shalt in truth come to me.

—Bhagavad Gita (9:34)

So far, with three major crises during the last 20 years, this has been a century of serial misfortunes for the world. Each one of them has left a lasting negative effect. The 9/11 terror attacks led to some disastrous foreign policy choices by the US. The decisions made in panic resulted in long, wasteful and, ultimately, unsuccessful wars in Afghanistan and Iraq.

The financial crisis of 2008 that followed brought about the recession. The rise of populism in western democracies is traced to it, and it strengthened autocratic leaders in many countries. While the western response to the financial meltdown was tardy, China's policy measures were quickly backed by a massive stimulus package. China has not looked back ever since, and its furious economic pace has led many to believe that it is well on course to become the world's economic leader.

The Covid-19 pandemic is the third and latest in this unfortunate series. Far more than the previous two crises, this has been marked by incompetence by most leaders. It is widely acknowledged that the effect could have been mitigated somewhat if Chinese President Xi Jinping and former US President Donald Trump had not responded with denial and misinformation. Instead of encouraging global cooperation in tackling the virus and taking a lead role in it, both the US and China chose to engage in diversionary propaganda battles. On its part, China blamed the US military for the presence of the virus in Wuhan. Trump, always keen to pick up a fight and take it to the opponent's corner, called it the 'Chinese virus'. Whatever its nomenclature, this virus has thrown the world into utter chaos, the likes of which has not been experienced for many generations. If Mao Zedong were alive, he would have taken it as an opportunity for China. As he once said, 'Everything under heaven is in utter chaos, the situation is excellent.'

Had China been upfront about the origin of the virus, and had the world been united in facing this challenge, the apprehension of the unknown and the fear of its consequences might have lessened somewhat. While China has not been fair with the world, America's behaviour has become a case of mistaken generosity towards China.

The Thucydides Trap

Such American acts of indulgence towards China predate its missteps during Covid-19. If China were ever to acknowledge its gratitude to people who catapulted it to greatness, two names would head that list. Henry Kissinger would be the obvious choice. In power and out of power, he has had the ear of the sitting US president on matters concerning international affairs. His words in China's favour have shaped the benign spirit in the American policy towards China.

Kissinger's fascination for China is long-standing. On 18 December 1969, in a year-end review with the press, he said:

> The Chinese people are obviously a great people. They have the longest unbroken record of government in one area of any of the existing civilizations; and secondly, 800 million people representing 25% of human race are a factor that cannot be ignored. They will influence international affairs whatever...policy we adopt. And their policy, for good or ill, will determine the possibilities for peace and progress.[1]

Kissinger may have been an exceptionally successful secretary of state, but it is difficult to endorse his conclusion that 'China will influence international affairs...(irrespective of) policy we adopt.'[2] The fact is that China, on its own, could not have achieved the great power status. If the US and its western allies had done nothing to help China to industrial greatness, its influence in international affairs would not have been as large or as menacing as it is now. It was the western investment and transfer of technology that catapulted China to the miracle it has become.

Moreover, if the size of population was a critical factor in Kissinger's conclusion that China 'cannot be ignored', then why did he pointedly work against India, which was almost equally populous? There were clear contradictions in Kissinger's assumptions, and their flawed foundation has cost the US heavy.

The other person who was consistent in promoting China and its leadership was Richard Nixon. He wrote in the *Foreign Affairs* magazine in 1967, 'The world cannot be safe until China changes. Thus our aim, to the extent that we can influence events, should be to induce change.'[3]

When he became the US president, Nixon set in motion the chain of events that would transform a poverty-ridden, poorly educated nation into a great power. Neither Kissinger nor Nixon was willing to consider the possibility that one day a risen China might confront the US with the Thucydides trap.

Kissinger, in particular, was besotted by the brilliance and subtlety of Chinese leaders, no matter who they were and whatever their flaws. As Jasper Becker comments:

> Even when he meets Mao – senile and dribbling – Kissinger can't help being blown away by his supposed brilliance… Yet Mao was by then recognized even by his followers as a mad monster. He had managed to make enemies of practically everyone in China, starved up to 50 million people to death, repeatedly purged the army and party, imprisoned or exiled millions, and ruined the economy.[4]

When Kissinger took Nixon to China in 1972, it was weak and vulnerable. It was largely in isolation internationally; its relations with the Soviet Union were fraught to the extent that in October 1969, Mao, fearing an immediate war with Russia, instructed the Chinese leaders to disperse around the country.

At that point in the early 1970s, China's per capita GDP was below that of Uganda and Sierra Leone. Even a decade later, in 1980, China had just about 10 per cent of America's GDP on a purchasing power parity (PPP) basis; 7 per cent of its GDP at the US dollar exchange rates; and a little less than 6 per cent of its exports. The foreign currency held by China was barely one-sixth the size of America's reserves.

Since then, something truly astonishing has happened as we witness in our lifetimes the biggest and fastest industrial revolution ever. By 2014, the dismal figures of 1980 had changed dramatically; China's GDP became 101 per cent of the US's GDP on PPP basis; 60 per cent at US dollar exchange rates; and 106 per cent of exports. China's reserves now are 28 times that of America's.[5] Naturally then, people around the world began to talk in awe about the rise of China.

All along, China has played a weak hand brilliantly. It has propelled itself from a situation in which it accounted for barely 2 per cent of the global economy to one in which it will soon be the biggest economy in the world. It would then have overtaken the US, which has dominated the world since 1872.

If China's march to primacy was facilitated by the Nixon–Kissinger combine in the twentieth century, then it can also be said that China's rise in this century was driven by its embrace of world trade. In fact, one major reason why China's economy has changed profoundly was its acceptance of the market norms and the rules of international trade. Far too late in the game, Washington now realizes that letting China into the World Trade Organization (WTO) was a mistake. Though not directly related, the statistical data, too, shows that China has been on the upswing since it entered the WTO in 2001. Its $1 trillion economy in 2001 has become a $15 trillion giant today. Its $220 billion in foreign exchange reserves have ballooned to a very impressive $3 trillion.

Some economists say that China's GDP will overtake America's in dollar terms by 2035. This, however, is overstating the case because the size of economy does not give a complete picture. China should have a per capita GDP of about four times its current level, besides a technological base that is robust under its own steam, before it can match the size and the diverse strength of the US.

While China can justly be proud that its power has grown formidably by almost every measure, it is not yet time for China to bring out the celebratory trumpets. Its internal problems are many. These challenges will ensure that it is not destined to dominate the world in some kind of unending process of astronomical economic growth. In fact, it faces increasing problems of demography and debt. China's workforce is projected to decline by 177 million people from the current levels by mid-century. The level of its debt should be the stuff of national nightmares, but China seems to carry on with a surprising show of calm. According to one report at the end of 2020, 'China's foreign debt…stood at roughly $2.4 trillion. Corporate debt was $27 trillion, while the country's total public debt exceeded 300 percent of GDP. China's public debt is already 60 percent higher than the average across other countries…'[6]

Viewed against this background, the US has the advantage of a stable system tempered by time and tested by trials. Important philosophical differences, too, separate China from the US. Both have a sense of manifest destiny, but American exceptionalism is missionary (or was missionary till recently), where it held that the US has an obligation to spread its values to other parts of the world. In contrast, China's exceptionalism is cultural. It does not proselytize or claim that its institutions are relevant outside China. Its approach is self-centred, and it tends to grade other countries as tributaries at various levels.

Still, if and when a future Edward Gibbon sits down to write a history of the decline and fall of the US, he might conclude that it was a case of self-harm—that the American obsession with China and its leadership was the cause of America's decline and China's rise.

However, if one believes fatalistically in destiny and feels that all is preordained, then the simple answer is that China was destined to become a great power, even the greatest power. However, more realistically and viewed on a practical plane, China was pushed to greatness. But it need not have been so. Had Nixon and Kissinger not made the move in 1972 to court China and to save it from possible Soviet aggression, the history of the world might have turned out differently.

According to Jasper Becker, '(I)f Beijing and Moscow had gone to war, surely it would have been to America's great advantage. America might have emerged victorious from the Vietnam War and saved Cambodia from the horrors of Khmer Rouge rule. The long-standing threat to South Korea and Taiwan might have disappeared...'[7]

US lost that chance. China, on the other hand, made up its mind to grab the opportunity by whatever means. Its strategic hawks egged on the leadership to manipulate and mislead their American counterparts in order to acquire or steal technology in economic and military spheres. Michael Pillsbury writes about it with a sense of betrayal: '(T)hese hawks had been advising Chinese leaders, beginning with Mao Zedong, to avenge a century of humiliation and aspired to replace the United States as the economic, military, and political leader of the world by the year 2049 (the one hundredth anniversary of the Communist Revolution)…This plan became known as the Hundred-Year Marathon.'[8] Like many others, Pillsbury is surprised that the Chinese ambitions should have been scaled up so high so as to outpace and outmanoeuvre even the US.

The fault, however, lies in the world's gullibility and its inability to read the Chinese intent. This was clear to people who could understand China well and decipher its ways. Lee Kuan Yew was one of them. He had forewarned the world that it was no longer possible to stop China's march to greatness. This was also the subject that an apprehensive Barack Obama raised with Xi at their Summit in 2015. The background was the newly reminted Thucydides trap.

Obama expressed the hope that despite the new situation caused by China's rise, 'the two countries are capable of managing their disagreements.' Xi worded his response with ambiguity: 'should major countries time and again make the mistakes of strategic miscalculation, they might create such (Thucydides) traps for themselves.'[9] This exchange is indicative of the great Chinese confidence about its position in the world.

Friends, Foes and Frenemies

In contrast to its so-far one-sided and beneficial to China relationship with the West, a long, complex and contentious history dating back to the 1800s is the background to China's relations with Russia. Imperial Russia's eastward expansion then, across Siberia and the Russian Far East, resulted in China giving up over 1.5 million sq. km of territory to it.

They remained uneasy neighbours for most of the nineteenth

century. Some thaw set in after the Communist Party of China (CPC) took over in Beijing in 1949 and Moscow dispatched technical aid, financial assistance and political advisers to China. However, this bonhomie did not last long.

In 1969, clashes along the disputed border left scores of Chinese soldiers dead. An uneasy peace was followed by years of negotiations, after which China received almost 340 sq. km of territory from Russia in return for Beijing dropping all other land claims against Moscow. In 2001, Russia and China signed the Treaty of Good-Neighbourliness and Friendly Cooperation, which laid the basis of a bilateral relationship grounded in mutual respect of sovereignty and territorial integrity, non-interference in internal affairs, equality and mutual benefit. Since then, the China–Russia relationship has gathered consistent strength. This is reflected at the personal level as well. For instance, Xi and Putin have met 38 times since 2013. As Putin noted in 2018, the only leader in the world with whom he had ever celebrated his birthday was Xi. On his part, Xi is equally exuberant about their relationship. In awarding Putin China's Medal of Friendship, Xi called the Russian president his 'best, most intimate friend'.[10]

But this bromance apart, China has not changed its ways. Rather, it has invariably succeeded in bending others to its will. The Chinese classics stress the value of violent solutions to security conflicts and of offensive over defensive strategies. They also call for flexibility, for using non-coercive means when confronting a more powerful enemy, but only as an expedient, until China could be sure of prevailing. As professor Warren Cohen notes, 'Insofar as the present times are concerned…the PRC was involved in eleven foreign-policy crises from 1950 to 1985. It resorted to violence in eight of them, or 72 per cent of the time—far more often, proportionally, than any other major power in the twentieth century.'[11]

China shares land borders with 14 countries. No other country except Russia has as many contiguous neighbours. None of China's neighbours consider its core national interests as congruent with Beijing's. Rather, they include five countries with which China has fought wars in the past 80 years—India, Japan, Russia, South Korea and Vietnam.

Outwardly, China claims it has peaceful intentions, that it has not committed aggression against other countries. But its record shows otherwise. It attacked India in 1962. A dispute with Russia in 1969 led to violent clashes. In 1974, it seized Vietnamese islands in the Paracels. This escalated to a major conflict in 1979. The two nations clashed again in 1988, this time in the Spratly Islands.

Currently, China has land disputes with Russia, India, Nepal, Bhutan, Laos, Mongolia, Tibet and Myanmar. It also has sea disputes with the Philippines, Vietnam, Japan, Malaysia, Indonesia, Brunei, South Korea, Singapore and Taiwan. This makes it a total of 17 countries with which it has a live dispute, while there are others where China's claims are causing unease to countries in central Asia.

Take, for instance, the Chinese record in the first-half of 2020. Its forces rammed a Vietnamese fishing boat, 'buzzed' a Philippines naval vessel and harassed a Malaysian oil drilling operation, all within their respective Exclusive Economic Zones (EEZs). Earlier, in June 2019, it conducted ballistic missile tests in the South China Sea. In 2009, it unilaterally put forward the nine-dash line to declare the South China Sea as its territorial waters. This claim is neither treaty-based nor legally sound. In fact, in 2016, the Permanent Court of Arbitration in The Hague ruled that China has no 'historic rights' over the waters of the South China Sea. It added that China did not have historic rights to the waters under the nine-dash line and ruled in favour of Philippines over its claim on the islands falling in its EEZ. China has been imperious in its rejection of that judgment.

China also intimidates to ensure its sway. That's why it was initially taken by surprise when, in 2017, India resisted its push into Doklam. But it backed off only to gain time and to regroup.

On its part, India had not thought the move through; some critics maintain it was impulsive, based on a false sense of bravura. Had it considered the implications carefully, it would not have resorted to a military push from which it was eventually pressured to withdraw. Nor should it have undertaken a self-congratulatory media-blitz claiming strategic victory because China rebutted every such claim by asserting that India had been taught a lesson.

Since then, China has advanced even deeper into the Bhutanese territory at Doklam, posing a quandary for India. Having lost the strategic advantage it had before the Doklam crisis, Indian strategists must be wondering if preferring the military confrontation over quiet diplomacy was a wise course to adopt.

On its part, China's conduct before, during and after the Doklam crisis, and later, in 2020, over the ingress in Ladakh, is in line with its strategic thinking, which views the world order as a hierarchical construct. It believes the world is stable because of hierarchy and not because everyone is created equal.

As a present-day giant in almost every respect, it suits China to promote this hypothesis. But all along, the world misread China's long-term intent. Otherwise, it could have done a lot to ensure China did not become the giant it has become.

In all these relationships, ranging from extracting the maximum from a willing West to managing relations with a comradely but apprehensive Russia to teaching India a lesson, China was repeatedly walking a thin line. Now that it has added considerable military, technological and economic substance to its giant geographical size, it is in a far better position than ever before to set the terms of its external interaction.

The Biggest Player

China has historically been hegemonistic. In the expansionist phase under Mao, it more than doubled China's size, making it the world's fourth-largest nation by area. Xi has not altered that tone; rather, he has repeatedly asserted China's intent to take back every inch of land that it claims is historically China's.

It is then natural that it should have added muscle to its resolve. All along, China firmly kept in view the historically proven fact that the nations that remain great powers best harness their economic potential to build up military strength. And so, starting with the 1980s, it has been pursuing, with great determination, the two ambitions of modernizing and becoming an economic power. Once it had the economic means, it began to methodically build its military muscle. By the end of the 1980s, it started to divert considerable resources into upgrading its defence forces. In the five-year period between 1988 and 1993, its military expenditure doubled. By 1993, China was spending nearly $12 billion annually on defence forces. By 2021, its military budget of $209 billion was more than all of its neighbours combined and almost three times as much as India.[12]

Since America is widely regarded as the greatest military power ever in history, the strategic community wonders if China's ambitious programme will make it an even bigger power. Singapore's leader Lee Kuan Yew thought as much in 1993, 'It is not possible to pretend that this is just another big player. This is the biggest player in the history of man.'[13]

Within three decades of this statement, the world is beginning its search for a new balance. It may still take another 10 to 15 years for this ferment to settle into a definite strategic shape, but there is no doubt that a new military order will be upon us by 2035.

But it will not mean a content China. As China becomes stronger, it will develop new needs and a set of new insecurities. There is also the possibility that civil unrest and eventual economic slowdown could lead it to expand outwards. Or to take its present posture, its strength will lead it to settle historical boundaries as it perceives them and to its satisfaction, be it the matter of islands in the Pacific Ocean or the disputed land in the Himalayas.

This Chinese ambition might be the spark that ignites the

next big conflict in the world, involving China's aggression against India, Taiwan or Japan. America might bide its time before getting directly involved in a China–India conflict, but it will find it difficult not to defend Taiwan or Japan.

An aggressive China will be the democratic world's biggest geopolitical test of the twenty-first century. Its autocratic leader Xi is no respecter of commitments given solemnly or that of the rules the rest of the world wishes to go by. There is, therefore, good reason for India, as also for Taiwan and Japan, to be on guard.

Whether the apprehensive world terms this behaviour lack of principles or that of scruples, it hardly matters to a country consumed by the idea of its greatness. Accordingly, the change in the world that China wishes to put in place will be Soviet in substance, where its authoritarian word forms the law and its interests determine the form.

This Chinese reluctance to take the established world order as the eternal horizon is understandable but not excusable because China's notion of a sudden leap into a new global regime is a fantasy of Hitlerian proportions.

In the confidence that its time to straddle the global stage is fast approaching, China's ambitions are growing by the year. It has set about methodically making its land forces a leaner and agile fighting force. In 2017, China's People's Liberation Army (PLA) embarked on a structural and operational transformation billed as the greatest in its history. It aims to create a more mobile, modular and lethal ground force. This modernization seeks capabilities that can match and degrade US operational and technological advantages. For instance, look at its plans to fundamentally change the range of its artillery guns. By using electricity and magnetism instead of gunpowder for propulsion, China has developed a rail-gun that can fire projectiles at speeds of almost 7,500 km/h up to distances of 200 km with great accuracy. Designed for use against land and naval targets, this is due to be put into service by 2025.

However, China is no longer content in being a formidable

land power. It wants to dominate the military aspects of air, space and the sea forces as well. To support its increased naval commitments abroad, China has grown to become the largest ship-producing country in the world. Its navy grew from 328 in 2017 to 350 ships in 2018. It commissions nearly three submarines each year, and by 2023, it will have more than 70 in its fleet. At the current rate of manufacture, it could soon be operating 400 ships. Within the next 15 years, roughly by 2035, China could have 430 surface ships and 100 submarines.[14] In contrast, by 2025, the US submarine fleet will have declined to 48, and by 2030, the active US naval fleet will be down to 237 ships.

China's air force, too, has begun to pack a deadly punch. The Chinese air force totalled more than 2,700 aircraft in 2018. Of these, 2,000 were combat aircraft and over 600 of these combat aircraft were fourth-generation fighters. But China has moved on even further, and it is rapidly inducting its fifth-generation J-20 and FC-31 jets. In space, China wants to acquire counter-space capabilities. These include kinetic-kill missiles, orbiting space robots and expanded space surveillance capabilities.

However, China is still not content with the formidable military capabilities it has already acquired. It is multitasking with the technology it has learnt, purchased, borrowed or stolen from foreign universities, research institutions and commercial enterprises. Look at how it intends to use tiny drones in the battlefield. Besides reconnaissance, swarms of drones can overwhelm existing air defences and destroy aircraft carriers. Flying one of these devices into the air intake of a fighter jet could take it down easily and at a very low cost to China.

China's military and technological rise has been greatly facilitated by its secret services, which have helped it obtain the latest and best in defence and information technologies from the West by means fair or foul. Their modus operandi has been to stay out of sight and operate quietly under the surface. They are obviously successful at it because a vast majority of people in the world cannot name any one of China's intelligence services. Yet, the overwhelming majority around the world would have heard of the Central Intelligence Agency (CIA) and the Federal Bureau of Investigation (FBI), and known that James Bond worked for MI6 (the British intelligence agency). They would have also heard in awe the exploits of Mossad (the intelligence agency of Israel), the fierceness of the Inter-Services Intelligence (ISI) and the KGB (the Russian intelligence service). But does anyone even wonder why there is next to nothing about the Chinese spy agencies? This is what has made the Chinese agencies so effective in recruiting agents, stealing technologies and in influencing opinion-makers abroad.

This combination of enormous economic and military power is a heady cocktail. Adding adrenaline to it, China is now led by a Rambo-like figure. Unlike his risk-averse post-Mao predecessors, China under the authoritarian Xi is no longer a status quo power. It pursues coercive foreign policy, and, ominously, Xi has declared that those who get in the way of China's ascent will have their 'heads bashed bloody against a Great Wall of steel.'[15]

Accordingly, there are serious reasons to prepare for a terrible 2020s. It will be so because this is China's window of opportunity. Its military advantages may not endure beyond this decade. Moreover, its strategic culture emphasizes hitting when it perceives gathering dangers. Such calculations have led China to war in the past. Alas, it could happen again.

The Great Leap

Besides its remarkable performance in the economic, defence and technological sectors, China is also the trendsetter in the scale and size of its aid projects. Despite chaffing under the strings that China attaches to its aid, the recipients do not see credible alternatives to working with China. It delivers aid fast; its projects are big and it executes them with remarkable speed. The only passable regional rival to it is India, which is ponderously slow in the execution of aid projects and has no counter-narrative to a giant scheme like China's BRI project.

Against the background of its overall performance, one could ask rhetorically if China's rise was inevitable.

It is often also asked as to when China started its march to greatness. The answer perhaps is the beginning of the 1990s, when the internal shock of Tiananmen Square and the events abroad leading to the collapse of communist regimes in East Europe combined to shake up the Chinese leadership. After the 1989 Tiananmen Square crackdown, Beijing kept its political system closed but liberalized its markets to attract foreign investors. This was the beginning of a plan that succeeded in turning China into the world's factory.

Taking a lesson also from the collapse of the Soviet Union, Deng Xiaoping outlined in 1990 a 24-character strategy for China: 'Observe calmly; secure our position, cope with affairs calmly, hide our capacities and bide our time, be good at maintaining a low profile, and never claim leadership.'[16]

This served China well for nearly three decades. But in 2013, Xi, as the newly appointed leader of China, announced his wish to 'make China great again.'

This was the public articulation of China's intent but since 1999, China's investment in research and development (R&D) has grown by an average of 17 per cent annually. In 2017, the total US spending on R&D was $549 billion (PPP), while China came a not too distant second with $496 billion.[17] This is 20 per cent of total R&D spending in the world, and more than Japan, Germany and South Korea combined. More students graduate with science and engineering degrees in China than anywhere else in the world. In 2017, the Chinese government outlined its road map for turning itself into the 'premier global AI innovation centre' by 2030.[18]

Xi has refined this plan further; he has now sketched out

a new strategy to suit the changed times and China's changed status. What this means essentially is a two-step approach. After achieving prosperity for all, it should use the next 15 years to complete a basic modernization project by 2035. After another 15 years, in 2050, China aims to become a major world power. Incidentally, China will be celebrating the hundredth anniversary of the founding of the People's Republic of China (PRC) in 2049, and if it meets the target set by Xi, its economy will be thrice the size of America by then.

Reshaping the Global Order

Despite its successes, China is consumed by its grievances. To avenge the 'Century of Humiliation' that China endured at the hands of western imperial powers from roughly 1839–40 to 1949, it adopted a one-size-fits-all approach. It is arrogant with all it deals with. Chinese envoys talk of being a responsible, globally minded major power, yet they stoke nationalism at home and play the bully abroad.

On a note of caution, a historical fact should, therefore, be flagged—when the ambitions of countries overtake the feasible and they over-extend their reach, the splurge of their spending exceeds their capacity. Then this desire to sustain a strategic edge leaves more productive parts of the economy starved of capital. It marks the beginning of their decline.

This is what had happened to China when its fifteenth- and sixteenth-century naval ambitions became exorbitantly expensive for its economy to support. This could happen now too. Its expenditures in pursuit of greatness are already the subject of envy and anxiety. But, so far, the world led by the US seems helpless to stop that march.

However, Covid-19 could be an inflection point. The revulsion that China's role in the pandemic has provoked throughout the world might have repercussions that China's ambitions had not factored in. If, as a result, the US-led West doggedly decides to shift its investments out of China and then puts up a wall of barriers to its exports, China may once again find itself going back to the stage in the seventeenth century, when it burnt hundreds of miles of its coastal territory to signal the end of its naval ambitions.

It is early yet to predict if the Covid-19-led revulsion of China and the disruption of supplies during the lockdown will mark a long-term shift by foreign investors out of China. But this trend has already begun, and manufacturers are diversifying their supply chains away from it. This economic decoupling will correspondingly lead to the reduction of economic ballast in the US–China relationship.

If and when China begins its decline, there would be multiple analyses as to why it happened and many diagnoses for it. One among them is bound to be the excessively ambitious BRI. This infrastructure scheme rivals the Taj Mahal in expenditure, though it lacks its serenity. Taj soothes and stuns with its beauty those who behold it; BRI terrifies countries with its economic trap. As is the case with the Taj Mahal, BRI's utilitarian aspect remains in doubt. It is being said that $1.5 trillion of expenditure on infrastructure projects over the next decade across Southeast Asia, South Asia and Central Asia may doom the recipients and China alike.

Critics begin their doubts with the fundamental premise of BRI that transportation is the ultimate panacea. They maintain that today land transport is cost ineffective. Besides the issue of different gauges and delays at multiple customs points, there is also the question of physical limitation. These are compounded by the cost-effective existence of giant container ships capable of carrying almost $1 billion worth of cargo.

In contrast, take the case of total value of freight carried between Yiwu and Europe by rail in the first four months of 2018. It was just $330 million. China's top four ports processed this value of cargo every three hours.

All this is true, but big powers with grand ambitions do not get motivated by commercial considerations alone. Had that been so, the conquerors of the world, like Alexander or Genghis, would not have left the comfort of their palaces. The desire to dominate and leave a mark on eternity motivates the actions of not just people but countries as well. BRI must be viewed in that context.

Its scope is not just the domination of the developing world but parts of the West as well.

BRI's expansion westward greatly increases Chinese access to the world as a whole, and indirectly Chinese control over what was once part of the Soviet Union without, in any way, intimating that they're seeking control over these parts and asserting their domination. This approach is very hard to oppose because there is nothing strategically offensive on the face of it. But in practice, it is principally strategic in dimension; it could alter the balance of power between China and Russia, and with the West, immensely.

Still all is not well with this project.

Defaults on investments cause problems for creditors as well as debtors. In this respect, BRI could well become the example for future historians to quote. It is an open-ended scheme largely of rail and road projects, and infrastructure projects by themselves cannot be self-sustaining. They need a complete menu of supporting industries and commercial projects to act as economic feeders. Only then can they become commercially viable.

Yet, indebtedness of others may be a costly but calculated Chinese plan to quietly extend its strategic power around the world. It has invested in small European countries as a matter of state policy. These stakes have given it critical influence over those governments and, through them, a role in EU's affairs.

The bigger challenge that China poses is about its attempts to reshape the global order. Xi wishes to cast the world to his design. He would like to flip a switch and replace the existing order with the primacy of the state, where institutions, laws and technology reinforce state control. In sum, he would like the world to mirror the authoritarian system he has put in place in China—a new world order of which it determines the rules.

To try and prevent that from happening will mean taking on China on the security front. It will involve strengthening allies and friends, blocking Chinese acquisition of strategic technology, preventing Chinese 'influence operations', which have already been exposed in Australia and New Zealand, punishing the worst offenders in China's vast array of state-owned enterprises and even denying student visas to sons and daughters of the CCP elite. This is a tall order, and despite vigorous efforts in this direction by the US, it may not be an easy battle.

Christopher Wray, former FBI director, outlined this threat in these terms, 'One of the things we're trying to do is view the China threat as not just a whole-of-government threat, but a whole-of-society threat... and I think it's going to take a whole-of-society response by us.'[19] This, however, will not be the first such confrontation of our times. The East–West confrontation lasted over a generation from the early 1950s to late 1980s. The big difference then was that the West, led by the US, was united and better prepared having thought the process through. The often quoted evidence of it was the 'Long Telegram' issued by George Kennan in February 1946.[20]

This time, the West is not united. To complicate matters for itself, the US is confused. As a new version of the Long Telegram called 'The Longer Telegram' mentions, 'The principal US interest has often been how a particular announcement might sound to the US domestic body politic, rather than the effectiveness... in changing Beijing's political mindset and associated policy behavior.'[21]

Like the East–West face-off, this time, too, the struggle is between free and open societies and a closed authoritarian system. This new confrontation might be bitter and long, its results uncertain till the very end. Unlike the last time, the US can no longer assume that it will prevail in this contest because China has learnt so much from the West. It has imbibed and improved upon many western best practices in economics, politics, science and technology. And, unlike the Soviet Union, it is not cash-strapped. Instead, this time the US has reason to be concerned; its recovery post the 2008 crisis, driven by 'quantitative easing' and 'consumer spending', is fragile.

China, on the other hand, can claim that all is well with its economy, and much of the credit for it can be traced back to the system of 'collective responsibility' introduced by Deng and followed by his successors till Xi took over.

Xi Takes Centre Stage

When Xi became China's president in 2013, Lee Kuan Yew had said about this unknown figure, 'Watch this man.'[22]

Whether it is the domination of tomorrow's world, controlling the international transport lanes, setting global standards, maintaining order in the world or starting a war, the man to watch is Xi. He controls all the strings of power in China and, through it, of some of the world. It is, therefore, important to understand the man.

Xi had watched in his youth his father's fall from grace in the CCP—from the summit of hierarchy to a lowly job—because he had chosen the wrong side in the political struggle between Mao and the others opposing him. Xi learned from that experience never to reveal his cards. Silence was his companion during the long journey to the top.

He was selected in 2012 as a compromise candidate between the Shanghai faction led by Jiang Zemin and the Youth League led by Hu Jintao. The party elders and other senior leaders thought that he would be pliable to their pressure. But they have been disappointed by the way Xi has obliterated the reforms and intra-party democracy introduced by Deng. Xi has also usurped all powers. Since he began the anti-corruption campaign in 2012, nearly 1.5 million have been killed, imprisoned or removed from their jobs, without a fair legal process.

A personality cult now surrounds Xi, who has tightened the party's grip on ideology and eliminated what little space there was for political speech and civil society. Today, China is a totalitarian country like the mid-twentieth-century Soviet Union.

There have been endless political purges in the name of an anti-corruption campaign that has silenced Xi's political challengers. Yet, the same strict standards do not apply to him and his coterie. All this has not gone without notice, and the internet echoes with messages of resentment. To make matters even more delicate for Xi, the contrast between outward confidence and inner apprehension is growing in China. This combination of ambition and fear explains why Xi is obsessed with control.

The challenge for the world is to deal with a Chinese leader who has been oppressive in Hong Kong, genocidal in the Xinjiang region, aggressive in Ladakh, threatening to Taiwan, ruthless on human rights issues, obdurate on trade and insincere on almost everything. Can the 'cold war' with China still be kept cold or would some part of Asia be plunged into a war with China before others get sucked into it?

After the outbreak of Covid-19 and the global reaction blaming China for it, the Communist Party's leaders believed they had a narrowing window of strategic opportunity to strengthen their rule and revise the international order in their favour. But its conduct with the world and its authoritarian methods internally during the Covid-19 rampage has not endeared it to many. Rather, this is taken as proof that China has no intention of playing by the norms of international law, trade or commerce. Instead, China's strategy may rely even more on coercion.

However, this pandemic could also act as a signal to the omen-conscious Chinese. From the imperial times, Chinese have believed the withdrawal of the 'Mandate of Heaven' to an emperor is signalled by a natural catastrophe. The Tangshan earthquake of 1976, which killed over half a million people, was followed by the death of Mao and the fall of the Gang of Four. Covid-19 is the biggest natural disaster that has happened since Tangshan. This cannot be a good sign for the superstitious Chinese. Will it lead to the diminution of Xi's power and the reduction of China's military and economic swagger? Perhaps it might.

Is it then possible that there could be a change in China?

It will be difficult, if not dangerous, for outside powers to intervene and affect a change because China is far too big and militarily formidable for any offensive external influence. It is equally unlikely that change will come from below in a broad, grassroots movement. Given the CCP's existing level of control and the sheer size of the country, it would be hard to coordinate a mass mobilization. If a change were to come, it would have to originate within the upper reaches of the party itself.

In such a period of turbulence, China might opt for a diversionary military engagement abroad. It is already difficult to challenge its aggressive moves in the South China Sea and elsewhere, soon it may become hazardous. China has gone past the stage of 'hiding its strength and biding its time.'

Even if a war does not break out, a matter of near-term strategic concern would be China's ability to manipulate global supply chains for its geopolitical benefit. It could create artificial market scarcities or simply block Japan's and India's energy supplies from the Gulf through its naval capabilities in Gwadar.

There are other factors that indicate a restless China. In his idea about the 'Clash of Civilizations', Samuel P. Huntington asserted that the conflicts in future would not be ideological, political or economic, instead, they will be cultural. Since then, the issues that divide the world have become more complex. If and when a contest happens, it would be much more than a 'Clash of Civilizations'. The struggle will be about the shape of a new world and its changed order. The two broad possibilities in this clash will both involve China on one side; ranged against it on the other side might be the US with or without the rest of the West in the first case and India in the second.

This thought about the challenge that China poses worried a former US defense secretary sufficiently to write:

> What does China's choice mean for U.S. policy? First, it means the rebalance begun under President Obama should continue, especially the military aspects of the rebalance. We must continue to invest in the innovative systems and ideas required to counter China's military capabilities. We must have the quality and quantity of forces necessary to prevent Chinese aggression if we can, and counter it if we must.[23]

However, there are some who quote historical precedent to assert that all is not lost, that there are still ways other than military aggression. Hu Shih, a philosopher and a former Chinese ambassador to the US, had once said, 'India conquered and dominated China culturally for 20 centuries without ever having to send a single soldier across her border.'[24]

This is noble sentiment. But is the state of India–China relations such that a current-day Chinese man of significance would have the courage to repeat in some sincerity words to the same effect?

More importantly, given the present state of China's defence preparedness, is there a realistic chance that an Indian soldier will be able to cross the border into China? Or for that matter an American soldier?

On the other hand, the prognosis might be grim. It is quite possible that by 2035, with or without achieving the greatness that Lee Kuan Yew had predicted for it, China may plunge the world into a great war as global as the Covid-19 epidemic, longer lasting than it and far more destructive.

4

RUSSIA: RACING ALONG

The pleasures that come from the world bear in them sorrows to come. They come and they go, they are transient: not in them do the wise find joy.

—Bhagavad Gita (5:22)

Russians can justifiably claim to have saved Europe twice—first by pushing back Napoleon's forces and then by confronting Hitler's armies. Just to take the example of the Second World War, the US involvement was mainly confined to Western Europe, but some of the war's most savage fighting occurred on the Eastern Front. There, the Soviets bore the brunt of Hitler's killing machine, losing more than 27 million people, including an estimated 11 million soldiers. In all, they took 95 per cent of the military casualties of the three major powers—the US, Britain and the Soviet Union. Yet, if one goes by the western mass media, especially Hollywood, the war was won by the American heroes and their sacrifices.

Russians remain resentful that despite this enormous war effort, the Soviet Union became the prime new target of strategic plans by the West led by the US. While a tired world was putting in place a new global order, some diplomats were busy divining the dark in silver clouds.

The most famous of these efforts was George Kennan's 8,000-word Long Telegram of 22 February 1946, which he sent from Moscow to Washington. As the single best-known dispatch in America's diplomatic history, it analysed the sources of Soviet conduct and advocated its containment; the substance of the telegram being to understand the Soviet Union in order to counter its ambitions.

In March that year, Frank Roberts, the British chargé d'affaires in Moscow, sent a series of reports and telegrams to London outlining Anglo-Soviet incompatibilities based largely on ideological grounds. His basic premise differed from his American colleague. Rather than countering it, he wanted the United Kingdom (UK), as a weakened and exhausted power, to understand the Soviet Union in order to work with it. Roberts could sense the Soviet resentment that despite its wartime sacrifices, it was being excluded from the Anglo-American club. Unlike Kennan, he was clear that all Soviet tactics are short-term, but their strategy, although flexible, is definitely long-term. More importantly, the long-term strategy did not include going to war. Accordingly, he reflected in these dispatches the Soviet wish to resurrect the Big Three (US, UK and the Soviet Union) for reasons rooted in geography, history as well as prestige.

In a remarkable coincidence, a few months later, in September 1946, the Soviet Union's ambassador in Washington, Nikolai Novikov, sent a telegram to Moscow about the likely shape of the American economic and military domination worldwide. In this indirect counter to the Kennan telegram, Novikov warned that the US had emerged from war economically strong, and to protect its interests, the Soviet Union needed to secure its buffer zone in Eastern Europe.

The stage was now set for the long East–West Cold War that followed.

But it wasn't just the diplomats who were working furiously to assess what the future held and how best to prepare for it.

The politicians, too, were defining the contours of this new age. Winston Churchill was no longer the British PM, still his word counted. On 5 March 1946, he delivered the famous Iron Curtain speech condemning the Soviet expansion in Eastern Europe. He thundered that from Stettin in the Baltic to Trieste in the Adriatic, an Iron Curtain had descended across the continent. He was warning thereby that though the Allies had spent six years fighting for freedom from fascism in Europe, they now risked having half the European continent under Soviet dictatorship.

A year later, in March 1947, President Harry Truman spelt out in the US Congress what later became known as the Truman Doctrine: '(I)t must be the policy of the United States to support free peoples who are resisting attempted subjugation by armed minorities or by outside pressures.'[1]

This was followed by the Marshall Plan, designed as much for reconstruction in Europe as to check the spread of communism by its economic success.

Meanwhile, Kennan kept cogitating. In 1947, as a public follow-up of the Long Telegram, he published the article 'The Sources of Soviet Conduct in Foreign Affairs'. The substance of it was the containment doctrine by which the objective of the American policy was to keep the Soviet Union inside its box. All the US had to do was to ensure that Soviet influence did not spread beyond the eastern borders. Kennan believed the US did not have to intervene in Soviet affairs because communism was bound to collapse due to its inefficiency.

Once again, subsequent events proved Kennan right.

The Soviet Union began to falter in the 1970s. Among many reasons for it were the vast sums dedicated to military spending. This was compounded by the negatives of a command economy, where Moscow expected to hear only the good news from its provinces.

There was also a Soviet version of the BRI, the enormous expenditure on the infrastructure development of Siberia, which hosted just a fraction of the country's population. Yet, it used up about a third of the Soviet Union's heavy construction equipment as Moscow pumped in capital to develop gas fields, coal mines and aluminium plants.

The Soviet Union also found it difficult to manage the vast territories it had acquired during the Imperial era. A declining economy is one of the prime reasons cited for their eventual shedding off.

Though this amputation was the end result, the Soviet experiment by Lenin had started on high hopes. To recall briefly, Karl Marx and Friedrich Engels claimed that communism would change not simply the history of Europe and the West but the history of the world as well. Their conviction that this would be so was given the formal status in the *Communist Manifesto* (1848). For a while, all seemed to be going as they had planned. Revolution became the carnival of the oppressed. In its full bloom, the communist Soviet Union lent organizational and financial support to whoever seemed willing and capable of organizing a communist revolution in his part of the world.

So great was the enthusiasm about this new world that, in 1956, Nikita Khrushchev, Stalin's successor, declared at the 20th Party Congress, 'The new period in world history which Lenin had predicted has arrived, and the peoples of the East are playing an active part in deciding the destinies of the whole world...'[2]

That hope sustained the Eastern Bloc for another 33 years, before collapsing in a collective heap in 1989.

Communism was banished overnight and the statues of its beacons were brought down throughout the Soviet Union and the rest of Eastern Europe. But the western hope that these new political societies coming to birth in the East will be replicas of those in the West was misplaced. The mutual mistrust persists, and Russia remains the outsider for the West.

Besides historical grudges that add to its bitterness, the constant scrutiny by the West of Russia's intentions does not augur well. These slights provoke Russia, and it continues to be restless.

Differences Set Them Apart

As with the Soviet Union, Russia continues to be a uniquely 'Eurasian' power, sprawling across two continents but never entirely at home in either. Viewed geographically, the part of the European continent that stretches east from the Bosnian Serb Republic in the west, through the eastern Balkans all the way to the Urals in Russia and across Siberia as far as Vladivostok on the Pacific resembles only superficially the western half of Europe. Its unforgiving landscape is in sharp contrast to the green pastures of Western Europe.

That sense of being different from the West extends to religion as well. Catholic and later Protestant Europe lost touch with the Orthodox Eastern Europe almost a thousand years ago. Over these centuries, this orthodox part of Europe became an entity whose separate values, traditions and, therefore, history have either been denigrated or ignored by the West.

Though it spans both Europe and Asia, its contacts with neither were prolific. Despite its unique status of being a major Eurasian power across two continents, it was not accepted as one of their own by the first and it was reluctant to be identified as a part of the second.

As a matter of fact, detailed geographical maps of the countries to its east started being made in Russia only in the beginning of the nineteenth century. Till the time the Russian Emperor Paul I ordered his Cossacks in 1801 to march towards Central Asia, the Russian maps did not show anything beyond Khiva.

Insofar as its neighbours to the west were concerned, the religious differences and the barrier of snow kept the orthodox Christian Russia at a distance from where both regarded each other warily. The Russian word for security is '*bezopasnost*', which means the 'absence of threats', but the Russian sense of isolation bred insecurity.

To an extent, this sense of insecurity was self-imposed by feudal Russia. It did not want its poorer, largely rural population to be exposed to the more economically advanced western societies.

This sense of insecurity continued during the Soviet period, when the country was hermetically sealed behind an iron curtain and contact with the western way of life was taboo. Yet, the forbidden magnified the western charms in Soviet peoples' eyes, and the desire for *perestroika* (restructuring) and *glasnost* (openness) seemed, at least in the heady days of 1989, a sign that the western way of life had finally brought the iron curtain down.

That turned out to be a short-lived hope. Though the Russian society is a lot more open now, at the governmental level, the suspicions and distrust have remained even after the Cold War. The West, on its part, does not trust Russia. The US, in particular, wants it as a pliant adjunct rather than as competition.

In the years following the disintegration of the Soviet Union, the West followed the strategy of squeezing Russia to the maximum while it lay wounded and helpless. In the 30 years since the collapse of the Berlin Wall, the North Atlantic Treaty Organization (NATO) alliance has expanded more than 1,000 km to the east of the former frontline dividing Germany. At first, the West was careful to temper its elation with magnanimity. In 1989, James Baker, America's secretary of state, gave an assurance to Gorbachev in Moscow: '(T)here would be no extension of NATO's jurisdiction…one inch to the east.'[3]

Yet a bloc that once shared only a slender border with Russia in Norway's northern fringes, now encompasses the Baltic states, former Soviet territories within 200 km of St Petersburg and 600 km of Moscow. Seven of the eight former members of the Warsaw Pact have become part of NATO.

Once again Kennan issued a warning. This time he wrote that the Clinton administration's decision in 1996 to expand NATO towards Russia's borders was the "'most fateful error of American policy in the entire post-cold-war era.' He predicted that the consequence would be a Russia that would "likely look elsewhere for guarantees of a secure and hopeful future for themselves.""[4]

Kennan's warning went unheeded yet again, and ever since, Russia has continued to feel threatened by the West as it had been during the Cold War and in the centuries before that. As a consequence, it has chosen to walk into the willing arms of China.

Putin, the Saviour

In Russian fairy tales, the hero often finds himself at a crossroads and reads less than encouraging signs. 'If you go left, you lose your horse, if you go right, you lose your head, if you go straight, you find nothing', is the familiar conundrum.

Vladimir Putin, extraordinarily lucky to have risen from obscurity to the presidency of Russia in a short span of time, must have felt somewhat like this fabled hero when he came to occupy the highest chair in Kremlin in 2000.

While the western world was popping champagne to celebrate the new millennium, the average Russian was unsure about his next meal. The Russian soldier was surly because his miserably low salary was overdue by many months. In oil-rich Russia, its air force could not keep the fighter aircrafts flying because the state did not have the money to buy fuel. Though Russia has an almost mystical tolerance for suffering, the country was in an unbelievably bad shape in every manner. It had indebted and doomed itself in the 1980s, when Moscow began the arms race with the US. A more recent humiliation came with the fall of the Berlin Wall in 1989 and the dismemberment of the Soviet Union. The Russia of the 1990s, under President Boris Yeltsin, was one that the West admired. But it was no longer a proud and sovereign country. It was a chaotic state, kept on life support by the International Monetary Fund (IMF) loans. This Russia that

Putin had been asked to preside over was truly at a crossroads littered with problems.

Very few were willing to give the new president the benefit of a novice's luck. The overwhelming opinion was gloomy, and the deck was stacked against him. A lesser person might have cracked, overwhelmed by the pressures of the unachievable.

Putin was untested—he had no previous administrative experience, and he did not know the ways of Moscow. He was a political beginner, and his statecraft till then was limited to outwitting western spies. But he had the determination to succeed and a nationalistic zeal; he wanted Russia to be great again.

Putin was Yeltsin's chosen successor, but he was not cast in his benefactor's mould. He did not accept the status of a large but second-rank European country that the West had assigned to Russia. Putin wanted the western world, and particularly the US, to acknowledge Russia as a sovereign country that valued its security. He wanted them to recognize that Russia defined and defended its vital interests as it saw fit. It was not going to be some 'has been' power that could be pushed around by others. In essence, he wanted a secure and proud Russia, recognized as such by others.

For this, Putin set himself a goal that defied tradition, history and even geography.

He has succeeded in restoring the Russian pride in itself, and Russia's image abroad as a stable power. There have been major improvements in the armaments industry, and its energy sector is robust. But some signs of concern persist. After the break-up of the Soviet Union, the Russian economy was not expected to transform magically in a generation, but the snail's pace of change is far below even the most modest expectations. Between 1992 and 2016, the real compound annual growth rate (CAGR) of Russian per capita GDP has been 1.5 per cent. In contrast, India (5.1 per cent) and China (8.9 per cent) have performed far better during this period.

Russians lay the blame for their poor growth on the economic siege imposed on them by the US. The sanctions put on the Russian entities have stymied economic growth and slowed down its exports. The western investment in Russia had seemed promising once, but now it has virtually dried up.

The West, prodded largely by the US, maintains that Russia's 2014 annexation of Crimea, its war in eastern Ukraine and its interference in the 2016 US presidential election have all been the reasons for imposing sanctions on it. But have the sanctions worked? The IMF has estimated that the sanctions linked to the 2014 invasion of Ukraine had cost Russia 1–1.5 per cent of its GDP by mid-2015.[5] Whether statistics always reveal the complete picture is open to doubt.

Insofar as Moscow is concerned, it has not changed its ways. Sanctions did not stop Russia from being a controversial factor in the US elections and its politics. Nor have they stopped Moscow from joining the war in favour of Syria or from abetting North Korea's efforts to bypass international sanctions. On the other hand, sanctions have alienated the Russian population, which was otherwise positively inclined towards America.

Naturally then, the question that the perplexed observers ask is this: why does Russia trigger such intense reaction in Washington?

This remains an abiding mystery. To give a more recent example of this puzzling paradox, 15 of the 19 hijackers involved in the 9/11 attacks were from Saudi Arabia. When, in revenge, the US decided to attack the Taliban in Afghanistan, Russia helped the US get bases in Central Asia and facilitated the American troops' transit through that air and land space. Yet, it is Saudi Arabia that is the American favourite, while Russia continues to be squeezed with sanctions.

There are other Russian grudges as well.

In 1997, the Group of Seven (G-7) major countries invited Russia to join it at the high table. The decision was appreciated by the wider world as appropriate to Russia's stature and as an act that could help promote some slack in their tensions. But the effort at conciliation did not last long.

The G-7 decided in 2014 to revert to its former configuration of being minus Russia. This was not a prudent move. Thus rebuffed, Russia has largely abandoned the hope for some sort of alliance with the West.

This was compounded by the public humiliation of Putin in 2014 at the G-20 Summit in Australia, where the western countries, led by Obama, treated him like a pariah. Putin had virtually no one to talk to, and as a result, he left the summit prematurely. Obama called it the western anger over Russia's pressure tactics against Ukraine. He said, 'I had naturally several interactions with President Putin during the course of the APEC Summit and then here at G20. I would characterize them as typical of our interactions, which are business-like and blunt.'[6] UK's then PM David Cameron was quick to add: 'This is going to be a test of the stamina of political will of the United States and the EU. I think we will meet that test…President Putin can see he is at a crossroads.'[7]

Since then, very few of the western leaders who were at the summit continue to be in positions of power. Obama is in retirement; Cameron had unwittingly led Britain to Brexit. But Putin remains firmly in his Russian saddle, and he is unlikely to forget those slights. Pushed thus into a corner, Russia will try to punch its way out of the West-imposed isolation and challenge the US hegemony.

Russia and China: More Hype than Realism?

If Obama insulted Putin at almost every major international gathering, President Xi went out of his way to show respect to Putin every time they were seen together in a multilateral setting.

In diplomacy, these signals matter, and the result is obvious in multiple ways. For instance, China and Russia are coordinating their positions at the UN. In the United Nations Security Council (UNSC) voting, they agree 98 per cent of the time, and Russia has backed every Chinese veto since 2007. If the US national security documents designate Russia and China as America's strategic competitors and adversaries, the Chinese and Russian national security documents term their bilateral relationship a 'comprehensive strategic partnership'.

Together, they are effective as partners against the West. Russia and China have combined to dilute human rights norms; they back each other to defend strategic interests in multilateral forums. Their joint advocacy is creating new norms around the cyber and internet domain.

Overall, Russia is amplifying America's China test. This synergy between Russia and China will be most problematic in the way that it increases the challenge that China poses to the US and its global leadership.

But Russia feels anguished that though it is not a communist country anymore, it is China, led by the Communist Party, that was being courted by the West till the disillusionment about Covid-19 set in.

All this while, the West was gloating that Russia lay panting on the mat. To ensure that it kept lying there, the West ignored the fact that China is the real challenger to American power and it is China that has infiltrated US institutions to a far more harmful extent, by stealing defence secrets and co-opting the best US corporations. China did it comprehensively and to a much greater extent than the Soviets ever did or the Russians ever can.

Moreover, after the Cold War, Russians are facing a double challenge. Besides having to deal with the aftermath of communism, there are also the issues of adjusting to an alien western culture and the muscular Islamic world.

But NATO misread Russia's deep-seated craving for respect, taking it as a given that there is a sort of historic evolution that will march across Eurasia. It did not understand that it might encounter something very different to a Westphalian entity. A risen and nationalistic Russia under Putin was bound to push back against this challenge to its identity, and it did.

Rebuffed repeatedly by the West, Russia had no alternative but to turn to China. It need not have been so because Sino-Soviet relations were not always smooth. After the founding of the PRC in 1949, they fell into two contrasting phases. A decade of 'eternal friendship' was followed in the 1960s by an era of 'eternal enmity'.

Even now, Russia continues to be wary of China. It is also apprehensive of the Chinese demographic expansion in eastern Russia. It watches suspiciously as China spreads a network of energy pipelines, roads and rail networks across Central Asia. During the Soviet era, the network of oil and gas pipelines in Central Asia was laid in such a way that it all led up north to the Russian centre. This was also the case with the rail and road network. These still exist, but a new Chinese-built network throbs with energy. These oil and gas pipelines are laid in the east–west alignment, just as the recently laid Chinese rail and road networks are. Chinese companies now own almost a quarter of Kazakhstan's oil production and over half of Turkmenistan's gas exports.

Russia feels even more uncomfortable as the BRI programme extends China's economic influence deeper into Central Asia. This in a region that until recently was a part of the Soviet Union. Even now, Russia continues to consider the Central Asian countries as within its sphere of influence, but the region's economic interests are now more aligned with China. As early as 2013, China overtook Russia in terms of regional trade, totalling $50 billion in commerce with the five former Soviet Central Asian republics compared with Russia's $30 billion.

Besides the historic distrust, there is more hype than realism about their current partnership. The wariness in their relationship was papered over by a mutual need in the last decade. After Russia annexed Crimea in 2014, the US, EU and Australia imposed sanctions on it. An unintended consequence of this decision was to turn Russia reflexively towards China. Over the next year, Russia struck a $400 billion deal for Gazprom to supply 38 billion cubic metres (bcm) of gas annually to China. This energy supply arrangement is not the only result of the western sanctions. The trade between the two countries has increased from $64 billion in 2015 to $147 billion in 2021, making China the largest trading partner of Russia.

However, theirs is not yet a formal security alliance against the West nor is it an ideological partnership. Rather, there are still issues and priorities that divide them. China's main security interests lie in Asia; Russia's are in Europe. Russia does not wish to reorder Central Asia or rearrange its boundaries, but it has deep security interests in Europe.

By the current standing, the Russia–China relationship is not a marriage made in heaven nor is it the sign of intense cooperation that exists between the US and its military allies in Europe and Japan. These latter relationships have the foundation of trust, but in the Russia–China relationship, both sides are wary, forever watching their back, and they have yet to pass the test of hard times. Moreover, as the smaller economy with GDP the tenth of China's, Russia is loath to become its junior partner.

There are other points of contention between them, and the recent bonhomie has been brought about largely by a common thread of friction with the West. It is, therefore, possible that the relationship between Russia and China may gradually start eroding because they have ethnic, political and economic challenges of a fundamental structural nature. Yet, they have found it convenient to ally for the moment.

As containing and balancing the US is one of the key missions of Russian foreign policy around the world, American behaviour still determines how Russia responds. In the absence of positive signals from the US, Russia continues to believe that it can be a global power only by limiting the influence of the US. It has accordingly built an anti-hegemonic consensus with China. But Russian leaders also remain concerned about China's long-term intentions.

For this reason, it would not mind if the US were to succeed in constraining China in Asia. As a result, the Russian objectives in Asia are preventive in nature—containing the US and China, while maintaining its influence in the region.

It is partly in consciousness of this that the US's National Security Strategy (NSS) brought out in December 2017 mentions: 'The combination of Russian ambition and growing military capabilities creates an unstable frontier in Eurasia, where the risk of conflict due to Russian miscalculation is growing.'[8]

A Place in the World

Russian strategic thinkers also spoke about the possibility of a military conflict. They warned repeatedly that NATO's creeping expansion was sure to lead to confrontation if Ukraine was to be included in NATO's embrace. On its part, Russia was not seeking limited sovereignty over central Europe. It knew this was no longer possible with its reduced means and the overall rise of those countries. Russia's protests were about the countries on its periphery that were aligning with NATO. Since an accommodation with its expectations was not reached, a confrontation was bound to be the result.

Behind the invasion of Ukraine, Putin's broader aim was to alter the balance of power that he feels was imposed on Russia after the Cold War. For Putin, it was the humiliating equivalent of the Versailles Treaty's impositions on Germany after the First World War.

But NATO is not Russia's only strategic worry. Its other long-term concern relates to the Far East and the Western Pacific. Some Russian experts hint darkly at the possibility of a war breaking out between Russia and China over the Russian Far East, and a war between China and a US-led regional coalition for supremacy in the Pacific, with Russia somehow getting sucked into it. Neither of these may happen in this decade, still Russia is undertaking a capability upgrade east of the Urals.

On its own, Russia would not like to engage the West militarily. While global military spending grew in 2017 to a total of \$1.7 trillion, Russia's fell from \$69.2 billion in 2016 to \$66.3 billion, making it the first time Russian military expenditure fell since 1998. That, incidentally, was the year when Russia defaulted on its debts. Currently, Russia's defence budget consumes 4.3 per cent of its GDP, but there are plans to cut it to below 3 per cent in the next five years.

Moreover, Russia's resources continue to be far inferior to the US in military and economic terms. Therefore, besides its desire to avoid direct confrontation while it is still struggling with the task of national development, Russia may not like to engage in an unequal battle. Apart from this muscular aspect, there is also the civilizational angle. In any other relationship, this factor should have been a strong bonding glue between the two countries—after all, Russia is a Christian country, and it was a US ally in the Second World War.

However, if pushed, Putin could catch the West off guard and fight dirty. This could even include crossing the nuclear threshold or at least the threat of it. Some analysts feel the resort to nuclear weapons will not be necessary and the sense of civilizational responsibility will ultimately keep the Russian finger away from the nuclear button. One commentator, Franklin Foer, writing in *Slate* went so far as to suggest that Putin has 'a plan for destroying the West—and that plan looks a lot like Donald Trump.'[9]

More serious observers feel there are many ways in which Russia and the West have antagonized each other. The UK complains bitterly about the poison attacks on its soil by Russian agents. And the US continues to be bewildered by the fact that a foreign agency could manipulate and influence its presidential election.

There are others who look beyond the present state of friction and see hopeful signs ahead. Zbigniew Brzezinski was sanguine about the post-Putin future, not because of some change in Russian intentions but because he felt that Russia will lack other options '...with its declining population, with people moving out of the Far East, with an enormously powerful China in the east, I think the real destiny of Russia is to become closer to the West.'[10]

That may well be the case in the future. For the moment, however, Russia is keen on countering the US and cutting into its sphere of influence in Russia's neighbourhood and in Asia. This brings up the issue of Russia and China coming together in an actual war against the West. According to independent experts, the present American policy of pushing Russia into the guilty corner may lead the West into a two-front war, precisely the possibility that many previous US administrations have worked hard to avoid.

That possibility apart, the East–West schism is a fact that both sides acknowledge. Sadly, neither side feels the gap could be bridged. While the contest between Russia and the West may not revert to the tensions of the Cold War, military strength and its occasional exercise will mark or mar this relationship. Putin understands well that power may not be the sole purpose of policy; still history is proof that military power determines the political influence of nations. All the rest are add-ons. Economic strength is vital, so are the diplomatic skills, and likewise for the smart and soft power, but what are they if a country gets run over by a stronger adversary?

Putin is determined that Russia should not get run over. It is an ancient civilization, proud of its past. As Putin sets about retrieving that pride for Russia, he may well be reminded of a similar circumstance in the mid-nineteenth century. Russia had just been defeated in the Crimean War, and the other European powers were conspiring against it. In that gloom, the Russian foreign minister Alexander Gorchakov had famously said, 'Russia is not sulking. She is composing herself.'[11] Once more, it is engaged in composing itself, and the aim of present-day Russia is the consolidation of its place in the world, with or without western support.

5

AMERICA FIRST

I am the Father of this universe, and even the Source of the Father. I am the Mother of this universe, and the Creator of all. I am the highest to be known...

—Bhagavad Gita (9:17)

It is said the collapse of the Soviet Union was a defining moment in global affairs. If that was so, 9/11, too, was a deep wound. If the contraction of the Soviet Union to Russia represented the rise of the US as the sole superpower of the world, 9/11 was an attempt at puncturing that swagger. These attacks were not random; they were a violent reaction to America's pre-eminence.

To read the tea leaves, if the humiliating withdrawal of the Soviet forces from Afghanistan in 1989 was the shabby end of ambitions that defined the Great Game in the nineteenth century, the US withdrawal from Afghanistan in 2021 was the West's admission that there are no winners in the Great Game.

This does not denote America's retreat into the sunset. As Mark Twain said, 'Reports of my death have been greatly exaggerated.' When he belted out this denial, he was the toast of the literary world and America's shining star. Since then, Twain has passed on, as even gifted mortals do. And America risks sliding down from the global top perch it had occupied for nearly a century, as all great powers eventually do.

But it will not be a sudden, steep fall, just as it was not an easy climb up. People have short memories, otherwise they would have remembered that America had to work its way through to the top and wait patiently below the summit before it could take the final step and claim the leadership position. Its economy had overtaken Britain's in absolute size in the last quarter of the nineteenth century. Still, that was not enough for America to be the world's central power. It had to mark time till the end of the Second World War, when Britain lay exhausted and America was raring to order the world to its design.

In anticipation of that position, the term 'American Century' was first used by Henry Luce in an editorial for *Life* magazine on 17 February 1941. He insisted that 'the world of the 20th century, if it is to come to life in any nobility of health and vigor, must be to a significant degree an American century.'[1]

This American Century began after the Second World War, and the US did work with evangelical zeal to help in the reconstruction of Europe, to better human condition in the Third World and to promote democracy throughout the world.

The new international order based on universal rules and values was built around the US but grounded in multilateral institutions like the UN, the World Bank and the IMF that were designed to promote collective interests over narrow ones. Subsequent American administrations supported and strengthened this basic framework that had pitched the US as the world's first reference point. In this role, the US was forever busy solving everyone else's problems in its own fashion.

There is no doubt that America's central role in the world and the globalization that it was the architect of still comes from its enormous military and economic power. Almost 88 per cent of currency trades use the United States Dollar (USD) as the medium. Credit card transactions are carried out mostly through Visa. America and its companies control over 50 per cent of the world's cross-border bandwidth, venture capital, phone-operating systems, top universities and fund-management assets. There is no other country, or a group of countries, anywhere remotely near this vast monopoly. As a matter of fact, ever since the late nineteenth century and till the dawn of this millennium, the US had not faced a competitor or even group of competitors with a combined GDP larger than its own.

Therefore, this millennium began on a comfortable note for America—it was the unchallenged superpower of the world; it led the technological revolution; and it was the leading light of free trade. But in quick succession, it was challenged on all three fronts—first by 9/11, then by the financial crisis of 2008 and finally by China.

China surpassed the US in PPP in 2014.[2] If it maintains its current pace of growth, it is expected to have the world's largest GDP in absolute terms by 2030. In comparison, at the height of its power, the Soviet Union's GDP was roughly 40 per cent the size of the US. It is, therefore, China that poses a grave challenge in the long term. When that finally happens and China surpasses the US, the American Century, proclaimed so triumphantly in the mid-twentieth century, may lie tattered and fading.

The first sign that the American giant was beginning to falter appeared in 1975, when the US admitted that it had failed in Vietnam. Since then, its military record has been mixed. It may have pulverized a hapless Iraq twice, but the victory resulted in the rise of an Islamic State of Iraq and Syria (ISIS) that continues to poke its finger in the American army's eyes. Rather than ordering Iraq and the region around it to its design, the US has left the entire area in an unresolved mess.

After an equally resultless 20-year war in Afghanistan, the US withdrew from it stealthily in the dark of the night. As its army retreated, it saw in its night-vision rear-view mirror the marching Taliban hordes that it had vowed to eliminate.

Even as these costly military misadventures were underway

abroad, the economic bruising of the US was beginning at home. The resulting loss of prestige meant two things—that the financial behemoth called the United States of America was no longer infallible and that it, too, was prone to the same mistakes, mismanagement and temptations like other, more ordinary countries.

Still, unlike many countries which tend to remain financially wounded after a major policy misstep, the US has managed to rise through the institutional debris of 2008. But it is no longer the dominant global economic power; its share of the global economy has steadily decreased. Its portion of the global GDP has declined from 40 per cent in 1960 to 22 per cent presently.[3]

There is more bad news for it. Some financial experts are predicting that at the rate the US Federal Reserve has been printing money, its currency may face a decline by as much as 30 per cent. Some add darkly that China could withdraw a bulk of its massive investment in the American treasury bonds, but that apart, the US itself is charting a hazardous course. Since 2008, the US has made quantitative easing its rationale to print money, doubling the dollar supply to 80 trillion. This helped put more money in American pockets, but it did not result in significant economic regeneration.

A declining or stagnant economy is only a part of the story. As a fading superpower, the US will be increasingly challenged by China and Russia for control over the oceans, space and cyberspace. The world, therefore, seems to be between orders, and it means this generation must find its goal. The arrangements that emerge will result in the shuffling of the existing world order.

At this critical juncture, the US needed a visionary at the helm who could carve a safe course out of the present turbulence. Instead, Trump as its president was a divisive and whimsical street fighter. After him, Joe Biden is a risk-averse president who is trying to set America on a regenerative course. His steady hand, it was said, would lead to a massive shift in international affairs.

It has indeed happened sooner than expected, but not in the fashion that the optimists were predicting. The 'America Only' approach in the messy US withdrawal from Afghanistan has left people wondering in disbelief. Is it the same America that had once held out a ready helping hand to the world? They add grimly that going by the current slide, the age of American domination may be over by 2035.

From Cowboy to Cowering Diplomacy

A clear sign that America is no longer the king of the global jungle would be the rupture of the economic system it had put in place for the world, and of which it was the presiding deity. The dollar as the symbol of American might may not remain the only reserve currency of the world, and the rules-based international order that emerged after the Second World War may no longer be the same.

But why blame Trump alone? A series of presidents prior to him have not inspired America to great heights either. His predecessor, Obama, has been criticized for his hesitations. In actual practice, he began the trend of the US becoming an island content with itself. He did not explicitly say so, but his disinterest and an ambivalent attitude ensured that the national mood in the US started to veer towards a reduced involvement in the struggles of the world.

This disinterest became obvious after the Russian invasion of Georgia in 2008. America did make the noise and protest, but in effect, its reaction was muted and low-key. Around this time, the programmes of military cooperation with Poland and the Czech Republic were also given up by the US to appease Kremlin. To the outside world, Obama's conciliatory approach appeared to reward Moscow's aggression.

Separately, Obama's messaging on Asia was giving contradictory signals. Though he had declared that American strategy should be geared toward Asia, the US allies were left wondering as to how reliable its commitment might be when facing the challenge posed by China. All this contributed to the dim view that observers took about his foreign policy. In a scathing indictment about him, *Time* noted, '(The US has) moved from the cowboy diplomacy of George W. Bush to the cowering diplomacy of Barack Obama—from unthoughtful hawk to self-pitying dud.'[4]

Eventually, history may be kinder in its judgment, but the assessment by some others before the end of Obama's presidential innings was not flattering: '...Obama, convinced of his "Solomonic wisdom and Spocky calm" will continue to wallow in self-pity—thinking of himself as the helpless prisoner of events—rather than make a decision about what to do.'[5]

The courage and the readiness to assert the American will was not in short supply once. Then America was decisive, and the considerations of morality in policy did not stymie it. Overall, in the first-half of the twentieth century, US military forces intervened in South America on more than 30 occasions to settle economic or territorial disputes on terms favourable to Americans. The list can go on to include its later wars in Iraq, etc., but the point is not the enumeration of the fights that the US got into over the last two centuries but to record the dividing line that it has drawn now. The once-agile US is in a ponderous mood today.

This combination that has alternated between bravado and indecision has been the confusing signal from the US leadership for some time. George Bush and Bill Clinton epitomized the two extremes in this respect. After them and Obama, the US needed a president who could sagely mix diplomacy and the threat of force to halt the growing disintegration of the world order. Some commentators, therefore, began asking questions about the direction that America should take, and to what strategic end. To that should be added the fundamental premise that the American Century started after the Second World War—that

America should lead a rules-based world order, in which global institutions will play a guiding role.

In his 2004 book, *The Choice: Global Domination or Global Leadership*, Zbigniew Brzezinski wonders on this note, 'Ultimately, the central policy question confronting America is "Hegemony for the sake of what?"'[6]

Had he asked the Bush administration's neocons who had driven America to a needless war in the Gulf, they would have responded, 'Hegemony, to control the world's energy resources.' But this was a limited and short-sighted objective. Over the years, America itself has become a major energy producer, and its priorities have undergone a change.

The response during Trump's tenure to the same question was self-centred. In his view, 'America First' was the solution to all ills. As a direct result of this new vision, the world became secondary to the project called 'America'.

Fortunately, this desire for American glory was not laced with nationalism. Were that to happen, it would make the world an even more dangerous place than it presently is. Still, the self-interest in slogans like 'America First' is damaging enough. Moreover, the effect of such a radical policy shift takes some time to become obvious. America may not be interested any longer in pursuing hegemony, but will the world let it retreat into a self-sufficient cocoon?

Ultimately, the answer to Brzezinski's question about 'hegemony' must be sought in the debris of the Second World War.

The global order devised in its aftermath had catapulted the US to the pole position, and the US had taken it upon itself to lead the world towards a stable, more prosperous environment. A rules-based world order was then built up with precisely these objectives in view. The question, therefore, that the doubters of today should answer is this: is the world stabilized and prosperous enough to be on autopilot?

A related issue is the vastly changed global picture since 1945.

To cite just two examples, in 1945, there were 51 member states in the UN. That number has nearly quadrupled to 193 now. Most new states lack resources, advanced technology, economic strength and military power, meaning thereby that one power or the other will muscle in to order their affairs in its fashion. Even more importantly, the technologies of this century are global not just in their distribution but also in their consequences. Therefore, the hegemony is no longer just military or economic in scope, it is also led by technological compulsions.

Disregarding all the evidence in favour of American engagement with the world, President Biden decided that America must retreat into its shell. The retreat of troops he ordered from Afghanistan was abrupt in operation, disastrous in consequence and universally viewed in shocked disbelief. There was a bleak candour and unblushing self-interest to Biden's decision, and a strange obstinacy to stick with it. If the desire to reduce military commitments abroad continues, Americans may not want to fight other countries' battles. But they would still want to prevent China and Russia from becoming regional and trans-regional hegemons. The US could conceivably try and make do with networks of missile launchers and drones, but they are unlikely, by themselves, to contain Chinese and Russian revisionism.

Unfortunately and puzzlingly for America, it may then dawn on it that the ungrateful world is no longer amenable to its will.

'Rambo Ran Away'

At stake now is a more contentious situation where the US is not the unchallenged power. In this emerging complex world, there will be events, like the Ukraine crisis, that pull the global system in new and sometimes contradictory directions.

Consequently, its priority of 'America First' does not rest well with its reduced leadership position or with the Russian aggressive behaviour or the economic and strategic revisionism of China. The contest for America, therefore, is as much ideological as practical.

Can it still try to shape a new global system based on shared interests or should it use its sovereign power primarily to entrench its own security? This fundamental question is at test now.

It may be early, but the first signs are that this strategic pause may be nudging the US towards a reduced global role. Trump had a prescription for how the US should do it. Instead of regarding the world as an arena of continuous competition, the US under Trump moved towards a largely transactional style of foreign policy. But the US needed to remember that 'transaction' requires two parties; and there is no guarantee that only America will end up being the winner in every transaction. If this untested phase was to continue, and if Biden, too, continues to treat America's allies as marginal to its interests, and China and Russia as future enemies, its relations with these powers will be increasingly perilous.

However, this isolationist approach bypasses one of the long-standing fundamentals of the American policy. It was the American belief that the continuation of international liberal order depends on the presence of a strong and active US in global affairs. In this fundamental concept lies another answer to Brzezinski's question: 'Hegemony for the sake of what?'

Except for an odd bump or two, US presidents, be they Republican or Democratic, have followed the policy that maintaining global order is the watchword. Whatever you do, don't rock the boat—this was their broad line to their foreign policy aides. It was grounded in the conviction that for a country to become a truly global leader, it has to assume responsibilities on a vast scale. And even now the size of the American military presence abroad is proof that responsibility requires engagement. It is fighting terrorist organizations in at least 14 countries, and in 2017, its special operations forces were deployed in 149 countries.

A consequence of military engagement on a nearly global scale was the increased military influence on American foreign policy.

All along, as America's military interventions increased,

its National Security Council (NSC) kept growing in size and influence. Steadily, it crowded out the diplomatic voices. The resulting militarization of US diplomacy received support in the White House. Over the years, the NSC has become a crisis-driven centre for foreign policy, which has repeatedly opted for rapid military solutions for deep diplomatic problems.

As a result, today's America is acutely conscious of the fact that its humiliations in some of the ventures abroad have exposed the quixotic nature of some of those decisions.

Whatever consternation this desire now to step back may cause within the US foreign policy establishment, and their internal resistance to it, is America's own affair. But strategic experts outside America are concerned over the likely ill effects of this policy abroad. For example, they worry that the US withdrawal from Afghanistan will ruthlessly condemn it to anarchy and possible fragmentation. They also point to the fact that by leaving Afghanistan, it abandoned a unique strategic space. After all, Afghanistan borders China, Iran, Pakistan and the former Soviet states of Stans. Moreover, if the US wishes to keep its army in Iraq to watch over Iran, it made equal sense to maintain the US military presence in Afghanistan to watch over China, Iran and Pakistan.

Still, even after abandoning Afghanistan, America will do well to recall some earlier chapters of history in the region.

In 1843, after he had subdued Sindh, General Charles Napier is credited to have sent a one-word telegram to London saying, 'Peccavi' (Latin for I have sinned, i.e. I have Sindh).[7] Aping him, in 1989, the CIA telegram from Islamabad confirming that the Soviet troops had pulled out of Afghanistan simply said, 'We Won.'[8] It is quite possible that after the last American soldier had left Afghanistan, the telegram by the ISI station chief in Kabul to his bosses in Islamabad may have unimaginatively read 'Rambo ran away.'

In an ironic twist, the wider world, which was otherwise

used to blaming the American dominance for its troubles, is now feeling uneasy, as if America's steadying hand has been withdrawn all too abruptly. This unease turned to concern from the time America was led by Trump, who seemed to be serious about frivolous things and frivolous about serious ones. Critics now accuse Biden of being guided by Obama's briefings and his own confusion about America's place in the world. It is America's good fortune that these shortcomings have not yet turned into disaster.

Life Is Not Fair

In 2018, the US outlined a shift in its National Defense Strategy: '… Inter-state strategic competition, not terrorism, is now the primary concern in U.S. national security'[9]

This policy shift makes inter-state strategic competition, primarily from China and Russia, not terrorism, the primary concern in US national security.

There is no doubt that their challenge has become a real matter of concern to the US, but it will be a mistake to discount the threat from terrorism. ISIS is not dead yet and the Taliban's successes in Afghanistan are proof that they are once again a potent force.

It is also true that the US has been engaged in fighting insurgents and minor powers like Iraq, Syria and the Taliban in Afghanistan for a long time now. The expenditure of billions of dollars annually in these engagements and the diversion of men and material there has meant a reduction in the availability of resources for important defence projects. As a result, the scaling up of the US's military capabilities has suffered. Cumulatively, this has led to a neglect of the main threat, which was from the two major powers.

In an alarming report, the US's National Defense Strategy Commission noted, 'If the United States had to fight Russia in a Baltic contingency or China in a war over Taiwan, Americans could face a decisive military defeat.'[10] This assessment is significant because up to the beginning of this millennium, it was thought that China did not pose a threat to America's vital security interests and so an aggressive approach against China would be offensive and unnecessary.

This soft approach towards China worked well so long as it remained relatively weak and preoccupied with internal developments. But with the transformation of China into a major power, the US–China relationship is being subjected to unprecedented strains.

The world is changing for America in many other ways, and howsoever much may America bemoan this shift, the reality of power is that life is not fair. When America was the single dominant player, its influence was the currency in global affairs. China and Russia are now cutting into that monopoly, and America is learning that to decline is to lose relative influence.

Many countries, in varying degrees, are turning to China just as in America's heyday they had pivoted to the US. For Australia, a close American ally for long, China now accounts for nearly 30 per cent of its exports. This is vastly more significant compared with only 5 per cent of its exports going to the US. Consequently, and despite the recent strains, Australians still talk of America as 'our ally' and China as 'our good friend'.

Some countries in Europe, like Greece and Hungary, have gone a step further. Having received considerable Chinese investment, they hesitate to endorse measures by the EU that could be viewed as anti-China. To give credit where it is due, China courts assiduously the countries it wishes to woo; it invites African leaders to large summits just the way it has started doing for the countries covered under the BRI. In contrast, America lost interest in Africa a few years after promising to keep it in sharp focus. To the outside observer, its relations with the countries in South America also seem fractious.

It is true that in the long term China may prove to be Shylockian in behaviour with the countries it promises to be generous to. It is equally true that far from being transactional, America can often be recklessly generous towards countries it decides are its allies. Yet, presently, China seems to be the preferred flavour in large parts of the world, even as America is a reminder to them of a former fling.

This diversion and the division of loyalties may continue. But secular trends alone are insufficient for predicting pre-eminence. History suggests that there can be unpredictable turns in national affairs that can take a country in an unexpected downward slide. Internal convulsions could cramp China's growth. Its deceptions and misinformation during the outbreak of Covid-19 have alienated much of the world, and this bitterness may outlast the virus by many years. However, till recently, China seemed to be on an ever-forward, ever-upward march in every respect.

Another area where the US has ceded ground is in its previous near-monopoly in soft power. From the 1960s to the 1980s, American soft power soared. From Hollywood movies to songs, jeans, food and even Marlboro cigarettes, 'Made in America' was the preferred brand in the world. America successfully created the impression of a country that was doing well domestically and enjoyed vitality in the wider world. The American soft power, more than anything else, was the straw that cracked the Soviet back. A lot has changed in the world since then. American soft power does not have the same irresistible pull nor is the US any longer a picture of its previous vitality.

Still, it is not a toothless giant. The US dollar is a powerful weapon that it can use to bring its allies and adversaries in line and conform to its wishes. Since foreign banks and institutions cannot avoid using it, America has been able to sanction and pressurize countries that for one reason or the other have fallen foul of it. These sanctions have worked best when they were supported and endorsed by multilateral institutions like the UNSC. But the US's new preference for independent salvos has weakened the effect of the dollar's force and the impact of sanctions.

So, if the US seems a shadow of its eminent past in ordering the global affairs, will Russia or China fill up the space vacated by America?

Russia is selectively increasing its footprint in countries like Syria and Iran. In fact, it has also symbolically sent its nuclear bombers to distant Venezuela in a potent signal to the US. But Beijing has not shown any clear intent for filling this vacuum entirely. China's ambitions may have taken it to different parts of the globe, grabbing strategic space for itself, but it has so far not shown the willingness to fight other people's battles. This may be because China's ambitions for the coming years are narrower.

In contrast, for the last seven decades, the US's grand strategy had revolved around maintaining its military, economic and political preponderance globally. Until recently, most Americans had acquiesced in this strategy. The complaint against the changed mood now is not about the rethink of American strategy but its abruptness and its intent of complete renunciation.

The other big flaw in the strategy of isolationism is the loss of precious strategic space that had, so far, worked in favour of the liberal order. Moreover, there was a tactical lacuna in this US approach to get away quickly. In their hurry to withdraw from Afghanistan and stay away from other people's battles, American policymakers announced their intention in advance. This deprived US negotiators of the bargaining power, putting them at a disadvantage. Still, American administrations, starting with Obama's, seem to have done exactly that. What, for instance, was the point of announcing a troop surge in Afghanistan if the Obama administration was simultaneously going to announce the date of their withdrawal?

The Taliban gleefully took note of the date of that withdrawal and sat it out patiently before resuming their operations with full force! As a result of such mistakes, the US let itself be led by the nose by Pakistan, whose proxies the Taliban are. Opportunism of this variety is a well-trod theme in geopolitics, one that Pakistan's military understands well.

This is not the only mistake that the US has made in recent times. Central Asian states, with a helping nudge from Russia, had hosted the US forces and allowed it to set up military bases soon after 9/11. Instead of consolidating its hold and aiming for a long stay, it began to focus its probing prism on the human rights abuses in these states. This alarmed the authoritarian regimes there, and thereafter it did not take long for the US to lose goodwill and vacate the bases.

Time for an Image Makeover?

A related mistake that the US often makes is the liberal use of sanctions. This is a double-edged weapon that should be used sparingly because while it hurts the offending state economically, it hurts America economically and politically as well. In fact, the damage to the American reputation among the people under sanctions lasts long after the sanctions have been lifted. At a practical level, too, sanctions can be effective if they are total and universal. On the other hand, if there are gaps, then those breaches make the sanctions less effective. This is what has happened in the case of the sanctions imposed against North Korea, where Russia and China stepped in to defy America. Yet, the US has used sanctions repeatedly.

A similar approach concerns Iran. America's desire for a regime change in Iran through sanctions is an illusion. Its desire to bring down Iran's oil exports to zero is bound to fail in the long term, just as it had failed earlier because Iran began to sneak in secret oil supplies to its neighbourhood. Among many other reasons, Saudi Arabia and the United Arab Emirates (UAE) cannot sustain higher production levels for long, and Iran's heavy oil, which many countries need for refined oil products, cannot be replaced by Saudi Light Crude. Moreover, Iran enjoys the support of Russia and China, and faces no organized opposition internally. It is nothing short of a fantasy to think that sanctions could get rid of its regime. Instead it might accelerate Shia–Sunni tensions, bringing the region closer to an armed clash.

The sanctions have not hurt at a bread-and-butter level too. So far, there have been 26 rounds of American sanctions on Iran. It has forced the exit of over a hundred corporations from Iran. More than 20 countries have ended all oil imports from Iran. But in the end, all it has resulted in is the loss of only $10 billion in revenue to the Iranian government!

Some critics maintain that it is because of this arbitrariness that America is losing friends abroad. The question then is: what else did America do wrong? Well, the list is long if viewed from an outsider's perspective. During the American Century, there were periods when America was supporting dictatorships and demolishing weak democrats. There were also phases when it crippled other economies by selling them costly projects. In the years stretching from the 1950s to nearly now, the overwhelming American image abroad has been that of an overbearing giant.

Still all is not lost, and power, like love, is resistant to reason. America still has the material wherewithal and an immense pool of human resources. It could easily re-emerge at the pole position. After all, as Churchill once said, 'You can always count on Americans to do the right thing—after they have tried everything else.'[11]

To do so, the US will have to make adjustments—starting with an image makeover to a more likeable version of itself. Moreover, it must learn to be generous all over again because grand strategies cannot be shaped on a shopkeeper's transactional ledger. It will also have to build up the capabilities of its friends, especially of those on China's periphery. The plain fact is that the US cannot defend its interests in Asia without support from its allies. But this is unlikely to happen in the transactional world where American representatives see in every meeting with a foreign leader an opportunity to drive a hard bargain in favour of selling some American product.

Let's turn back briefly to the question as to why America should pursue 'hegemony'. If a state can maintain itself as the only great power in the international system, it is theoretically possible to say that it will enjoy something very close to absolute security. But, history is proof that such monopolies do not last long. As Kissinger noted, 'Hegemonic empires almost automatically elicit universal resistance, which is why all such claimants have sooner or later exhausted themselves.'[12]

Sadly, America's foreign policy missteps have been many. It could have turned out differently though, and the world may have been a calmer place.

For instance, the desire for a world at peace with itself missed an opportunity during the Cold War. The mistaken belief that the Soviet Union was an existential enemy bent on America's destruction led to a costly arms race. It prevented the candid negotiations that could have ended the US–Soviet struggle in the 1950s. Instead, mutual suspicion led America to invest in a massive system of about 800 bases around the world.

There was a second chance for stability after the dissolution of the Soviet Union. It was vital at that stage to be sensitive to Russia's concerns. During the Cold War, no American president had considered Eastern Europe important enough to American security to risk a war with the Soviet Union. But with an enfeebled Russia, it was mistakenly assumed in the 1990s that the risk had vanished. During Clinton's presidency, the US moved to admit Poland, Hungary and the Czech Republic into the NATO. At that time, Kennan had warned the move would 'inflame the nationalistic, anti-Western and militaristic tendencies in Russian opinion.'[13] As a result, ever since 1991, periods of dialogue, progress and optimism in the relationship between Russia and the US have been followed by tense interludes, stand-offs and mutual criticism.

The American complaint is that Russia has always been an expansionist power. It will not give up anything and concede nothing. But that is not how it looks to the outside world. To the foreign observer, Russia is a mirror image of the US. Like America, it wants to have a veto on international issues. But the reality is more nuanced.

The legacy of the Cold War, the different world views and the shifting power dynamics create structural tensions that are more powerful than the inclinations of whoever happens to be occupying the White House or the Kremlin. The only chance of their being on the same side in the next big war is the American apprehension of the two-front war, and the Russian fear that sooner or later it will have to take on China all by itself.

Since all this is in the realm of uncertainty, how should we assess the success or otherwise of the present state of the American foreign policy? One measure of that is the effect it has on the US internally, as was suggested by Walter Lippmann in 1943. He wrote that the goal of American foreign policy was to serve as the 'shield of the republic'; its purpose was to shape an external environment that protects freedom and prosperity at home. If that is taken as a measure to determine foreign policy success, then the growing federal debt, stagnant income growth and degrading infrastructure mean that the US has not fared well.

A lot else is not going the way Americans would have wanted. Following the 2008 financial crisis, there were confident predictions that America would consolidate its leadership, China would remain inward-focused and Europe would grow more unified. Nothing of the sort happened.

But this time, post Covid-19, it will be different. The myth of America's global superiority that it could outsmart its enemies was laid bare even as it was laid low by the onslaught of the pandemic. The disease has finished off the post-Cold War period, a time of peace, prosperity and globalization. In this new phase, the US will have much to be humble about, and the world, more uncertain.

The liberal international order will become less liberal and less ordered. International institutions will weaken further. Nationally, the slide into nationalism or religious extremism will be a convenient option, and new technologies will solidify authoritarian control and challenge democratic governance.

At the larger, global level, the stability after the Second World War was a combination of globalization and the policy of containment. The two together in their own but different ways successfully ensured that the big power differences did not get out of hand. That era of confidence is past us. The domestic priorities will determine the external agenda to a far greater extent now. In this environment, the isolationist approach of the US will be ruinous as a policy and damaging for America's global gravitas.

But there is time still, and it does not take long for fortunes to shift. This change could easily take place over the next 10 or 15 years. The US's new strategic agenda could, therefore, include some of the following elements:

- Deepen ties with democratic governments,
- Make efforts to promote western unity,
- Enhance assistance on a fast-track mode, militarily and technologically, to some countries bordering China, and
- Find a way of reaching an accommodation with Russia.

This is not a tall order for a country the size of America, with its determination and vast resources. All that is required is a shift from isolation to selective engagement and cultivating the habit of being patient with those well-disposed to it.

More importantly, and as Alexis de Tocqueville noted, 'The greatness of America lies not in being more enlightened than any other nation, but rather in her ability to repair her faults.'[14]

6

INDIA'S LONG WAIT

My mind is in confusion because in thy words
I find contradictions. Tell me in truth therefore
by what path may I attain the Supreme.

—Bhagavad Gita (3:2)

When the acerbic V.S. Naipaul wrote about a 'million mutinies' in India, he may have exaggerated. Or, he may have impetuously opted to write the smart word rather than wait for the politically correct note to strike him. Yet, it must also be acknowledged that India is not an easy place to govern. It exasperates the most indulgent foreign observer with its contradictions and complexities. For its people, India's past is constantly the referral point, the standard by which they strive to guide its today and shape its tomorrow.

Since long, the idea of India has been plural and inclusive, making it a huge melting pot that absorbs every foreigner and every foreign idea that falls into it. Consequently, as a spiritual rainforest, it has, for long, teemed with religions and their mutations. Because of this fusion, India incorporates a greater variety of religions and sub-religions than any other country. The results are obvious in its daily life. It has a Sikh majority state in Punjab, three Christian majority states in Nagaland, Meghalaya and Mizoram, and two Muslim majority Union Territories in Lakshadweep, and Jammu and Kashmir (J&K). The idea of acceptance makes this possible.

But this diversity provoked Marx to wonder:

> A country (India) not only divided between Mohammedan and Hindu, but between tribe and tribe, between caste and caste; a society whose framework was based on a sort of equilibrium, resulting from general repulsion and constitutional exclusiveness between all its members. Such a country and such a society were they not the predestined prey of conquest?[1]

Marx may have come to this conclusion on the basis of repeated invasions and conquests of India in the last millennium. Besides, a country teeming with people is bound to have many fault lines. Today, it has the world's second-largest population, but you rarely hear of India's planners fretting too much about this growing mass and the difficulties of catering to that enormity. This vast population is divided into hundreds of ethnic groups speaking hundreds of languages. In a quaint fashion, the linguistic incomprehension of the other may be aiding the spirit of tolerance. Sometimes frowning foreigners fault this fatalistic acceptance for India's ills. Like Marx, they then remark in frustration that India's patchwork quilt has begun to fray at its political edges.

Governing this vast and diverse population has indeed been difficult for India's rulers from the beginning. But all along, Indian people have used the limited options available to them to their best advantage. As a colony, they could not put up a decisive fight against the greatest empire then in the world, so an accommodation of sorts was arrived at. The ruler was tolerated but not allowed to overwhelm the indigenous, as it had done in Latin America. Later, as a newborn state, India did not have the military means to ward off the two superpowers, so it opted for the safety of non-alignment.

On a somewhat similar but slightly cynical note, Kissinger feels that India employed methods that served its interests best:

> ...India had survived its turbulent history through an unusual subtlety in grasping and then manipulating the psychology of foreigners. The moral pretensions of Indian leaders seemed to me perfectly attuned to exploit the guilt complexes of a liberal, slightly socialist West; they were indispensable weapons for an independence movement that was physically weak and that used the ethical categories of the colonial power to paralyse it.[2]

Such myth-smudging apart, Kissinger overlooks the fact that Indians and the newly independent India did not have the luxury of time. In the older democracies of Europe, nation-building preceded democracy by almost 200 years. A principal instrument they used was war. But India uniquely used democracy for nation-building. In the process, it had to accommodate and make compromises. As a result, even its adoption of technology, at times, had to pass through the conservative filters of tradition.

Lee Kuan Yew, Singapore's first PM, barely hides his impatience when he remarks in his book *From Third World to First*:

> On my early visits in 1959 and 1962, when Nehru was in charge, I thought India showed promise of becoming a thriving society and a great power. By the late 1970s, I thought it would become a big military power because of its size but not an economically thriving one because of its stifling bureaucracy. It was sad to see the gradual rundown of the country, visible even in the Rashtrapati Bhavan (president's palace.) The crockery and cutlery were dreadful—at dinner one knife literally snapped in my hand and nearly bounced into my face.[3]

In a final verdict, he concludes, 'India is a nation of unfulfilled greatness. Its potential has lain fallow, underused.'[4]

Since he wrote that book, India has changed and not just in the quality of its cutlery! But there are still many miles to go. Meanwhile, Lee Kuan Yew's verdict keeps hurting because of its continuing validity.

For example, let's consider India's performance in exports. In 2020, the export of goods and services contributed about 18.7 per cent of India's GDP.[5] In contrast, exports made up over 36.4 per cent of South Korea's GDP.[6] Similarly, in 2006, when China was growing at nearly 13 per cent, the share of exports in GDP was more than 36 per cent.[7] For India to achieve double-digit growth, exports will have to be a crucial part of the strategy. But its current performance is short of that marker.

In 2017, India ranked a low 146th out of 190 economies on the World Bank's 'trading across borders' component of doing business, which measures the time and cost (excluding tariffs) associated with documentary and border compliance, and domestic transport procedures for trading goods. Indian exporters, on an average, took nearly four times the time taken by Chinese exporters to comply with border compliance requirements in 2017.[8]

With such a procedural web, is it any surprise that the share of India in total world merchandise exports was just 1.71 per cent in 2019?[9] This is a level it has more or less maintained since 2011. India says it plans to double its exports, though no date has been set for achieving that target. Let us assume that it will do so by 2025 or even by 2035.

But this promise to double exports requires work on a scale for which present conditions do not hold much promise. Existing exports are barely able to hold on to their market share, and unless innovative manufactured products are added to the basket, India will stay far short of what it is aiming for.

There are other challenges as well. A McKinsey report of April 2010 titled 'India's Urban Awakening' had predicted, 'India's urban population soaring from 340 million in 2008 to 590 million in

2030...at a speed unlike anything India has seen before. It took India nearly 40 years (between 1971 and 2008) for the urban population to rise by nearly 230 million. It will take only half the time to add the next 250 million.'[10]

The report also sets some benchmarks:

> ...to meet urban demand, the economy will have to build between 700 million and 900 million square meters of residential and commercial space a year. In transportation, India needs to build 350 to 400 kilometers of metros and subways every year, more than 20 times the capacity-building of this type that India has achieved in the past decade. In addition, between 19,000 and 25,000 kilometers of road lanes would need to be built every year...India needs to invest $1.2 trillion just in capital expenditure in its cities over the next 20 years.[11]

The alternative would be massive chaos.

To complete the list of critical domestic issues that India may face in the coming years, it must continue to make massive efforts to keep feeding its enormous population. A failed monsoon or an administrative misstep could spell disaster.

Moral Mirror

It is not just internally that India must multitask and wrestle with the daily odds just to stay where it is. Its external environment, too, is prickly. But regardless of how the foreign strategist views India, the writer, the poet and the curious foreigner have all been generally rapturous about it. Romain Rolland wrote, 'If there is one place on the face of earth where all the dreams of living men have found a home from the very earliest days...it is India.'[12]

This is ecstatic to hear, but at a more practical level, does India have a workable strategic plan beyond dreams? It is important because India's history is marked by foreign invasions.

As a Russian general of the nineteenth century put it, 'Of the 21 attempted invasions of India over the centuries from the north and the west, 18 were successful.'[13]

It may not have been with this background in view that the Pentagon asked the RAND Corporation in 1992 to comment on India's security strategy. The report prepared by RAND Corporation concluded, '…India did not have a cohesive strategy because its foreign policy since 1947 was loosely based around the teachings of Buddha and Gandhi.'[14]

Later, in 2006, the US government ordered another review of India's strategic culture. This report also pointed out the Buddhist and Gandhian moral foundation of Indian foreign policy. It went on to add that there was also the guiding political framework of Kautilya's *Arthashastra*.

The suggestion in both these reports was that India holds the moral mirror to the world. This must have puzzled the Americans, who are more comfortable living in a here and now materialistic age.

Critics also add that India interprets, rather uniquely, the rules of the global economic game, and, for too long, the Indian policy establishment has viewed economic growth as a substitute for grand strategy. The thinking has been that as the Indian economy grew, its weight would automatically resonate in the international system, and they expected India to be wooed then by major powers! Mulling over this logic, some critics have caustically wondered if India really needs to have a foreign policy strategy, a policy that could be pursued consistently and over the long term. Wouldn't bonhomie, bluster, a few hugs and the impression of a bouncing economy suffice?

Let us add to this list the hope that booming trade could give a boost to foreign relations. China's annual trade with India in 2021 amounted to $125 billion, compared with $28 billion with Pakistan. Turkey's trade with India stands at $8.6 billion against $1 billion with Pakistan. Malaysia–India trade at $14 billion is

14 times more than the $1 billion of goods and services Malaysia exchanges with Pakistan. Despite the enormous difference that these figures show, it is Pakistan that is the preferred flavour for China, Turkey and Malaysia.

The discerning offer yet another view of India's stumbles. According to Lee Kuan Yew, 'There were three reasons the world's largest democracy has not done better: central planning; the caste system; and "endless conflicts and wars with Pakistan."'[15]

Lee Kuan Yew's observation may offend the Indian reader, but years after it was written, it remains largely valid. Centrally dictated plans and their shoddy implementation continue to be a drag on India's growth. Otherwise, India's GDP, at under $3 trillion, should not have lagged so far behind China's $14 trillion.

Insofar as Lee Kuan Yew's lament about caste is concerned, it remains a social sore point, though not to the same degree as when he wrote about it. The modern and everyday life in India is no longer shackled as hopelessly to caste as it once was. India today is more carnivalesque in appearance and liberal in attitude. Though the caste system has not entirely been eliminated, development and mobility are regularly eroding its authority.

His third point about 'endless conflicts and wars with Pakistan' is as valid now as when it was written. Insofar as Pakistan is concerned, there is an existential disjuncture. As a result, no matter what India does, Pakistanis treat it with disdain and suspicion. The picture becomes even more complicated when others step in, as the US mistakenly and the UK mischievously have often tried to do.

From the early 1950s, the Pakistani leadership has been highlighting to the US and UK its strategic location close to the Soviet Union, China and the Persian Gulf. This was the peg on which it premised the quid pro quo for the American support to it vis-à-vis India. Ever since, this strategy has worked without any major disruption for Pakistan. This locational argument more or less established US's policy as far as the South Asian region was concerned.

Once this policy was set in motion, the distrust between the US and India kept growing. After the Chinese invasion of 1962 had exhausted India, the US saw in India's predicament an opportunity, and sent a joint US–UK delegation led by Averell Harriman, a prominent US diplomat. But as the then US ambassador to India, John Kenneth Galbraith, acknowledged, 'The Indians perceived that the United States was exploiting Nehru's post-war weakness to push India to the table. This left Nehru with only one option to reaffirm India's pride and power: refuse to budge on Kashmir.'[16]

That the US should have thought of exploiting India at its most vulnerable is bad enough, that it should have done so under a liberal and otherwise India-sympathetic President Kennedy was a warning. The element of suspicion introduced in the Indian mind in those early days continued to plague the relationship for long years. This despite the fact that the two largest democracies were made for each other—at least their people and the Indian media thought so.

Had the US not acted on British nudging, and if it had not fallen for the Pakistani allurement about its strategic location, the history of the region and perhaps of the world may have been different. And 9/11 may not have happened. The US need not have faltered into the Afghan trap, and India may not have slid into the Soviet embrace. But, as it turned out, India and the Soviet Union were drawn to each other by the circumstances and the lack of strategic alternative.

Almost from the beginning, the Soviet Union stood by India on the Kashmir issue; however, the overall relationship had its bumps. Analysts remember that the Soviet Union had tilted towards China during the 1962 Sino-Indian War, partly because it wanted China's support during the Cuban Missile Crisis.

The role of the Soviet Union after the 1965 Indo-Pakistan War is also a matter of some contest. The Soviet Union viewed it as an opportunity to act as a mediator in the dispute, thereby adding to its great power status in global view. It positioned itself as a neutral broker between India and Pakistan by hosting the summit at Tashkent. But it is said the Soviet Union leaned on PM Lal Bahadur Shastri to make concessions to Pakistan. Thereafter, it gave military assistance to Pakistan in 1968.

These were episodic aberrations in an otherwise close relationship in which there were more reasons for applause than any real need to raise eyebrows in enquiry.

In 1969, the Soviet Union proposed signing a bilateral treaty with India. The substance of this treaty of friendship would have gone against the spirit of non-alignment. So, stalling for time, India advised its ambassador to Moscow, D.P. Dhar, to continue to talk without any finality. This was cleverly bureaucratic but an irritating brief to any practitioner of diplomacy. It was this reality and the fast-developing tensions with Pakistan that made the Indian decision-makers rethink the wisdom of procrastination.

P.N. Haksar, the then secretary to the PM, wrote a note to Mrs Indira Gandhi spelling out his reason for relying on the Soviet Union rather than the US:

> ...The Soviet anxiety which is so manifest at present, may change overnight. We have, therefore, to calculate our self-interest and not proceed on the assumption that time is on our side and that we can dilly-dally at our pleasure... It would be a tragic mistake to work on this assumption... Situated as we are in South Asia, with our entire Northern borders covered by China and USSR, we have to live with this geographical configuration. America can give us little comfort in such a situation...[17]

The fact of American indifference generally to India's concerns and the escalating human tragedy in what was then East Pakistan tilted the balance in favour of a treaty with the Soviet Union. The formal treaty was signed in August 1971, and Soviet support was invaluable during the December 1971 war with Pakistan.

There continue to be many in Russia who consider the Indian relationship to be precious. Yet, in the last few years, India has let it slide. One indication that Russians are miffed about it is Putin's steadily briefer visits during Indo-Russian summits. These are among other signals that all is not well with India's relationship with Russia. Indo-Russian strategic linkages demand that these concerns should be quickly addressed, but India has been busy wooing the US. The US, on its part, expects that India should come up with a shopping list of arms every time a high-level visitor comes to Washington.

It becomes difficult to nurture such a relationship. But even if the US wishes to pursue a transactional relationship with India, it has to recognize the basic rule of transaction—that there are two parties to it. A relationship where only one side is expected to place high-value purchase orders cannot, by definition, be termed transactional. As a result, doubts crop up and questions are raised by the Indian analysts: why did the US act so generously by transferring high technology and making huge investments in China? Why did the US lavish money and arms on Pakistan? In stark contrast, why is it so mercantile and demanding when it comes to dealing with India?

Worry Lines

Closer home, and just across the once-insurmountable Himalayas, lies China. Over centuries, it had remained a distant, slightly mystifying neighbour. But this changed dramatically in 1950, as put succinctly by India's consul general in Lhasa, Sumal Sinha, in his message to New Delhi, 'The Chinese have entered Tibet; the Himalayas have ceased to exist.'[18]

Ever since, China has worried the Indian security establishment deeply. There are valid reasons for it, and the memories of the humiliating Indian defeat in 1962 continue to haunt the country. A top-secret CIA report of 2 March 1963 concluded that the

Chinese diplomatic effort was a five-year masterpiece of guile executed by Chou En-lai:

> Chou played on Nehru's Asian, anti-imperialistic mental attitude, his proclivity to temporize, and his sincere desire for an amicable Sino-Indian relationship. Chou's strategy was to avoid making explicit, in conversation and in communication with Nehru, any Chinese border claims... Chou sought to create an impression with Nehru that Beijing would accept the McMahon line but again his language was equivocal, and what was conceded with his left hand, he retrieved with his right.[19]

This CIA report also quotes a letter by the then PM of Burma, U Ba Swe, written to Jawaharlal Nehru. He had warned Nehru to be cautious with Chou in dealing with the border issue. But Nehru replied that Chou was 'an honourable man who could be trusted.'[20]

The Chinese doublespeak has continued over the years. Take, for instance, a much-quoted quip by the Chinese leader Deng Xiaoping. In 1988, he told the then PM Rajiv Gandhi that the next century will be Asia's century. But he left undefined as to who would be the dominant force in that Asian Century.

If India and China were friends, the shape of the region around them would have been vastly different—at peace with itself and vastly more developed, with flourishing regional trade. Together, they could have been a calming influence on the world. But they are not friends, and unlikely to be in the near future.

Far from being the dominant force in Asia that Deng had ambiguously spoken of, India may have to live with the emerging geopolitical reality that it will no longer dominate even its neighbourhood. This area that was so far its 'sphere of influence' in South Asia will now have to contend with the shadow of China's influence.

India and China have the largest territorial dispute in the

world, covering an area the size of North Korea. And they have two of the largest armies in the world, armed dangerously to the full. If the two lurch into conflict, the consequences will be terrifying. But India's military objective against China isn't offense. It is deterrence and defence. Sadly, it does not remove the threat; rather, it lures India into taking false steps, like agreeing in 2021 to a disengagement of troops in Ladakh that placed it at a disadvantage.

Most assessments, including those by Indian strategic experts, assert that the disparity between the two is so large that India cannot counter China's military power by itself. On the whole, there is serious and growing asymmetry between India and China. To begin with, let's compare their geographical size. China's landmass stretches over 9.6 million sq. km, dwarfing India's 3.29 million sq. km by a factor of three. It leads India in all other respects—from military and technological to economic; from efficacy of governance to social discipline; from assertive self-confidence to amoral pursuit of goals. India faces negative asymmetries on all these issues. If effective diplomacy is the art of optimizing resources to one's benefit, then India has miles to go before it can come anywhere close to what China has achieved already. Despite this negative asymmetry, India can make up for this handicap through nimble diplomacy and by biding its time.

Strategic thinkers like Kautilya and Sun Tzu have recommended that the weaker side in any such relationship should never engage in unequal engagements but pick those it believes it can either win or derive benefit from. It should husband resources to choose the time and place for the engagement that enhances one's strength while nibbling away at the adversary's.

However, the road ahead might test India at multiple levels and in many ways. The situation looks bleak already. There is criticism that India has not learnt from its blunders at the negotiating table. Its soldiers won the strategically vital Haji Pir Pass in the 1965 war with Pakistan. Yet, Shastri agreed to return this territory at the talks with Ayub Khan in Tashkent. Mrs Gandhi was far more hard-nosed than Shastri. Yet, she, too, conceded to Zulfikar Ali Bhutto at Shimla what should have been kept as negotiating reserve.

Recently, history repeated itself to India's disadvantage, yet again. Indian soldiers succeeded in neutralizing the territorial gains made by China in Ladakh in 2020, by moving into the heights overlooking those areas. But for reasons shrouded in mystery, India agreed to pull back forces from its territory in Kailash heights, leaving the area open for a quick grab by China at a later date. To make matters worse, after negating India's advantage, China refuses to withdraw from about 1,000 sq. km of territory it has captured in the region.[21]

It is against this background that critics assert India's conception of policy may sound apt but it falters in implementation. This has, for long, been the world's complaint against India—that it talks too loftily. Moreover, smaller South Asian states are increasingly playing smart games to hedge between China and India. They obtain high levels of economic and military assistance from China, forcing India to offer them increased aid as well. But the amount of Indian economic and infrastructure aid, and the speed of its execution, is nowhere near China's.

Worse still is the fact that the earlier adulation for a democratic India in comparison with autocratic China has now been replaced by practical considerations. The cheers for being a vibrant, even if somewhat chaotic, democracy have been replaced by the many disappointments with India's performance.

At a time when China's plans span decades, India is struggling to look beyond its next election. To the external observer, the Indian government seems to be constantly struggling with domestic crises, leaving it little energy for long-term strategic planning. India also appears more polarized than ever before, and the trust in its governance model is at an all-time low.

On the wider global front, India has sometimes been told that in articulation of its policies, it veers between being preachy and moralistic. More damagingly, and especially in recent years, the perception has gained ground that India is conducting foreign policy without many instruments at its disposal. And India's neighbours think it will somehow reconcile these contradictions in its mind without actually doing anything.

The world around India is impatient with stasis because it is changing at a rapid pace. Even the smallest of countries around it are no longer obligingly compliant as they once were. They see in China a convenient trump card to flaunt in India's face.

More worryingly for India, its vulnerabilities have increased steadily even on the security front. This episode about India's past is illustrative:

> Oleg Kalugin, who in 1973 became the youngest general in the FCD, remembers India as…'a model of KGB infiltration…' Kalugnin recalls one occasion when Andropov personally turned down an offer from an Indian minister to provide information in return for $50,000 on the grounds that the KGB was already well supplied with material from the Indian Foreign and Defence Ministries: '…It seemed like the entire country was for sale; KGB—and the CIA—had deeply penetrated the Indian government. After a while neither side entrusted sensitive information to the Indians, realizing their enemy would know all about it the next day.'[22]

The foreign hand in the Indian bag of secrets was manifold like that of the mythical Goddess; American, Soviet and Pakistani spy agencies were merrily dipping into it. Now China is a formidable new addition to this list. It can also penetrate, disrupt and disable India's power, telecom, financial and even security establishments. This is a reality that India is struggling to find a counter to, but its response, so far, has been knee-jerk, and every time it thinks it has found a counter to a security challenge, a fresh one crops up.

India's relationship with Pakistan is trickier still. Despite its avowals that its foreign policy is no longer cramped by one country, India's worry lines till recently were largely Pakistan-centric. And its dilemma in dealing with Pakistan continues to be along the long-familiar lines. Stumped by the imponderables of a flare-up, it has invariably opted for no action or limited action. Though after the surgical strikes in 2016, PM Narendra Modi has pursued what could be called a strategy of 'deterrence through uncertainty'.

If one lives in a dangerous neighbourhood, one must be prepared to protect oneself from troublemakers rather than relying on someone else to do so. This rule applies as much to societies as to countries. But India wishes to act like an exception to this rule. It has invariably looked to others to cajole and try to discipline Pakistan on its behalf. This strategy shows weakness and leaves India vulnerable to pressure by both the country it has turned to for intercession and by Pakistan as well.

Yet, successive Indian leaders have chosen to repeat the mistakes of their predecessors. As a result, India has been short-changed by the brokers it turned to—from the UK to the Soviet Union to the US. Only once, during the Kargil crisis, Clinton truly stood by us. In more recent times, during the Balakot crisis, we even turned to China. Having tried the big powers, India then turned to what can most generously be described as mid-rank powers—Saudi Arabia and the UAE. Why not, the optimist would argue, what is the harm in trying?[23]

Half-Front War

Unfortunately, we have been trying whimsically and experimenting with the national destiny far too often over the years. Along the way, arbitrariness has crept into India's policymaking, institutions have decayed and the economy's structural deficiencies have worsened. Animal spirits have been sucked out of all but a handful of firms. The government compounded this pain by handling the Covid-19 pandemic with the same inept authoritarianism that had come to define its approach on economic, political and social issues.

As a result, unlike any other period in living memory, 2020–21 was memorable for all the wrong reasons. It was a bewildering time that tested the nerves of the people of the country to the extreme. People, especially those who had to walk back hundreds of miles to their homes, tried desperately to make sense of their woes. At the national level, India faced public health, economic and strategic challenges that few could have imagined possible.

Internally, it is also on the brink of a worrying phase, which, if unchecked, could turn into a half-front war. This can be crippling and sometimes more telling in its blows than the casualties of war. India's half-front is expanding exponentially through divisive narratives and the rising feeling of persecution among the minorities. Such feelings of exclusion eventually form the substance of a resistance. Since many wars start with the setting off of a spark on the half-front, strategic prudence demands that corrective action should be taken well in time before the internal poison has the time to ripen and spread over the national body.

India's chaotic democracy has, sadly, produced a class of politicians who are adept at winning power but irresponsible in using it. Sometimes it strains belief that despite all this, Indians should be so patient and forgiving of all the ills of their government. But the young of the country are tired of the old idioms of patience, and their inaction may not forever remain valid. It is from among them that heroes might emerge, just as they had emerged to wrench freedom from the colonial grip.

At its present juncture, India is unhappy and is in need of heroes. It also needs them quickly because time is running out, and India finds itself virtually friendless in the world. There is no longer the assurance of a 1971-type of treaty with the Soviet Union to turn to in the time of need. The US and the Quadrilateral

Security Dialogue (QUAD), both are a faint glimmer, but that's just about it. As it limps towards 2035, this largely friendless India faces the prospect that, at least in the initial stages, it may have to fight a two-front war (with China and Pakistan) all by itself.

7

PAKISTAN: THE PUPPETEER

They torture their soul with insatiable desires and full of deceit, insolence, and pride, they hold fast their dark ideas, and they carry on their impure work.

—Bhagavad Gita (16:10)

Pre-Socratic Greek philosopher Democritus had deliberately blinded himself because his eyes interfered with total concentration on his thoughts. Pakistan, too, is single-minded in its objective. It is blind to all other aspects of nation-building because it wants to concentrate on the single issue of proxy war with India. Through it, Pakistan hopes to grab the territory it covets in Kashmir.

Its other great lament is its smaller size: why is it spread only over 800,000 sq. km when its rival, India, occupies over 3.29 million sq. km of South Asia? It has wallowed in self-pity ever since its unexpected birth in 1947, but it has never taken a pause to enquire whether its birth was legitimate.

The doubt about legitimacy is its third great lament because it lacks the past that provides a country the sense of belonging, a reference point to take lessons from. Accordingly, Pakistan is often called a country of sighs and regrets, one that is still wondering if it should have come into being. Consequently, for Pakistan, history is constantly starting, stopping and restarting. When

General Mohammad Zia-ul-Haq was alive, Pakistani wisdom maintained that he was the greatest man alive. After he died, history began again, and Pakistani text books were rewritten. Now, in a new claim, it is being asserted that after Mohammad Ali Jinnah, Imran Khan is the greatest Pakistani ever!

The reference to 'ever' should not take them very far in history, but if wishes could materialize, then Pakistan would want to roll back time to where history started for India. Pakistan's leaders feed their people the illusion that the wonder that was India was actually them; and to those who doubt, they point to Mohenjo-daro and Harappa as evidence. But in this Janus-like aspect, Pakistan looks back at a chimera, even as its future seems economically precarious and its standing in the world little short of a feared aberration.

Economically, since the 1960s, Pakistan has just about managed to keep its head above water. Politically, over the years, Pakistan has been slowly calcifying under different types of authoritarian regimes, elected or otherwise. It will, however, remain safe from outright collapse because Pakistan has convinced the West, China and its Arab allies that its strategic location benefits them. In return for that nebulous promise, Pakistan successfully obtains from them regular infusions of financial aid.

Long after he had given up office, former PM Manmohan Singh recalled for my friend his experience of dealing with Pakistan. The subject turned to Kashmir and the possibility of an acceptable solution. Dr Singh claimed that he was close to reaching an agreement with Pervez Musharraf. When my friend asked him if the army was with Musharraf, Dr Singh said this was the exact question that he had asked Musharraf, and he had replied, 'I am the army chief. The army is solidly behind me.'

The issue for an outsider is not whether the generals in Pakistan are unanimously behind their chief—that is the Pakistani army's internal affair. The question that a foreign leader should ask is this: is the Pakistani leader, or the army chief, levelling with me? Can I trust his word?

Carlotta Gall provides a clue to the issue in her book *The Wrong Enemy: America in Afghanistan 2001–2014*:

> A few days after 9/11, Musharraf invited several political analysts to a meeting, among them the retired lieutenant general Talat Masood...Masood told the General that he should cease support for the Taliban and all militant groups including the Pakistani ones that operated in Kashmir. 'Yes, I think we should stop supporting the Taliban but we will continue supporting the jihadis in Kashmir,' Musharraf told him.[1]

These twin obsessions of Afghanistan and Kashmir will not let Pakistan become a state content with itself and with what it has. In almost every conversation that a Pakistani leader or a general has with a foreign leader, the subject of Kashmir is brought up like a mantra, in the belief that this repetition boosts Pakistan's claim.

In October 2010, in the White House, Pakistan's army chief, General Ashfaq Parvez Kayani, handed over to President Obama a 15-page paper that he claimed to have written himself. While the paper was about Afghanistan and the Pakistan–America cooperation in stabilizing the country, a major point in it concerned India: 'We will require your help in settling Kashmir and other strategic problems between Pakistan and India.' His recommendation on Afghanistan was, 'They beat the Russians, they beat the British, they are beating you.'[2] In essence, it meant that Pakistan was in a position to end the imbroglio that the US found itself in.

Kayani had a point there because America's frustrations in defeating the Taliban in Afghanistan could be traced back in their entirety to the shelter and support that Pakistan provided the Taliban. Three months after 9/11, and a couple of weeks after being defeated by American forces in Afghanistan, the ISI was plotting a grim chapter against the West. In December 2001, the Taliban leadership assembled in Peshawar in a meeting to determine the future course of war. This was happening despite Pakistani avowal of support in America's war against terror. Gall describes it thus in her book, 'Discussion focused on how to confront the American military in Afghanistan and their Afghan partners. The Taliban leaders divided Afghanistan into separate areas of operations, assigning command of each geographical region to different men who would direct an insurgency. The plan…was to "trip up America." The Taliban comeback was underway.'[3]

All this while, Pakistan was putting up a friendly face to the US. At first, in the immediate post-9/11 anger, Americans were firm as they presented their seven demands of cooperation from Musharraf via their newly appointed ambassador to Pakistan, Wendy Chamberlin. Just two days after 9/11, on 13 September 2001, she read out from the list American demands and asked, 'Are you with us or against us?'[4]

Musharraf nodded grimly and assured Chamberlin that Pakistan was with the US. But he did not give her the categorical assurance that she sought on the issue of her demands. He said he needed to consult his commanders and the cabinet before making a commitment.

Though Musharraf was the army dictator, he still needed to take the nine three-star generals along. Several of them were opposed to the idea of abandoning the Taliban and to side with the US as it prepared to attack a fellow Muslim country. But as Musharraf was to rationalize later, 'We were on the borderline of being…declared a terrorist state—in that situation what will happen to the Kashmir cause?' Two days later, when they met again to discuss the issue in greater detail, Musharraf made it clear that 'terrorism in Kashmir should not be equated with that in Afghanistan.'[5] Eventually, Pakistan wasn't with the US on Afghanistan either. Its immediate assurance of being with the US after 9/11 was tactical rather than absolute.

ISI's Diabolical Ambitions

George Bush is said to have remarked, 'In almost every conversation we had, Musharraf accused India of wrongdoing.'[6] If this was just an irritating habit, it could have been dismissed as a petty nuisance. But it is much more—it is a successful tactic that relentlessly keeps India on the back foot via messages of restraint and concession from international interlocutors.

These complaints also ensure that Pakistan comes out of every meeting with the US after squeezing out of it another monetary infusion or arms aid. It is not only at the leadership level that Pakistanis relentlessly keep up this pressure, they do so at the operational level as well. ISI as an institution is well-practised at manipulating the CIA and the Taliban simultaneously. A former Afghan ambassador, Javid Ahmad, spells out ISI's objective in Afghanistan as diabolical in scope and frightening in its detail:

> (ISI) operates under a philosophy that it needs enemies to remain relevant—and in control. This paranoia has allowed the service to manufacture pet militant groups and imaginary threats to drive its motives. To do so, the service allegedly maintains a roster of nearly one hundred thousand militant fighters at its discretion…ISI support networks (in Afghanistan) have been designed to break Afghanistan into pieces and then remold it into a pliant state. The objective is to complicate Afghanistan's security landscape and drive its political climate into an uncharted constitutional territory…[7]

Ahmad's is not the only voice narrating the reality as it is. Americans dealing with Pakistan have repeatedly expressed their mixed feelings of frustration and helplessness. David Kilcullen, the unconventional warfare specialist advising Condoleezza Rice, on a tour to Afghanistan and Pakistan in 2008 found that:

> The Taliban clearly had professional help…Their indirect

> fire from mortars and rockets had become more accurate. They had acquired heavy sniper weapons and optics... the Taliban forces operated a rotation system—training in Pakistan, field deployment, and then rest and recuperation back in Pakistan. Pakistan Army and Frontier Corps troops along the Pakistani border were firing on American border posts to provide covering fire for the Taliban to infiltrate into Afghanistan and return—the same tactics Pakistani forces employed for Kashmiri militants along the Line of Control.[8]

That was in 2008. Since then, the Pakistani army had perfected the technique, its soldiers were embedded in every major battle where the Taliban were engaged. In one instance, in August 2018, hundreds of Pakistani army's Frontier Corps men were said to have participated in the battle with Afghan and US troops for the control of the area around Ghazni. As many as 120 dead bodies of these soldiers arrived back in Pakistan for burial.

As the Bush term was coming to an end in 2009, its South Asia experts were closing their engagement with Pakistan as a dispirited lot. For them, the Mumbai terror attack was the last straw in a seven-year-old journey that began with counterterrorism engagement leading to disillusionment. As another advisor to Rice, Eliot Cohen, concluded, '...in some ways we were actually fighting the ISI.'[9]

In his last visit to Afghanistan, Bush gave a farewell hug to Hamid Karzai and conceded, 'About the ISI, you were right.'[10]

Bush was echoing what every Central Asian leader had been telling the US—that it was chasing shadows in Afghanistan. It was trimming the branches of terror there, whereas the roots of terror were located in Pakistan, where they kept sprouting more branches at will.

But the American political and military leaders were unable and unwilling to acknowledge the obvious. In August 2009, the US ambassador to Afghanistan, Karl Eikenberry, and commander of the US and NATO forces in Afghanistan, General Stanley McChrystal, met Karzai to brief him about the general's assessment of the war. At the end of the PowerPoint presentation, Karzai looked suitably impressed with its sophistication, but when asked to comment on the substance of its conclusion, he focused first on the term 'insurgency' used in McChryrstal's presentation before remarking bluntly, 'This is not an insurgency. An insurgency suggests…there are citizens of a country fighting against their government because they think the government is illegitimate… This is no insurgency. This is a problem of international terrorism and we, the Afghan Government and the US, are allies in the battle against terrorism.'[11]

Karzai, like many other Afghan leaders, believed that the essential issue was the reluctance of the US to confront the ISI and Pakistan. And, all along, sharply different lenses have defined the objectives of the US and Pakistan. For Washington, it is all about how Pakistan can help US efforts in Afghanistan. For Islamabad, it is all about minimizing the threat of India, though it knows that India is a friend, not a threat, to the US.

Finally, after 20 years of living in the shadow of Pakistani deceit, US moaned in defeat in Afghanistan. Pakistan, which had been exulting in unending supply of US arms and dollars over the last two decades, has reason to celebrate.

If Pakistan is relentless in pursuing its agenda abroad, it is ruthless in stamping out threats to its integrity. And the threats are many because Pakistan is a fragile state lashed by many mutinies. On top of this, if Afghanistan descends further into chaos, Pakistan will be seriously buffeted.

A Steep Price

In 2009, Pakistan was in a panic mode. Terror had finally struck home. After 18 months of fighting, beheadings and suicide bombings, 850 people were dead and more than 100,000 had fled the frontier areas of Pakistan. By April, the Taliban had achieved victory after fighting the Pakistani army to a standstill in Swat Valley. Pakistani Taliban along with Uzbek volunteers had taken Buner, just a hundred miles short of Islamabad. Once in control there, they did not lose any time to enforce strict Sharia laws. The threat that the advancing Taliban posed to Islamabad was grave enough for the Secretary of State Hillary Clinton to warn: 'I think that we cannot underscore the seriousness of the existential threat posed to the state of Pakistan by the continuing advances… of (the Taliban)…'[12]

At that point, General Kayani turned in desperation to the Americans because he had only five airworthy Mi-17 helicopters to fight the terrorists. The US was quick to respond—it helped Pakistan in multiple ways during this battle. Its drones circled overhead all day and night, killing thousands of Al-Qaeda and Taliban militants, and many civilians as well in collateral damage. Thanks to American efforts, Pakistan was able to escape disaster, but that did not dilute its focus on Afghanistan. ISI's campaign against the American forces continued as before.

Since then, Pakistan has systematically eliminated a large number of terrorists inimical to it, but extremist ideologies remain prevalent in the country. School textbooks, the sermons by religious leaders and the Constitution, which contains a clause designating Ahmadis as non-Muslims, are all signs of a society rife with hostile views about religious minorities, India and the West.

Its people are paying a steep price for the extremist path that Pakistan has chosen as a way of settling scores. A comparison with Bangladesh illustrates the point well. In 1951, East Pakistan's population was 42 million, while West Pakistan's was 33.7 million. Now Bangladesh has far fewer people than Pakistan; 165 million versus 220 million. Bangladesh's exports were next to nothing in 1971. They shot up to $35.8 billion in 2018. In comparison, Pakistan lags behind at $24.8 billion.[13]

This need not have been so. Till the late 1960s, Pakistan was a leading economy in Asia. Its domestic priorities reflected its developmental ambitions. Thus, during the 1970s, the real growth rate of development expenditure was 21 per cent per annum and the growth rate of defence expenditure was 2 per cent. But its priorities began to change by the mid-1970s, indicative of its drift towards becoming a security state. By the 1980s, the growth rate of development expenditure had dived sevenfold to 3 per cent and the growth rate of defence expenditure rose to 9 per cent!

The downward trend in developmental expenditure continued. As a percentage of the GDP, it stood at 1.8 per cent in 2018–19. Expenditure on education was 2.3 per cent of the GDP in 2019, which declined to 1.5 per cent in 2020. Its defence budget, however, was unaffected by the delicate state of Pakistan's economy. In 2019, military expenditure in Pakistan amounted to about 4 per cent of the GDP. In fact, the actual figure will be higher still because pensions and some other military-related expenditure are not reflected under the defence head.

While it will somehow manage to keep its army in the style and luxury that it has been used to, Pakistan will find it increasingly hard to juggle its financial figures. It will, in addition, have to cater some extra money for the Taliban government in Afghanistan. On the other hand, its earlier providers of vast financial aid, like the US and Saudi Arabia, have begun to ask questions. The IMF, too, is more rigorous now when Pakistan turns to it for yet another instalment of financial aid.

The reality is that the China–Pakistan Economic Corridor (CPEC) project with China hasn't been beneficial to Pakistan's economy and also beginning to add strains to its budget. Almost $20 billion in projects have been completed or are under construction. But rather than transforming Pakistan's economy, CPEC has worsened the country's pre-existing condition—perpetual economic disequilibrium fuelled by consumption-driven growth. On top of that, the time for repaying the high-interest loan has started.

However, there has been a significant, but less remarked,

change in Pakistan. While feudal Pakistan is still a major political factor, the growing middle class is a fact of everyday life. Its diaspora of doctors, scientists, academics and other professionals have become an increasingly important part of the global community. As a state, Pakistan has close religious, cultural and economic ties with other Muslim states like Turkey and Saudi Arabia. At a strategic level, it is China's twin. While Pakistan is not one of the principal global players, its network of relationships can be of some strategic benefit to any of the great powers.

Pakistan is presently engaged in an image makeover, where it is trying to present itself as a liberal state interested largely in economic development. But an image cannot be better than the original. The original remains largely the same as Jinnah had described it—a 'moth-eaten Pakistan'.

More Illusory Rabbits

Instead of a course correction, Pakistan shows no signs of actually veering off its tested path. Rather than follow a developmental agenda, Pakistan's external linkages continue to be governed by the muscular dimension and religion.

More than any other country, Saudi Arabia still influences Pakistan's body politic. WikiLeaks have quoted Adel Al-Jubeir, a former Saudi ambassador to the US, as saying, 'We in Saudi Arabia are not observers in Pakistan, we are participants.'[14]

Its relationship with China is equally deep. Since the mid-1960s, China has been strengthening Pakistan militarily to keep India under pressure. Over the years, China has been selling military hardware, nuclear weapons technology, warships, aircraft and missiles to Pakistan. Some reports suggest that it has also begun helping Pakistan develop aerospace capability. The establishment inside Pakistan of satellite stations linked to China's BeiDou Navigation Satellite System ensures that the avionics, guidance systems, etc., of Pakistan's military are tied to

Chinese systems. After the establishment of Gwadar as a naval base, it now plans to use Pakistan as the outpost for its extended global maritime reach. The CPEC is also an important part of this strategic design. As a result, their relations are graduating from all-weather cooperative partnership to one where Beijing is increasingly integrating Pakistan into its military system as a part of its global ambitions.

But military capability is not a substitute for good governance. On this score, Pakistan has been particularly deficient because even in the years that it was not under direct military rule, its civilian leadership was operating to the army's wishes. Since the army requires active support of groups like the Jaish-e-Mohammed (JeM) and Lashkar-e-Taiba (LeT) for its operations abroad, that synergy reflects in domestic affairs as well. And therein lies the contradiction because Pakistan's so-far close connection with Washington intensifies radical nationalist and Islamic fundamentalist opposition to this relationship. There is another growing wrinkle in their relationship. The US has, for long, given billions of dollars in direct and indirect assistance to Pakistan. Now the US faces the unpleasant prospect of a Pakistani backlash as it tightens its purse strings.

Pakistan's ties with the US or for that matter its so-far close bond with Saudi Arabia are not the only relationships undergoing a stress test. It could well extend to its other allies. For the moment, all seems to be going well in Pakistan's relationship with China, but there are risks that loom there as well. China's harsh treatment of its Muslim minority, particularly in Xinjiang, bothers Pakistan because of the linkages that the Chinese Uyghurs have developed with Pakistani extremist groups over the years. Moreover, China will find it difficult to be endlessly generous financially with Pakistan. While neither of these are a major concern yet, the potential for misunderstandings is significant.

This list would be incomplete without a speculative peep into Pakistan's connection with Afghanistan in the days ahead.

After the Taliban regime was re-established in Afghanistan, Pakistan has been intimately involved in managing its affairs. As this pattern holds, there will be expectation on the Taliban side that Pakistan will continuously provide it with financial aid. If it is unable to provide the economic support to the Taliban government, the result would be a fractious and incidence-based relationship. Besides, Pakistan hosts nearly two million Afghan refugees who may be reluctant to relocate to an uncertain situation in Afghanistan to start life all over again.

As for the ISI, even as it gloats while the Taliban move steadily to settle again in Kabul, it will have to reassign the nearly 100,000 terrorist fighters that it had at its discretion in Afghanistan. Kashmir could well be the next station of their operations.

The larger issue, however, remains the path that Pakistan might choose to follow in the coming years. Islam and the army, both in their separate ways, seem to be holding Pakistan together. Yet, they are also responsible for its divisions. If, as has been the case so far, it continues to repose faith in the army-extremist combine, then the prognosis for it and the region is bleak.

Message for India: 'Lay off and Stay off'

The leadership in India will, once more, mull over the dilemma that Nehru had pondered over in December 1947. This time, the struggle over the next step will be more complex because now Pakistan is equipped with a range of nuclear options, and this time a war with Pakistan could mean a long-awaited opportunity for China to join in and make it a two-front ordeal for India. Therefore, the odds that stayed Nehru's hand in 1947 were relatively minor compared to the formidable challenge that Pakistan has now become for India.

Back then, Nehru wrote:

> Are we to allow Pakistan to continue to train new armies for invasion and allow its territory to be used as a base for these attacks? The obvious course is to strike at these concentrations and lines of communications in Pakistan territory. From a military point of view this would be the most effective step. We have refrained from taking it because of political considerations. We shall have to reconsider this position because a continuation of the present situation is intolerable.…This involves a risk of war with Pakistan. We wish to avoid war, but it is merely deluding ourselves to imagine that we are avoiding war…[15]

After bleeding a million bodies, the blade of Partition had barely taken a pause when Pakistan invaded Kashmir. Therefore, Nehru must have written this note in deep anguish. But he avoided a larger war, hoping that peace and amity would prevail after the swords of Partition had been sheathed. Alas, it was not to be, and Pakistan kept perfecting its policy of inflicting a thousand cuts on India. It was a low-cost, low-risk, high-returns strategy that has worked well for it. There is little reason to believe that Pakistan will abandon it as a policy.

On its part, India, despite an occasional strike against terror targets in Pakistan, has not veered much off the Nehruvian line. Except for once, in 1971, its response had the uniformity of the timid. Some also ascribe this to the conviction of every new Indian PM that he would be able to do what his predecessor(s) failed to achieve in relations with Pakistan.

But it is not the leadership alone that has faltered repeatedly with a Robert the Bruce-type approach of trying again and yet again. Some Indian commentators, based on their understanding of Pakistan, also lead the chorus in its support. For instance, a mediaperson from *The Hindu* wrote laudingly in favour of backchannel talks on the basis of inane tittle-tattle like this—that a Pakistani backchannel representative knocked at the hotel room of his Indian counterpart to discuss a point that had happened to strike him at the midnight hour, or that the Pakistani government allowed the Indian negotiator's special aircraft to be parked next to their president's aircraft.[16]

The Modi government, too, has repeatedly tried to reach out to Pakistan, including through the backchannel, but its efforts have not resulted in any remarkable breakthrough. However, there is a difference this time because Modi can shift policy suddenly and dramatically. As the US's National Intelligence report for 2021 suggests, although a general war between India and Pakistan is unlikely, crises between the two are likely to become more intense, risking an escalatory cycle. 'Under the leadership of Prime Minister Narendra Modi, India is more likely than in the past to respond with military force to perceived or real Pakistani provocations...'[17]

Despite this categorical assertion, it will be unwise to rule out the possibility of a war. Yet, the fact of living dangerously and the feeling of being balanced on a razor's edge have sharpened Pakistan's instinct for survival. It has repeatedly used its wits to successfully wriggle out of difficult situations. Witness, for example, this exchange between Musharraf and an agitated Chamberlin a few days after the 9/11 terrorist attack:

> Musharraf emphasized his concern that the longer any military campaign went on, the greater was the possibility of negative feelings. A quick action and extraction of U.S. troops was in both countries' interests... 'We're compromising a hell of a lot (for you). This will undermine my personal standing.' As for India, 'Tell the Indians to lay off and stay off,' was the blunt message he wanted conveyed to New Delhi.[18]

Had he still been the president of Pakistan, Musharraf may have been worried about the internal state of Pakistan and its economy, but he would have had considerable reason for satisfaction that most of what he told Chamberlin had come true. Americans remained stuck in the Afghan swamp for no good reason; Pakistan and the US are still trying to find a way to work together; and Indians have been pushed off the Afghan map. But he would have also had reason to wonder: how long can Pakistan keep pulling illusory rabbits out of its bag? How long, indeed, can it keep living by its wits?

8

AFGHANISTAN: THE RETURN OF THE TALIBAN

What power is it, Krishna, that drives man to act sinfully…

—Bhagavad Gita (3:36)

Winston Churchill had witnessed fighting in Afghanistan in 1897. The Taliban were there even then, but those days they were known more elaborately as the Talib-ul-ilm (student of knowledge), a motley collection of holy men who lived off the hospitality of the local Afghan tribes.

Churchill considered them 'as degraded a race as any on the fringe of humanity…' and blamed the Talibs for keeping Afghans in the 'grip of miserable superstition'. It wasn't just a racist rant by Churchill; there were valid reasons for his outrage against the Talibs and their 'loose moral conduct'. According to Churchill, they (Talibs) '…enjoy a sort of "droit du seigneur," and no man's wife or daughter is safe from them. Of some of their manners and morals it is impossible to write.'[1]

The Taliban of today are no better in their rapacity. But instead of a begging bowl, they now carry a gun. Instead of wandering about aimlessly, they have the pick of the best house when they are in power. When Churchill had reported on the Anglo-Afghan war, the Afghans were the defeated party. This time the Taliban hold all the trumps.

Since their taking over again, Afghanistan has begun to slide back into the dark ages. For Afghans, and for many others in the world, it will be like living in times without mercy once more—when books like *The Kite Runner* ignited horror for Afghans; when terror set the terms for India in Kandahar; and when 9/11 shook Americans on their soil. To make the American humiliation complete, the Taliban swore themselves back into power 20 years later—as if time had stood still and the inferno of twin towers was a continuing chapter.

For Afghan women and children, it meant hope belied, the snatching away of the life they had begun to value. When it signed on the dotted line dictated by the Taliban in Doha on 29 February 2020, the US knew it had erred, and that it was signing in an age of shadows for Afghans. But the US was frustrated. Despite warnings of a dire Afghan future, it was in no mood to continue with an engagement that was draining it financially, with no end in sight. Annually, the US was spending more than $50 billion on war in Afghanistan, and since 2001, it has spent over a trillion dollars for its military and economic engagement there. In retrospect, there are complaints that much of those trillions lined up the pockets of politicians, contractors and officials.

The grim reality is that corruption wasn't a design flaw in the Afghan war. It was a design feature. The US did not build a nation in Afghanistan. It built over 500 military bases and the personal fortunes of people who were their contractors. Just about 12 per cent of US reconstruction assistance budgeted over 20 years actually went to the Afghan government.

All through this long chapter of corruption and inefficiency, the US had been acting like a regional gendarme to pursue the hopeless task of keeping Afghanistan together. The complexities involved in this job were numerous, and America's military presence in the region was in itself a source of instability, especially for the regimes on which the US relies.

To be fair, it should also be said that the US tried. It wanted the best Afghan army that money could buy and an able government under the academic Ashraf Ghani. It ended up with two ghosts, who disappeared at the first sign of the approaching Taliban.

After its retreat from Afghanistan in defeat, the US will now have enough time to reflect on the flawed fundamental premise on which it had first confronted the Taliban in Afghanistan—that it could bomb them out of existence without having to take on Pakistan.

The long war in Afghanistan has been a humbling lesson for the US on the limits of its power. While its technologically advanced military force can match the best in competition and win conventional wars, it flails helplessly like a puzzled elephant when faced with unconventional and asymmetric warfare. The Taliban, equipped, aided and supervised by the ISI, were an effective force frustrating the US army at every turn.

But the withdrawal of its forces does not mean the final goodbye. Afghanistan will continue to haunt the US in multiple ways. One immediate effect is that the nearly 300,000 Afghan army personnel, trained by the US and equipped with the sophisticated arms supplied by it, have become available for use. Add to it the highly motivated and well-armed cadre of about 75,000 Taliban fighters, and you have a very large lethal force of violent men. Since the Taliban government will not have the budgetary resources to keep more than 60,000–70,000 of these in the army and other security services, the bulk of them will be looking for employment elsewhere. Left on their own, without a job, they could cause problems within.

However, the ISI seems to have thought this through. For it, this could be a formidable force to settle scores and to launch operations outside the Afghan borders into the Central Asian states, or more likely in Kashmir. The Taliban have already christened one of their units Panipat, commemorating the battles of Panipat won by the Afghan forces.[2] There is also the risk that some of the Taliban cadres may have scores to settle with Pakistan. But like a gambler on a winning streak, the ISI does not seem overly bothered by the prospect.

Overall, Pakistan wishes to have its way in Afghanistan by having a predominantly Haqqani-led government. However, there is a fundamental contradiction between its wishes and the result thereof—it cannot have both a friendly government and stability in Afghanistan.

The Coming Churn: Another Somalia or Yugoslavia

A historical precedence must be added to this list. The East India Company's soldiers had initiated the Great Game in the mid-nineteenth century to expand and maintain western influence in Afghanistan. That enterprise brought this company to financial ruin. The subsequent pursuit of the same goal by the British Empire was, to some extent, responsible for its decline. Almost a century later, the Soviet Union's foray into Afghanistan in the 1980s was equally consequential for it. Its splintering into 15 states is partly ascribed to the disaster in Afghanistan. In this millennium, the US experience has been no less bitter. The humiliating withdrawal of its forces means that after two centuries of fighting, the western world has finally admitted its defeat and that, henceforth, the Great Game will be a regional affair.

Once, the strategic space of Afghanistan was considered essential to American calculations; by it, the US could check the Russian and Chinese ambitions in the region and keep a watchful eye on their activities. It could be argued that with technological advancement there is no need for the US to keep a human footprint in the region any longer; the same watch could now be kept by its eyes and ears in the sky. This argument has validity but only to a limited extent. There is no substitute yet for human intelligence nor for human feet on the ground. It is this ability that will be sorely missed by the US.

But the flip side of the argument is the continued US engagement that was draining its resources and demoralizing its troops. Therefore, it might be poetic justice if the ISI and the Taliban were now to get stuck in the Afghan quicksand.

Over time, a civil war could break out between the Pashtun-dominated Taliban and the other ethnic groups that together form a majority in Afghanistan. It is, therefore, possible that an ethnic war may take place, with the Pashtuns ranged against the Tajiks, Uzbeks and Hazaras. If their resistance succeeds, a de facto partition of Afghanistan could follow, with the Pashtun areas virtually separating from Afghanistan.

There is yet another way the events might shape up. If the external financing dries up and the Taliban government finds itself short of funds, then Pakistan's difficulties might be many. A new wave of refugees could stream into Pakistan, and the flow of drugs from Afghanistan may increase, leading to greater strife as warlords quarrel to seek supremacy. In that event, Pakistan's fence along the Durand Line may stem but cannot stop altogether this flow of people and drugs.

Whichever direction its destiny leads Afghanistan to, one thing is certain. As before in its history, the political pot in Afghanistan will keep simmering. And as in the past, sometimes the churn might be so rapid that an instant will become history. In this flux, one factor will remain constant and that is in the field of governance, or rather the cavalier manner of it.

In almost every parameter of governance, the Ghani government drew as close to minimum marks as possible. From rule of law to the government's efficiency, from political stability to control of corruption, the writ of the government simply did not hold. In fact, it was the Taliban who were in effective control, directly or indirectly, of 50 per cent of Afghanistan by early 2020. The Taliban's writ steadily expanded to other parts, till the Ghani government in Kabul caved in. That chapter of negatives is not going to fold up with the Taliban taking full charge in Kabul.

But, factually speaking, it was not just a victory of the Taliban. In almost all the major battles that the US and the Afghan security forces fought with the Taliban, the actual strategy and conduct of operations on the Taliban side was driven by Pakistani army officers. Having reinstalled the Taliban into power, the ISI officers and men are not going to melt away. They are already positioned in the most crucial departments of intelligence and security. And it needed the personal intervention of the ISI chief to discipline the squabbling Taliban factions, before their government could be formed.

Sadly, Afghanistan is a deeply fragile state, in continual conflict since the Soviet invasion of 1979. As a result, Afghanistan faces huge challenges. Its per capita GDP is among the lowest in the world, poverty is widespread and other social indicators are dismal. These negatives are unlikely to change for the better. Its governance, in all likelihood, will be paralysed by a weak and divided central government of the Taliban.

Afghanistan's economic figures tell an entire story. Its GDP remained stagnant at around $3.7 billion from the first year of occupation by the Soviet forces in 1979 till 1985. Then it dipped slightly and was $2.8 billion in 1987, just before the departure of the Soviet forces. Throughout the Taliban rule, and right up to 2001, the Afghan GDP remained around $2.7 billion. The upward movement started soon after the Taliban were defeated. From that rock-bottom position, it climbed steadily, over the years, to achieve a GDP of $20 billion in 2020.[3]

It was the same story in per capita GDP terms. From a low of $167 in 2001 it reached $508 in 2020. The exports reveal a similar picture—Afghanistan's exports in 2000, during the Taliban rule, were a pitiable $69 million. By 2020, they had reached a reasonably respectable figure of $777 million.[4]

The positives in these figures may return to the dismal state that the Afghans were used to during the previous Taliban rule.

For the moment, however, Afghanistan is somehow managing to hold itself together.

But for how much longer? This is the often-pondered question.

What will happen then? What will Afghanistan's future be like? These follow-up questions have no clear answers because the only thing consistent about Taliban is their inconsistency. They do not seem to have given much thought to the dangerous future that awaits Afghanistan if it continues down a slide. There is no regional consensus either on the way forward. Afghanistan, therefore, faces the real likelihood of morphing into another Somalia or breaking into a loose confederacy of statelets like the former Yugoslavia.

9

WEST IS RESTING

For all those who come to me for shelter, however weak or humble or sinful they may be they all reach the Path Supreme.

—Bhagavad Gita (9:32)

Viewed in terms of nature's bounties, Europe is a continent blessed by gods. Its population has remained manageably adequate—neither too large nor too small. It gets just the right amount of rainfall to cultivate crops on its rich soil. Physically, Europe's coastline is 23,000 miles long, which is almost equal to the earth's circumference. Its riverine topography has ensured that it is the only continent without a major desert. Europe's geographical features are one important reason why it has been a major presence on the global map for long periods of time. It was Rome that dominated the world almost continuously for six centuries from the third century BC onwards. Then, nearly all the way through the second millennium, Europe was the dominant power in the world.

If we restrict the term 'West' to West Europe, we could say that right up to the beginning of the twentieth century, it was the master of the world. Its word was law, and its arrogance in the colonies it ruled was boundless. Broadly speaking, the decline of the West started around the end of the nineteenth century. Like all such slides of major powers, it was gradual and imperceptible at first, but the signs multiplied as it engaged in wars within and as its colonial hold shrank. The two big wars drained it.

After the Second World War, as Europe lay battered and bruised, there was an attempt at resuscitation. 'Let Europe arise!' Churchill exhorted in 1946 in Zurich.[1] His speech then, to the European leaders gathered there, was about the possibility of a 'United States of Europe'. Someone in the audience took courage to ask him if Britain would join the 'Union' he was advocating. To which Churchill thundered that Britain would not be a part of the Union because it already had its empire and commonwealth.

But Churchill's bluster did not last long. Britain's empire began to crumble soon thereafter. The Commonwealth has carried on, but limply and in a lacklustre fashion. Britain joined the EU, only to decide to withdraw from it in a policy misadventure.

While the British uncertainties increased after the Second World War, the US became the economic powerhouse of the world. Despite the geographical distance with Europe, it became a part of the new broader fold called the West. This 'West' was envied by the rest of the world.

The 1960s were the time to be young in Europe. For the youth, it was a liberal, liberated age, a carefree utopia, an ecstasy without complication. Europe, too, fell into the mood of its people, content with what it had already achieved. This adrenalin shot lasted up to the 1980s. Then ennui took over—Europe was exhausted by its riches. Its will and the drive for more and even more began to decline. The ageing Europe wanted to enjoy the benefits of what it already had; it was no longer interested in plodding to work day after day in low-technology industries.

It convinced itself that the harder work could henceforth be done by the lower-income countries. By the 1980s, it had made up its mind that, environmentally, Europe needed to remain pristine and pure and so began to shift the labour-intensive and polluting industries to China and to a lesser extent to other countries in

Asia. Europe wanted to move on to the higher end of technology, and its labour wanted more wages for less work.

At this juncture, China became conveniently available, steadily turning itself into the factory of the world. By the time the West realized that its economic power was beginning to sap, it was too late. To give an example, the only sign that now remains of the famous Murano glass industry in Venice is its label; the manufacturing part has shifted to China.

By moving industries to China, the West became the instrument of China's rise. When it started dominating world trade, it also set in motion practices that bewildered the rest of the world. Overnight, it would flood their markets with cheap and subsidized goods, forcing the local industry out of operation. The wizards of the West forgot that industry drives the wheels of commerce. With reduced industrial production, its GDP became stagnant, and unemployment increased.

Much before the financial crisis of 2008, the signs of decline had started appearing in Europe. Over the next decade, real incomes declined in many countries. Even in countries that do not have a major unemployment problem, there are significant numbers of underemployed (PhDs flipping burgers).

To compound its misery, Europe got militarily ambitious at the wrong time. Egged on by the US, it became adventurous abroad by engaging in the Gulf wars, intervening in Yugoslavia and bombing Libya. All this was happening when it did not have the spare financial muscle to sustain costly military campaigns. A combination of factors, ranging from the ageing population to declining entrepreneurial drive and frequent military engagements abroad, brought it to a pass where it could threaten to swat others, without being able to cause much harm. Therefore, as in trade, so in matters concerning defence, Europe realized too late that it had dealt itself a rough hand.

European policymakers are not overly omen-conscious. Had they gone by the signs and put some faith in the occult, they would have been wary right from the beginning because one of the American diplomats involved in the creation of NATO was 'Achilles'. As the head of the US State Department's Western European Affairs office after the Second World War and later as the US vice deputy in the North Atlantic Council, Theodore Achilles was a lead player in drafting the NATO treaty. But the Europeans did not pay attention to that coincidence. Had they done so, they might have opted for a European Defence Mechanism, because the US may have the proverbial force and large financial resources, but it lacks the spirit of accommodation. It is partly a result of these slights and, in part, resentment at being pushed into wasteful wars, that Europe has been seeking a united force of its own.

However, people like T.S. Eliot had foreseen the European discomfort. He may have been reflecting on the state of present-day Europe when he wrote, 'If you will not have God, you should pay your respects to Hitler or Stalin.'

Charles de Gaulle may not have had Eliot's ease with words or had his pessimism for Europe in mind when he was talking to André Malraux after his retirement. Regarding Europe's reliance on the US, he said bluntly, 'Despite its power, I don't believe the United States has a long-term policy. Its desire, and it will satisfy it one day, is to desert Europe.'[2]

Despite this gloomy prediction, there are many threads binding the two together, and the US could still have made a difference, but it has been increasingly convinced that its destiny lies within. On its part, Europe was beginning to struggle with new ghosts of its own creation. Having joined the US, howsoever reluctantly, in its military adventures abroad, it was now reaping the whirlwind. Illegal immigration from Libya, Syria and Nigeria was a challenge to the free borders that the EU was proud of, and so was Islamic terror, a dilemma for the Europeans, who had thus far held the mirror of human rights to the rest of the world.

Europe was not just tired, it was confused too.

There was a touch of irony as well in this situation. Being

narcissistic by nature, the West had once promoted itself as the upholder of principles it did not keep, and of a morality it did not practise itself. In the age of increasing human interaction, Europe sought cultural purity. This was simply impossible in the face of a vast Muslim influx. After the shock wave of refugees, it is seeing the other viewpoint and making adjustments in its principles. It no longer uses human rights, as it used to earlier, as a weapon to shame others.

Europe's woes are not limited to disappointments with religious extremism and refugee influx. It is beginning to repent the societal fallout of letting the Chinese settle in vast numbers in countries such as Italy to replicate in Europe what they were doing in China, viz. producing cheap quality goods at low wages. Over time, they also brought in their social mores and standards of law and order. All this was somehow tolerated by a society that prides itself for excellence in design and quality. But Covid-19 was an unexpected and a rude shock to this policy of laissez-faire. Chinese immigrants are widely believed to have brought in the disease to Prato in Italy, causing havoc there and in large parts of Europe.

A Divided Union

Briefly, it seemed that the disintegration of the Soviet Union in 1991 had removed the only challenge to the West in the world. But even as America was celebrating its dominating role, the rest of the 'West' was beginning to stagnate. Over the years, the US seemed to have lost steadily its previous ardour for Europe. So, the God that Eliot had talked about was no longer available to it. Still, Western Europe had a chance.

Alas, it seems to have let that chance slip out of its reach. Fifty years after tanks rolled into Prague, and almost 30 years after the Berlin Wall came down, authoritarianism is back at the heart of the EU, a union founded on the promise of 'never again'. The lurch to the far right by parts of Europe may not be a general rule yet, but it is significant enough to make its people sit up in concern.

In each case of gain in elections by the far right, the message is uniform: far fewer migrants, stronger borders and a desire to take back control from the elite. More worryingly, this message is fed by hatred of freedom.

As hysteria increased, it benefitted the far right. But as is often the case with migration, the perception does not match the reality. Migration into Europe has actually come down. From 1.3 million in 2015, it was down to 417,000 in 2020.[3] The whipped-up hysteria against it is typical. Facts do not matter; they are just figures to be randomly manipulated. The masses don't do deep research before soaking them in and getting agitated. This serves the fascist purpose.

The historically acknowledged fact is that immigration produces energy and vitality, but there has to be a structure to it. A limit is necessary. But political leaders of the extreme shade do not have the patience or the inclination to digest plain facts. That's why when Europe began to face a larger influx of migrants from the Middle East and North Africa, Italy's leader of the 'League party', Matteo Salvini, sensed an opportunity. He broadened the League's message to include trenchant nationalism. Salvini exploited Italians' frustrations over their debt-laden economy, sluggish growth and a more than one-third youth unemployment rate. And he came up with a new slogan with Trumpian echoes: 'Italians first.'

However, it is not the migrants that pose a lasting society-weakening threat to Europe. In the longer run, the Chinese influx might worry Europe far more than the shelter that immigrants seek in it. China's BRI is trying to create an Indo-Pacific and Eurasian region that takes a China-centric view in its economic practices and political norms, and which excludes the US. Just as it seeks to weaken existing alliances and ease the US out of

Asia, the BRI seeks to weaken economic links between the liberal democracies on either side of the Atlantic.

Hungary, for instance, is a China enthusiast within the EU that also seeks to be Eastern Europe's 'gateway to China'. Realizing that political obeisance is a sure way to receiving financial largesse, Budapest has been arguing that the EU should grant China the market status. In 2017, it refused to sign a joint EU letter denouncing the torture of detained lawyers in China. In the same year, its near neighbour Greece blocked an EU statement on Chinese human rights violations to the United Nations Human Rights Council (UNHRC), making it the first time the EU failed to make a statement to the UNHRC. Both Hungary and Greece remain unwilling to criticize Chinese actions in the South China Sea, thereby preventing an effective EU stand on the issue.

On its part, China has impressed Europe by successfully reviving its ports. When China's COSCO Shipping Corporation took over the Greek container and passenger port of Piraeus in 2008, fewer than 900,000 containers passed through its facilities. In 2020, the figure reached 5.437 million containers, putting it at fourth place in the list of European ports handling containers.[4] Chinese firms are promising to achieve similarly impressive results for the other ports they operate in Europe. Chinese state-backed investors are estimated to own at least 10 per cent of all equity in ports in Europe. Some of these are in Greece, Spain, Italy, France, the Netherlands and Belgium.

Most of this investment makes sound commercial sense. For example, the maritime route through Italy's Trieste can cut costs dramatically compared with the northern ports like Munich. A shipment from Shanghai will take 33 days to reach its destination in Trieste, as compared with 43 days using the North European route. As it is, the economic map of Europe is ripe for a transformation, with the added advantage that railway links already exist and borders are irrelevant. By thus weakening EU unity, China can build strong bilateral economic relations with its members and improve access to markets and technology. As against China's clearly laid out objectives, EU is more divided than ever on China.

If Greece and Hungary are enthusiastic about cooperation, others like Sweden are lukewarm, while France and Germany are hostile to China's economic challenge. As rivalries between the EU member states surface over everything from the economy to immigration, China is relishing its increasing role as a player with stakes. But, more importantly, Chinese investments in European ports are linked to the BRI—a reason for Europe to be concerned.

There are other issues of longer-term worry. Chinese projects tend to exclude local and international participation. The past experience shows that 89 per cent of contractors participating in Chinese-funded projects are Chinese companies. Only 7.6 per cent are local companies, with 3.4 per cent non-Chinese foreign companies.[5]

While the Chinese interest in the ports is BRI-driven, and while it is true that it has both strategic and economic objectives, it is unlikely that a Chinese-invested port in Europe will be turned into a military base for the PLA. China's 35 per cent stake in the Euromax Terminal at Rotterdam, a 20 per cent stake in the Port of Antwerp and the full ownership of Zeebrugge port in Belgium will not bend European resistance to Chinese military presence.

There is a caveat; however, this is the present position. What if the economic condition of a European state deteriorates and its dependence on Chinese investment increases to cover large sections of its economy? It has happened to some extent already, and it could happen even more in the future. In that event, it is just a short squeeze for the Chinese to insist that PLA presence is necessary to ensure the protection of its investment. It might seem far-fetched to predict this as a real possibility at a time when Europe is fuming at China over the spread of Covid-19, but people have short memories, and policies can make about-turns without necessarily looking back at the litany of previous complaints. The driver ultimately is economic necessity.

But China and its ambitions are not the only worry for the West. There is no doubt that Europe today is a continent with a creased brow. It has major societal worries of unemployment—there are around 17 million unemployed people in Europe, including 35 per cent or more of unemployed young people in Italy, Greece and Spain. Economically, much of the EU languishes in the bottom quartile of global entrepreneurial activity. To complicate the economic picture further, its member states have fundamental differences about the path ahead.

Equally, there is concern about the direction in the realm of ideas. The essential spirit of the 'West' was inclusive liberalism. Critics lament that even though the western civilization is far from being destroyed, the process has been set in motion. It is steadily being diluted and dispersed. The vivacious and creative Europe of the 1960s and 1970s is beginning to vanish.

Fortunately, though, the picture is not uniformly bleak.

Not a Lost Cause

The three Baltic states—Estonia, Latvia and Lithuania—are among the most entrepreneurial in Europe. Then there are parts of Eastern Europe that have successfully integrated into the EU—Czech Republic, Slovakia, Slovenia, as well as parts of southern Poland and northern Hungary. They have become 'industrial hinterlands', the supply source for German and other European countries' engineering and manufacturing industry. But here as elsewhere in Europe, the middle-income trap looms, where wage increases run ahead of the rise in productivity, resulting in businesses and industries becoming increasingly uncompetitive.

Still, and on the whole, Europe need not despair. It continues to have the essential strength—a large, well-laid-out infrastructure, skilled population and the ability to rise again. More importantly, it is economically well grounded. In 2021, the EU's GDP, inclusive of the UK's, was estimated to be about $17 trillion, making it one of the largest in the world.[6] It could still have an important say in the world if it gathers the will to stand up and be counted.

The hope also lies in the statistic that though nationalists and populists have flourished at national levels in different points of time, historically they have always struggled to build durable, cohesive alliances at the European level. This time, too, the chances are that the far-right idea currently influencing parts of Europe would be both short-lived and short in its span.

Moreover, nationalists are not a united lot; their national interests are not identical. In fact, it will be a contradiction in terms if there was unanimity of objectives among nationalists of different nations. Thus, the French and Austrian far-right parties want closer ties with Russia, whereas Poland's Law and Justice party is staunchly opposed to the idea. Italy's Salvini complains about the lack of EU help to cope with illegal migration, but Hungary's Viktor Orban and Austria's Freedom Party are opposed to this assistance. Italy also complains that the EU left it to its own devices when it was being devastated by Covid-19, a fact that was later acknowledged and regretted by the EU.

Similarly, while the issue of Brexit had consumed the UK since 2016, the rest of Europe's interest in it waned steadily. From curiosity tinged with some alarm at the idea, the EU soon began to show signs of boredom with the issue. Moreover, the messiness of British party politics made the Brexit process look like a domestic dispute, which is sometimes a puzzle to the outsider. The consensus after Brexit is that its economic fallout will be felt far more acutely in Britain than in the EU, let alone in the wider world.

Brexit is one example. But Europe faces a variety of other problems, ranging from Russia to refugees. At this juncture, the drift in the Transatlantic Alliance is worsening, with the US looking for Europe to do more with less say. But the declining Europe is unable to comply with America's many demands.

Besides, it is caught between an assertive China, a revisionist Russia and an erratic America. Thus squashed, Europe fears it will become the grass on which the great-power elephants trample.

Despite all the gloom enveloping it today, Europe is not a lost cause. Some aberrations apart, there is also broad agreement in Europe that successful societies are diverse societies. In comparison with other regions around the world, it is still coherent, prosperous and effective on the world stage. Even now, Europe can be America's meaningful partner in upholding the post-war global order.

On the security front, too, Europe will not be helpless if it were to stand by itself against Russia. NATO's European members have a combined population of over 500 million, whereas Russia's population is about 146 million. NATO members of Europe have a combined GDP nearly nine times larger than Russia's $2 trillion. Moreover, NATO's European members spend three to four times more on defence every year than Russia does. Add to this the fact that France and the UK are nuclear weapons powers. Therefore, the idea that Europe lacks the wherewithal to defend itself against Russia does not stand up to scrutiny.

But NATO's expansion after the Cold War, from 16 member states to 30, has brought with it territorial disputes and ethnic tensions that have led to many European wars in the past. The war in Ukraine is the latest. Putin had warned about this possibility in March 2007. Addressing the annual Munich Security Conference Putin asked, 'NATO has put its frontline forces on our borders… (it) represents a serious provocation...we have the right to ask: against whom is this expansion intended? And what happened to the assurances our western partners made after the dissolution of the Warsaw Pact?'[7]

If that was Putin's worry, the fear of being abandoned by the US in a crisis influences the European debate. This is one reason why the idea of 'strategic independence' seems to be catching on. 'Europe can no longer rely on the United States for its security,'

Emmanuel Macron said in a speech to French diplomats, in August 2018, at what he called a 'crisis moment' for European politics. 'It is up to us to guarantee European security.'[8]

As a reminder to those who still doubt its capacity to defend itself, one should recall the words of Herman Van Rompuy, the first full-time European Council president. Ironically, while accepting the Nobel Peace Prize in December 2012 on behalf of the EU, he said, 'War is as old as Europe… Our continent bears the scars of spears and swords, cannons and guns, trenches and tanks, and more.'[9]

Overall, Europe may be looking tired and overwhelmed presently by multiple challenges, but its capacity to overcome them is not in doubt. There is also the inspiration of its past. As Eddie Izzard said, 'I grew up in Europe, where the history comes from.'[10]

10

EAST STIRS

The splendour of the sun, which dissipates the darkness of this whole world, comes from Me. And the splendour of the moon and the splendour of fire are also from Me.

—Bhagavad Gita (15:12)

Before he died in 1941, Rabindranath Tagore was reflecting sadly on the state of the world:

> I had once believed that the springs of civilization will issue from the heart of Europe. But today, when I am about to leave the world, that faith has deserted me. I look around and see the crumbling ruins of a proud civilization strewn like a vast heap of futility. And yet I shall not commit the grievous sin of losing faith in man. I shall wait for the new dawn, a new chapter in history when the holocaust will end and the air will be rendered clean with the spirit of service and sacrifice. Perhaps that dawn will come from this horizon, from the east where the sun rises.[1]

Tagore's disappointment with the West was in large part because of Hitler's atrocities; his faith in the East was rooted in its placid past. It took a few more agonizing years, but Hitler and his methods were defeated, and the West rose from the ashes of the Second World War. We are now living through the end of seven decades of western ascendancy, of western predominance.

All along, it has also been an assumption that as the West declines, the East shall rise. But the hope that every part of the East shall rise simultaneously is mistaken. There will be multiple stages of development, and states will rise after their own fashion and effort because from Turkey to Japan lies a vast region of political and economic complexity.

The situation in the Arab world is a typical example of it. The Middle East or West Asia, depending upon which part of the globe you are viewing it from, is a diverse region united largely by language and religion. However, Iran and Israel are the exceptions even to that minimum uniformity. From the Black Sea down south to the edge of the Arabian Sea in Oman, it extends to almost 2,000 miles. It is about half as much at a thousand miles if measured east to west from the Mediterranean Sea to the mountains of Iran. Its great natural blessing has been the discovery of oil and gas in the largest continuous desert in the world. But it also contains the fertile land called 'Mesopotamia', the land between the rivers Tigris and Euphrates.

For long, the outside powers, especially colonialists like Britain and France, have tried to mould this region to their will. Ever since Napoleon invaded Egypt in 1798, the West has made efforts to transform the Middle East, and to convert Arabs, Persians and Turks to the secular values of the European Enlightenment and to democratize them. But the Arabs have not been persuaded. Instead, new power centres developed in the Arab world.

Much of the mischief can be traced back to the Sykes-Picot Agreement of May 1916. This secret convention between Great Britain and France was made with Russia's assent. It was finalized by the British Colonel Mark Sykes and a French diplomat, François Georges-Picot. Their objective was the dismemberment of the Ottoman Empire, and they went about their task with a butcher's brutal knife. Their decisions were taken hastily, regardless of their effect. Before the collapse of the Ottoman Empire, the map-makers of the world did not have in their lexicons the names Syria, Lebanon, Jordan, Iraq, Saudi Arabia, Kuwait, Israel or Palestine. These states were new, and their foundations, fragile.

Sykes and Picot split the Ottomans' Middle Eastern Empire, drawing a diagonal line in the sand that ran from the Mediterranean coast to the mountains of the Persian frontier. The territory north of this arbitrary boundary was to go to France, and most to the south of it would go to Britain. It soon became clear that there would be plenty of time to regret this haste.

The position that the Ottoman Empire had occupied once was not passed on to anyone else; instead, there were different claimers to the leadership of the Islamic world during the Cold War. Egypt remained one for long, with Algeria, Iraq and Syria vying for influence as well. Even though the principal centres of worship were in Saudi Arabia, the region around it, being impoverished, did not count for much in the councils of the Islamic world. Moreover, many of these newly created states were engaged in the matters of internal consolidation.

The Saudi royal clan had gained power with the help of the Allied powers after the First World War. The 'House of Saud' quickly reached a practical pact with the fundamentalist Islamic clerics to enforce their dictates in return for receiving their theological endorsement. Consequently, compromises were made, and Saudi Arabia created a totalitarian state, enforcing strict religious, social and political codes.

The big change in Middle East politics came after the oil boom of the 1970s. Saudi Arabia, supported by other Gulf states and vast amounts of funds, gradually edged past Egypt to introduce a more rigid concept of Islam in the Middle East. Soon, Wahhabism became the signature tune of the region. Being the largest oil producer in the Gulf, and flush with funds, Saudi Arabia now began to matter the most geopolitically. Its version of rigid Islam began to replace the liberal interpretation preferred thus far by

Egypt. There were other changes as well.

Before oil wealth flooded the Gulf states, 'Arab nationalism' had resonated with the ideas of anti-imperialism, besides the slogans of state socialism and non-alignment. Gradually, both the Arab League and the Organisation of Islamic Cooperation (OIC) were in a shambles because 'nationalism in Arabia' replaced 'Arab nationalism'.

'Arab nationalism' was supposed to transcend national boundaries. As against this, 'nationalism in Arabia' has risen out of the debris of Arab unity; it is essentially about the interests of separate sovereign states in the Arabian Gulf. In the resulting structural shift in this region's politics, Saudi Arabia has been ranged against Turkey and Iran.

Iran and its Shia supporters in Lebanon, Syria, Yemen and parts of Iraq are, in effect, the alternate pole in the Islamic world. Add to this the fact that, given their long and distinguished history, Iran and Turkey are the most coherent states in the region. However, they are not destined to work in perfect harmony, and it is not just because of the schism in their faith. Turkey and Iran have restive Kurdish populations, and for Turkey, in particular, it means keeping them on a tight leash. Turkey's worst nightmare is losing control of ethnic-Kurdish areas in eastern Anatolia. Therefore, Kurdistan will increasingly provide the geopolitical battleground for Turkey versus Iran.

In the larger tussle for prime position in the Islamic world, the revenue from oil gave the Gulf sheikhdoms immense amounts of money to splurge; it also gave them a say in intra-Arab affairs. Since they needed a cause they could own, Islamism replaced nationalism, and the Arab power fount shifted from Egypt to Saudi Arabia.

This shift also removed the hand of restraint that an ancient civilization like Egypt represented. Instead, the tribalism of a newly consolidated Saudi Arabia began to steer the regional ways. This combination of vast amounts of easy oil money and resurgent religion led to ambitious proselytizing. After lying dormant for centuries, jihad became the new buzzword. The ultimate jihadi fantasy is the domination of the world by Salafi Islam, and for inspiration, they turn to the Arab accounts of their successes in the Thirty Years' War (1618–48).

This shift has come at a price, as Saudi ambitions to dominate the region clash with Iran's vision for it.

Eight Million Savages

The larger Middle East region, having embraced Islamism, was at odds over who had the basic proprietorial claim over it. Sunnis and Shias agree on Islamic unity but not on which sect should lead it or whose theology and laws should define it. This has added to the ferocity of the historic Sunni–Shia split. This grudge got further speed in the 1970s because there was plenty of oil money to support their strategic ambitions. Since then, Saudi Arabia and Iran have been locked in a struggle for influence over the Islamic world.

Therefore, today, it is a blend of Islamism and nationalism that defines Arab politics. Resurgent religious identities are pushing against the bounds of nation states that were conceived assuming the dominance of secular nationalism.

Parallel to it, there are other developments that reduce the financial comfort of these states. The world is changing, and oil is on a collision course with technology. Alternative energy is reaching an inflection point. Soon, it will make economic sense to dump combustion engines in favour of alternatives led by electricity. The oil boom has plateaued, and the Saudi economy itself is in trouble. It would need oil prices at roughly $90 a barrel to carry on spending as before and living its present lifestyle. But if oil prices remain subdued, there could be yet another change in the Middle East's politics. How this plays out over the next decade or so will have major economic and political impacts in the region.

Moreover, over the years, the number of oil producers in the world has expanded. As Norway, Canada, the US, Kazakhstan and Russia became significant oil producers, the ability of the Gulf states to wield oil as a coercive weapon has reduced. Saudi Arabia is still a major oil supplier, but it has lost its energy dominance. Its financial clout stands reduced correspondingly, and no outside power wishes to control the region for its oil deposits any longer.

This decline in Saudi Arabia's fortunes may not be unpleasant news for many. They detested its arrogant ways, and in general, Saudi Arabia's role in the wider world has not been a record of loyalty or consistency. Very few countries have delivered as much pain as Saudi Arabia did to the US by raising the oil prices in 1973, after which Kissinger had fumed, 'It is ridiculous that the civilized world is held up by 8 million savages,'[2] or over the Arab–Israeli conflict, and much later, over the 9/11 attacks. American lawmakers have also been repeatedly disillusioned by its despicable record on human rights, in particular, the Saudi state-authorized butchery of the journalist Jamal Khashoggi.[3]

Yet, the relationship has endured because the US considered Saudi Arabia a necessary geostrategic ally. This is no longer the need. If and when the confrontation of the US with Iran turns into a war, Israel rather than Saudi Arabia would be more effective militarily, especially after an ineffective Saudi performance in the war it imposed on impoverished Yemen.

The last few years, particularly after the Saudi Crown Prince Mohammed bin Salman became the country's de facto ruler, have seen yet another shift. Saudi Arabia made the attempt to liberalize even as Recep Tayyip Erdoğan nudged Turkey closer towards the rigid Sunni vision. Saudi and its Gulf allies do not resent Turkey's sharp turn towards rigidity in religion, but they are deeply suspicious of its neo-Ottoman ambitions. And Saudi Arabia has not forgotten that it was Turkey that offered to send 10,000 troops to defend Qatar when, in 2014, Saudi Arabia threatened to overrun it.

Watching all this with increasing impatience is a restive population, especially of countries like Egypt, Tunisia and Algeria. They are not organized enough, just yet, to launch a sequel to the Arab Spring. But their murmurs about authoritarian leaders and their inability to provide jobs and to improve the lot of the poor have alarmed the regimes enough for them to put in severe surveillance regimes.

One way or the other, whether it is flush with oil money or lacks funds, this region is destined for long-term turmoil. The American involvement in the region has been strong since the 1960s because of its desire then to checkmate the Soviet Union in the area, and due to the Gulf region's vast energy resources. But its intrusive interest in their domestic affairs and intervention in favour of some regimes has resulted in messy situations. This has sapped American energies. It is quite possible that in the next decade or so, it might give up in frustration its efforts to unravel the mess that defines the present-day Arab world.

In that event, China, besides Russia, may gradually step into the vacuum. India and Pakistan, for their own reasons, would also want to have a strong connection with the region. With the multiplicity of these external forces at play, a Middle East version of the Great Game is a possibility. When this happens, it will be bloody.

Not a Strategic Sideshow

With America tiring of its 'Middle East obsession', the developments in and around Southeast Asia are beginning to dominate its strategic thought. This region will increasingly occupy international attention, too, because of China's hunger for yet more space.

Lying at the other end of the Asian continent, it might be a geographer's convenience, but the term 'Southeast Asia' conceals a rich mix of history and culture. Moreover, in comparison with the turbulent Middle East, it presents a relatively calm picture, as it has steadied after the bloody decades of the 1960s and 1970s.

Among the prominent trends, a recent history of colonialism links the Southeast Asian states. Except for Thailand, other countries in the region were colonies of some western power or the other by the turn of the twentieth century. The Dutch East India Company arrived in Indonesia, then called the Spice Islands, in the early seventeenth century. Vietnam, Cambodia and Laos, commonly known as Indo-China, fell to France in the late nineteenth century. The British, in the nineteenth century, extended their rule to Myanmar and later occupied the Malay Peninsula. The US ruled Philippines as a brutally seized prize of the Spanish–American War of 1898. During the Second World War, Japan conquered most of these countries, in the process, conveying a message to the people that their western colonialists were not invincible. It is remarkable that, unlike China, this region does not carry grudges against the colonial powers.

It was only after the Second World War that the process of liberation started. For decades thereafter, Southeast Asia was one of the most backward regions of the world. Singapore was a swamp known for its disease-carrying mosquitoes. The rest of the region was locked in a series of, what seemed then, deadly wars. Moreover, communist insurgencies had led to violence in Cambodia, Vietnam and Laos.

With this diverse and differing background, when the Association of Southeast Asian Nations (ASEAN) was formed in 1967, it was greeted by sceptical observers as a half-hearted effort by its members to somehow bring the countries together in a debating forum. They were soon to be proved wrong. The formation of the ASEAN led to the beginning of a transformation; from confrontation and wars the region slowly moved towards cooperation.

Today, the ASEAN represents a market of half a billion people with a combined average GDP growth that is twice that of the global average. But its consensual approach and concentration on economic issues leaves it ill-equipped to tackle the strategic challenges together. Above all, the 'ASEAN way' is to talk through issues. Reaching agreement and understanding is more important than confrontation.

However, Southeast Asia will have to pay greater attention to the emerging great-power tussle. The sea lanes that pass through it, its proximity to and abutment of India and China, and its resources are giving it increasing geopolitical importance. Now, the region is much more than a strategic sideshow.

The frantic swirl of waters that surround the region suggest great turbulence in the days to come. The Indian Ocean is the third-largest body of water in the world, containing vital sea lanes that help feed some of Asia's largest economies. More than 80 per cent of the world's seaborne trade in oil transits through it.

The Portuguese, Dutch, French and the British contested for supremacy in the waters of the Andaman Sea in the centuries gone by, when they were just beginning to stake their colonial claims in Asia. The British hegemony in the Indian Ocean in the early nineteenth century and its tacit understanding with France and the Netherlands kept the Andaman Sea in a calm state. Since then, the principal players and their stakes have changed.

Over the years, these seas have become the principal arteries of the global economy; yet, two very different visions of Asia's future are now in play. Moreover, the broad term 'Indo-Pacific' does not comprise just the Pacific and Indian oceans. It has a wider embrace that includes the Bay of Bengal, Arabian Sea and the waters of Africa to the west, besides the East China Sea, South China Sea and South Pacific to the east of the Malacca Strait.

Since the defeat of Japan in 1945, and especially since the end of the Cold War, the US Navy had treated the Pacific almost as a private lake. It used that power to implement an international system in its own image, a rules-based order of free trade, freedom of navigation and, when possible, democratic government. In this period, China's preoccupation with internal consolidation helped too. The four decades since Nixon met Mao in 1972 have been the most stable and prosperous in Asia's modern history. One result of that meeting was the US endorsement of China's return to the family of nations and China's implied nod to American military dominance in Asia. This lasted as long as China was rebuilding and biding its time. But the understanding of 1972 now lies tattered, leaving these vast waters in ferment.

In recent years, there are other developments that bring the region to sharper strategic focus. To quote an example, the technologically deficient India and natural resource-deficient Japan have much to gain from a close relationship. As an island state and as a major economy, Japan is totally dependent on sea lanes for its energy, commerce and industry needs, besides its security. Yet, it faces serious capacity limitations in its ability to protect its seaborne trade and energy traffic. Apart from the tyranny of distance (a ship could take up to 18 days to cover the 12,000 km stretch from Japan to the Persian Gulf), it was, for long after the Second World War, also restricted by constitutional curbs on the maintenance of military/naval forces and their deployment overseas.

India, as a regional naval power with a dominant peninsular location overlooking the shipping lanes, plays an important role in ensuring maritime security in the Indian Ocean and its environs. But it needs to do much more. When India announced its intention, in 1991, for greater integration with the Pacific region, it termed that intent 'Look East'. Ever since, that coinage has served as an occasional placard. When a high-level visit takes place, either way, that placard is dusted out of storage and waved in public as a reminder that the East remains on Indian radar. But it is not enough.

On the ground, there is very little movement forward. Road connectivity, which was to be a lynchpin of trade and people-to-people contact, remains a distant dream. Trade and political relations remain largely somnolent. A new nomenclature was given by PM Modi to the 1990s' intent, following which 'Look East' became known as 'Act East'. This change has not helped much. In fact, after an initial spurt, the trade with the region has declined since 2011. Even in the case of a showcase relationship like that with Japan, India's exports reduced from $6.81 billion in 2013–14 to $4 billion in 2020.[4]

While economic and technological cooperation remains far below its potential, there is also a difference in perception about China. Japan is conscious of its own security concerns in the East and South China seas, and seems to play down the threats that India faces from China.

Still, the recent use of the term 'Indo-Pacific' rests on the assumption that its mantra-like repetition will put economic and strategic life into the two oceanic regions. One foundation of that belief rests on the hope that the economies of countries like India and Indonesia will grow and expand. But evidence suggests that there are continuing structural weaknesses in their economies, which will place limits on the roles that they can play in the region.

Moreover, the idea that the coinage Indo-Pacific acknowledges the shifting weight of economic and political power westwards in Asia, towards India, overvalues India. It underestimates the complex economic and political interdependence that China and the US have with mainland Asia. To add to the complexity of this picture, the unwritten understanding of the 1970s between Beijing and Washington on America's role in Asia is also beginning to crumble. China now wishes to recast its military and political dynamic in the region.

It is a pity that all this while successive US presidents opted to view China's aggression through forgiving lenses. A major lapse took place when the US did not stand for Manila during the Scarborough Shoal crisis of mid-2012. This encouraged China to assume that American commitments to allies in the South China Sea were hollow.

After 2013, President Xi initiated a major land-reclamation campaign in the Spratly Islands. Along with it, China began to build military facilities at these islands, ranging from ports to runways capable of handling fighter jets and bombers. It also installed radars, anti-ship and anti-aircraft weapons on them. The American response continued to be muddled and hesitant even after July 2016, when the Permanent Court of Arbitration in The Hague ruled against China's claims in a case brought by the Philippines. However, Trump ordered a course correction, and his relative hard line was codified in the December 2017 National Security Strategy. It termed China a 'revisionist power' seeking to 'displace the United States in the Indo-Pacific region… and reorder the region in its favour.'[5]

As the US began to sanction Chinese entities and target its technology companies, tensions rose dramatically. There were many unsafe encounters between their forces, invariably instigated by Chinese ships or air force planes. On his part, Xi had told his military as far back as 2018 to 'prepare for war'.

If the US fails to successfully contest China's dominance over the South China Sea, it will steadily lead to:

- The end of the rules-based order of the sea that the US had informally established in the South China Sea,
- A severe blow to its prestige among the Southeast Asian states, and
- An end to its ambitions of exploiting the underwater resources.

With the resulting corrosion of the rules-based system, the management of political and economic tensions could become problematic. If, over time, China displaces America, and the South China Sea becomes a Chinese lake, it will mark:

- A major blow to international law, and
- Beijing's seizure of a maritime entitlement five times larger

> than permitted by the United Nations Convention on the Law of the Sea (UNCLOS, which it ratified in 1996) and customary international law.

The effect of this, for other waterways, would mean anarchy where the powerful holds sway. From the Persian Gulf to the Arctic, nations like Iran and Russia could insist that their revisionist interpretations are the new maritime law. Meanwhile, China is delighted at America's inability or unwillingness, so far, to enforce the freedom of navigation and to defend the interests of its allies.

Whether China becomes a new menace to the world remains to be seen, but the US–China rivalry could be more volatile than that during the Cold War with the Soviet Union because there are more areas of potential disputes. As Halford Mackinder wrote, 'The temptation of the moment is to believe that unceasing peace will ensue merely because tired men are determined that there will be no more war. But international tension will accumulate again... Who among the diplomats at the Congress table at Vienna in 1814 foresaw that Prussia will become a menace to the world?...'[6]

Like then, and as in the two world wars, the Indo-Pacific Cold War will just need one spark to turn hot. When that happens, will the US have the will and the endurance to last till victory? That is open to doubt, if one goes by a previous instance in the region. In October 1972, Nixon asked Kissinger about the likelihood of South Vietnam's survival.

'I think there is one chance in four,' Kissinger told him.

'Well, if they're that collapsible, maybe they just have to be collapsed,' Nixon said.[7]

The question that the states in the Indo-Pacific region must ask themselves before joining an America-led war is this: has America changed? Or will it be just as whimsically fickle the next time?

11

THE AGE OF MANY WORLDS

By hundreds and then by thousands, behold, Arjuna, my manifold celestial forms of innumerable shapes and colours.

—Bhagavad Gita (11:5)

Following the end of the Second World War and till about the economic shock of 2008, American foreign policy was in some part directed towards maintaining its global supremacy. Its effort was to prevent the emergence of other great powers. The Soviet Union was certainly a great power while it lasted, but it was not a global hegemon in the American manner. It did not have the economic wherewithal to assume global responsibilities. Even for America, the Atlas-like effort of supporting the globe finally proved to be a frustrating and unendurable burden.

To begin with, the US and its allies in the West were fired by the twin ballasts of a desire to mould the world to their plan and an evangelical zeal to get the better of communistic East. This menu of global interaction was selfish but not entirely.

There was the desire that the scale of violence in the world wars should not be repeated. There were other factors like the steadily increasing prosperity, and armed with that force, a desire to make the less unfortunate of the world follow the path where democracy and prosperity combined could work miracles for their population.

It was through the infusion of $12 billion (roughly $120 billion now) of the Marshall Plan funds that the US helped Europe rebuild its devastated economies after the Second World War. It is equally true that the fusion of American idealism and exceptionalism were the driving forces behind a new international order. It is also widely acknowledged that a global network of security and economic partnerships was formed under the American leadership.

But it was not a mission of selfless charity that the US had embarked upon. America benefited economically, politically and in strategic terms from the pole position it had assumed in the world. Sadly, the US used this role selectively and, in some cases, ill-advisedly. Dictators were often let off lightly, and human rights violations in the oil-rich Gulf states were winked at.

But for many in the Eastern Bloc and in the developing world, the human rights forum of the world bodies was an ordeal where they were named and shamed by the US and its western allies. It was a deserved dressing down in some cases, but the selective application of the principle did hurt.

There were complaints about the ways of the Eastern Bloc too. Its people, wanting to breathe free, were chaffing at the restrictions imposed on them. This denial of freedom for individuals was replicated at the state level; the Eastern Bloc countries were resentful of the vice-like grip of the Soviet Union on their external affairs. Though they continued to present a united front to the world, the Bloc was in a constant state of suppressed ferment. Moreover, its image in the wider world approximated a pariah region that was heavy-handed in its dealings.

Therefore, even while there were two blocs in the world, and for all practical purposes, it was a bipolar world, the fact is that the democratic West was the preferred partner of the smaller countries—the fashionable consort to be associated with.

This two-power bloc of the US and the Soviet Union was feared as long as it lasted. But it had successfully provided stability to the world by being a hedge against the domination by the other. This system crumbled with the collapse of the Soviet Union. By the mid-1990s, the US also began to pant. It was beginning to slide from the peak of prosperity it had climbed. Still, it was powerful enough to relish being the sole superpower of the world, supported by its western allies.

In a unipolar world, like the one the US had then begun to dominate, one civilization leads, leaving others far behind. The main political, economic, cultural and social vectors are defined by that most influential state. As Themistocles said, 'I have with me two Gods; Persuasion and Compulsion.' It was through a combination of these two measures, 'persuasion and compulsion', that America forced compliance by the rest of the world to some of its whimsical decisions.

It gave up realism in its foreign policy for a grand strategy of hegemony. This was to cause considerable harm to it at home and abroad, prompting voices that Washington should return to the realism and restraint that had served it well. The ideal course would have been the hard-nosed approach to foreign policy that relied on diplomacy, rather than rushing to arms every time there was a crisis somewhere in the world.

Instead of that soft touch, unipolarity became a carte blanche for armed interventions by the US and its allies in the West. To give them legal sanction, they got the UN to agree that people needed to be protected from an oppressive regime or an irresponsible leader. This sugar-coated fig leaf was called the 'Responsibility to Protect'.

The US was still in an evangelical mode after the Cold War, but there was a subtle change in its priorities. Its spirit, this time, was not fuelled by the generosity of a Marshall Plan. In this phase, too, it wanted to mould the world in its fashion but without expending too much of its money. In fact, one of its major objectives was to control the energy resources of the world. Its military interventions were in part motivated by that aim, and its interventions abroad in the period after 1990 followed this broad objective. In pursuance of this, it engineered bloody regime changes in Iraq and Libya, and tried for one in Syria, after getting the UN to rubber stamp its approval. But the question that the world forgot to ask is this: are these countries in any better shape now?

There is no doubt that the devastation suffered by West Europe during the Second World War was far greater than that of Iraq in its two wars. On the other hand, it is also true that the level of human skills in West Europe was far greater than in Iraq. Besides, unlike Iraq, Europe did not have to go through the trauma of a civil war and an ISIS-like terror after the Second World War ended. Therefore, Europe could steady itself quickly. Still, let's make a rough comparison. The $120 billion (in today's terms) spent under the Marshall Plan brought new life and prosperity to West Europe. But America's expenditure of $1 trillion in Iraq, over the war effort and later for development, has not improved the lot of its people. Rather, it has left them chaffing at the imposition of war's misery under the label of 'Responsibility to Protect'. At the end of the war, there is a sense of befuddlement among the Iraqi people as to what or who they were protected from, if ISIS was to be the result.

There are other questions as well. Why is the world blind to the fact that the people of Yemen are being killed regularly by the Saudi army? If ever the principle 'Responsibility to Protect' needed to be applied somewhere, it was in Yemen, where women and children are being routinely targeted by Saudi bombs.

It is in uncomfortable moments like this, when global institutions like the UN become ineffective bystanders, that doubts begin to be raised about leaving the global fate in one domineering hand.

Wasn't the old-style East–West balance of forces a safer bet for a secure world? There were tensions even then in the world and there were occasional wars, but there were no major flare-ups;

the world was reasonably safe. No one got up in the middle of the night worrying about the zeal of America the next morning.

Many Cooks

It is the crux of sovereignty that states should be concerned about a predominant power's intentions. In fact, the imbalance of power in America's favour had begun to bother other countries well before 9/11. It was in part due to this factor that Russia and China found common ground in coming together to establish 'a multipolar world'.

Some others also contest the unipolar model and nostalgically speak of a semi-multipolar world of Cold War when the two blocs of East and West had the Non-Aligned Movement (NAM) standing in the wings. It wasn't a bloc by itself, but it had the power of numbers and a moral force of sufficient vitality to be given serious hearing. However, at a practical level, it must be added that a moral force can restrain, but it cannot be a factor of power by itself. Moreover, in the changed global setting now, a sequel to NAM is neither necessary nor feasible.

The world is, therefore, looking for an alternate model where an individual state's sovereignty has a chance to breathe free, and where convenient theories like the 'Responsibility to Protect' do not become an excuse for ready intervention in a country's internal affairs. Those who support a 'semi-multipolar' world do not want a single driving force dictating the global agenda. There is considerable merit in this view because during the years that it remained the sole superpower, the US did sometimes behave like a spoilt child.

So, what would this semi-multipolar or a wider nearly multipolar world look like (for the sake of convenience, let's use multipolar)? Should it have different ideologies as during the Cold War? The supporters of the multipolar world want to see a functioning democracy in world affairs, guided by the competing interests of various powers. They also argue that a multipolar world, where largely equal powers cooperate, is likely to be more peaceful and desirable than an imperial Pax Americana, where others chafe against its overwhelming power. Moreover, a multipolar world will be free of clashing ideologies and their passion.

It is partly for this reason that multipolarity has become a fashionable term in strategic circles. But discussions about multipolarity tend to be laced with biases. Some advocates of multipolarity talk wistfully of a nineteenth-century balance of power when the western world was calm. It is true that after the Napoleonic Wars (1799–1815), the rest of the nineteenth century was relatively tranquil. The absence of wars is one reason why the Congress of Vienna is sometimes spoken of as a model for stabilizing global affairs.

But this argument in favour of multipolarity ignores the essential point that Europe was tired after the Napoleonic Wars. Moreover, the common factor of Christianity was important in ensuring calm after the Congress of Vienna. It also ignores the bitter fact that this multipolarity was limited to Europe; much of the rest of the world could not breathe free, stifled as it was by the colonialism of these European powers.

These factors are not in play any longer. The world is angry and sullen. It does not have the calming effect of religion in post-Napoleon Europe. Quite to the contrary, religion now is a divisive force due to its multiplicity and nationally driven agendas.

In this setting of differences, people may want the world to evolve in the mirror image of what they wish, rather than how the world actually works. Such a hastily conceived alternate system may not be the answer to people's prayers. Therefore, multipolarity or a multiple division of power to determine the destiny of the world can be an open invitation to bickering.

On the other hand, China may find it convenient to advocate a multipolar world because it would like to have a greater share of power than it has now. Moreover, its objective is driven by ambition and commerce, and that can only be achieved at the cost of others. That may be China's aim, but would the world be content with China's mercantile mercenarism? Or its strategic demands?

On the other side of the spectrum are the countries that feel that every problem we face today—from financial missteps to terrorism—requires coordinated response. They add that the root of the world's problems is the level of power the US holds globally. Nor are they comfortable with the idea of a dominant and domineering China in a bipolar world. The suspicion of China's hand in the spread of Covid-19 and the apprehensions about its strategic agenda behind BRI has made people wary.

Therefore, those who feel they might end up as losers in a new system contest the idea of a bipolar world. But confounding matters, they also argue that a multi-power system, like too many cooks, will not be effective in a complex world of today. Take the example of Afghanistan, they say. Since 2001, a US-led coalition had tried to bring peace to the country and defeat the Taliban. Yet, almost two decades later, it is the Taliban who are once again the overlords of Kabul. Experts blame the multiple pressures from countries like Pakistan, the US, Saudi Arabia, Iran, Russia and China as the reason for this state of affairs in Afghanistan.

This example can be multiplied to support one side or the other of the argument. The crux is the complexity of the issue. Will it be wise to rush into change just because there is demand for change? The risk with such quick fixes is the disappointments that follow.

What we are witnessing today is jostling among the big powers; from global trade to areas of influence, from bases abroad to armed intervention, almost every region and each major strategic asset is under contest. In this rush, the objective of China and Russia is to somehow sap America's sinews.

It must be irritating for the US to be constantly under attack, but it is not the first country in history to have to deal with the rise of other states. Through most of the nineteenth century, Britain, as the world's leading power, had to contend with the rising US and Germany. Both were strong economies, with a rapidly rising industrial base, and both had ambitious, stable regimes; the first, a major democracy, and the other, a strong monarchy. Britain dealt with each differently; drawing the line, for example, over America's unrealistic claims over Oregon in 1845. Britain's task then was tougher because the colonial world that it was dominating was not rules-based. In contrast, the US has to contend with the ambitions of China and Russia in a rules-based world.

Still, decline for the US, in this context, does not mean melodrama of a tragedy where, at sunset, the principal protagonist falls into the sea. It means a shift from a position of unipolar dominance to becoming a heavyweight in a non-unipolar world.

Moreover, historical evidence suggests that no society remains permanently ahead of others. Still, even as America's relative share of wealth and power ebbs, it will long remain a major power. But it would also mean adjustments and accommodation of the other viewpoint by America. In a truly multipolar world, compulsion may not be the most effective option, or even possible all the time, because the balance of power may be nearly equal among the few bigger powers. Persuasion rather than compulsion may win more friends in such a world.

An Alternative

Regardless of what happens to the power play currently underway, there is a parallel development that is steadily working towards an international order of multiple stakeholders. The progressive reform of international institutions like the IMF, World Bank, etc., is an important step. Another effort has led to the creation of institutions such as the Shanghai Cooperation Organisation (SCO) and the BRICS New Development Bank (NDB).

All this points to the possibility that the world may be in a transition mode—from unipolarity to multipolarity—that could deeply influence the way the world runs in the twenty-first century. But is the idea of a multipolar world similarly understood in different parts of the world? Is the world ready to put up with a messy dispersal of power among many states?

These ifs and buts are only natural, and it must also be emphasized that no replacement can be perfect. Still, there is no doubt that a shake-out of the existing system is needed. For the sake of its overall growth, the world needs to look beyond the monolith and create new players.

Assuming that this would be so, there are two options available to the US—it can either continue pursuing geopolitical dominance on its own, for as long as it can, or it can parcel out its burden and maintain a rough balance of power by adopting a multipolar strategy.

A variant of this was the recognition, during the Cold War, by Nixon of the need for a policy of détente, which was a shift in style with substantive consequences. The Soviets and the Chinese were to be approached not as alien ideologues but as adults with whom the US should find it possible to work. Nixon's first inaugural address animated this sentiment, 'We cannot expect to make everyone our friend, but we can try to make no one our enemy.'[1]

In its expanded version today, it could be called 'offshore balancing'. This strategy embraces multipolarity in its broadest sense. It recognizes that the great power rivalries, messy regional conflicts, and the rise and fall of great powers is a geopolitical fact of life. Therefore, 'offshore balancing' is the acceptance of the reality that there are other countries in the world that have acquired capabilities to extend their power and influence beyond their borders, and even their regions. At a practical level, too, it is always the safest and cheapest option to get others to stabilize the turbulent regions they are a part of. In fact, by not pursuing the extravagant objectives of the 'preponderance' strategy, the US can minimize the risks of confrontation with emerging great powers.

Anticipating this, it is argued by the ambitious among developing countries that they, too, are strong enough to pose as one of the many poles in a multipolar world. This is where the bickering begins.

The moment one country lays claim to being the regional satrap, that claim is contested promptly by the other hopefuls from the region. They contend that had these other claimants really been so powerful, the world would itself have pointed them to their place on the global high table.

This, they add, is precisely what happened in the case of China. There was neither any contestation nor any counterclaim. China simply glided into its seat as a matter of right. But this is a flawed argument. China slid into greatness because the western countries wanted it on the high table as a counterweight to the Soviet Union. Moreover, India, in a fit of generosity, forsook the UNSC seat that was on offer to it in the 1950s in favour of its seemingly friendly neighbour China. The fact is that China's case was an aberration. For others, the world has yet to put in place a system that recognizes and automatically provides them a place on the high table.

Moreover, having benefited itself, China is averse to a further distribution of power amongst the rising in the Asian region. Instead, it wants a hierarchical order where China assumes primacy, first in the Asia Pacific and eventually globally.

The other lament among strategists is that neither the bipolar order of the Cold War nor the later unipolar hegemony of the US was successful in creating a harmonious world. Rather, the world became steadily more restless, unpredictable and dangerously complex. China benefited in this flux.

Unlike China, the current set of claimants to the big power status find the door shut in their face. Every time countries like Japan, Germany, Brazil, South Africa and India try to make their way towards a UNSC seat, they are dragged back by other nations with competing claims to the bottom of the pit, where they all lie.

The claims of these contenders, such as Pakistan, Italy, Egypt and Argentina, are contentious, but the effect of their complaints is that the setting of the global high table is unlikely to change anytime in the near future. The resulting lack of expansion means the world cannot be called multipolar till such time as it becomes truly representative of the term and of today's changed geopolitical realities.

There are obvious gaps and weaknesses in the global order as it has existed since the Second World War, yet the established rules have served the world well. It has watched over a reasonably well-regulated system of international trade, finance and cooperation, and it has prevented major wars from taking place. Therefore, people ask apprehensively: is tinkering or tampering desirable or even practicable in a complex and already divided world?

A rational way will be to fill the gaps, to expand and strengthen the rules in the face of a rising China, and to accommodate the aspirations of other deserving claimants. Will Durant had put faith in India to provide such a way: 'India will teach us the tolerance and gentleness of mature mind, understanding spirit and a unifying, pacifying love for all human beings.'[2]

Howsoever necessary this ideal and idyllic world may be, the fact is that we live in an impatient age, where gentleness, understanding spirit and pacifying love are alien and qualify as other-worldly concepts that are best left to an afterlife.

This makes the picture bleaker still. If unipolarity's time has passed; if the bipolar system with China–Russia providing the other pole is not desirable; if regional poles are not workable; and if moral alternative of the type dreamed by Durant cannot come about, then what other alternative does the world have?

Perhaps, in the years to come, we might see a de facto Russian–Chinese alliance that matches the de jure US–West European alliance, partitioning the world into two camps. This will not be a mirror image of the Cold War because many of the extreme contrasts of that time would be missing. Then the East was in purdah, and the contrast between the economies of the two blocs was enormous. On many other indicators, like the freedom of speech and a free media, the East lagged far behind the West.

This is no longer the case. The new equation is far more balanced in terms of economy, and despite some restrictions in China and Russia, social media is a great equalizer today. Still, the question that we started with will remain unresolved because these two blocs—one led by the US and the other by the China–Russia combine—will not be fully representative of today's world, nor will they be truly responsive to its needs. The world needs a third voice that is independent of the big power play.

Some say hopefully that we are entering a new age—where varying degrees of power would be exercised by five or six countries. They include, in this arrangement at the global high table, countries like the US, China and Russia, with India as a possibility. They also include in this list the EU.

But even this would not be representative enough. The world will demand something more, if for no other reason than as a safety valve for the lesser powers of the world to let off steam occasionally. Perhaps we may be moving towards a bipolar-plus system all over again. The question then is: what will be the shape of the third party? NAM, as mentioned earlier, may be difficult to rustle up again because the conditions are vastly different from the time when that first version came up. There aren't any longer emotive issues like racism and colonialism to rouse the developing world to a common cause. Nor are there two strikingly different big power ideologies for them to stay equidistant from.

In addition, there are interests that divide these other countries more than they unite them under a common cause. There are special interest groups like the OIC, whose religion-dominated agenda does not rest well with others. Within the Islamic world, countries like Saudi Arabia and Iran warily eye each other. Moreover, the turbulence of South America and the continuing travails of Africa do not exactly mesh with the ambitions of Southeast Asia. So, rather than hoping for a unified third group in the manner of NAM, it might be more practical to consider regional focal points who could articulate the concerns of a group of countries around them. Over a period of time, these focal points, like South Africa, Brazil and India, could provide that much-needed group of a third pole.

Will the world be more at peace with itself when such a multipolar system is in place? Will it lessen strife and interventions of the type that Iraq, Libya, Syria and Yemen have witnessed in recent years? Will the world agree again to abide by the rules-based order devised after the Second World War?

The chances are that there may still be ferment, and the world will continue to be poised occasionally at the brink, but there will be hope. In the age of 'many worlds', with more than one voice at play, the saner counsel might prevail, pulling the world back from the brink.

12

LET HUNDRED FLOWERS BLOOM

The destruction of a family destroys its rituals of righteousness, and when the righteous rituals are no more, unrighteousness overwhelms the whole family.

—Bhagavad Gita (1:40)

On winning the Nobel Prize for Literature, in 2001, V.S. Naipaul spoke of 'England my home, and India, the home of my ancestors.' When asked why no mention of Trinidad, he said he feared it would 'encumber the tribute.'[1]

The England that Naipaul paid tribute to, at the beginning of this millennium, has changed. Then, it was still the 'cool' Britannia, which prided itself on multiculturalism. Now, the idea of celebrating differences frightens it because the experiment has spectacularly failed. Its message is not being heard by some to whom it was addressed.

The idea of multiculturalism was introduced at a time when Muslims were embracing the transnational intensification of identity, and Britain wanted these migrant communities to integrate, without losing their identity. Its objective was that if all bloom and grow together, it will be good for everyone and the UK as well. But this wish soon began to clash with the supra-state that the Ummah (Muslim community across the globe) was advocating.

These contradictory pulls led to disappointments.

Finally, the Conservative Party under David Cameron rejected multiculturalism, citing it as 'a doctrine that tolerated segregated communities behaving in ways that run counter to our values.'[2] Later, as the British PM, Cameron said in 2011, 'Frankly, we need a lot less of the passive tolerance of recent years and much more active, muscular liberalism.'[3] There is no doubt that the idea of multiculturalism is under strain in the UK and in many other parts of the world. Instead of a society where all had a feeling of belonging, multiculturalism, in practice, became a convenient way of being comfortable in self-appointed silos, segregated and divided rather than being a part of the whole. The idea of blooming in togetherness was overwhelmed by the safety of the familiar. While multiculturalism is not dead, it is not vibrant either. That's why some fear that there is the risk that its decline may lead significant numbers towards hostility.

With multiculturalism dead, or dying, the latent sentiments against migrants have now emerged to the fore. Politicians, sections of society and many in the media are questioning the need of a policy that leads to more silos. Like England, the US, Germany, Poland, Hungary, France and Italy are putting up barriers.

Since Naipaul was a fussy critic, it is difficult to say whether he would have still proudly called this changed England his home. But about India, the land of his ancestors, his view may have remained the same because even he could not have changed what has already come to pass. From ancient times, India has been a land of inclusion.

That spirit of acceptance has been a positive influence, leaving the society that much more liberal and culturally vibrant. It is true that as elsewhere in the world, the Indian society has also periodically put up barriers. There were aberrations like the taboos against mixing with the invader, the odious Sati practice and orthodoxy in a society famed for Khajuraho. They were syndromes of an otherwise liberal tradition under test because the foreigner had invaded and conquered. But every time such tensions have gripped the Indian society, and the extreme view proliferated, the society has suffered.

Once again, there is concern that the secular tradition that India was proud of is under threat. The liberals hope that it is a passing phase till the next elections. The silent majority in small towns and villages is apprehensive—worried that the social fabric that has held together for centuries might start fraying. In that event, the disruption of a civil conflict would be enormous.

This protective reaction is not just peculiar to India. Every society under siege tries to insulate itself when its culture, beliefs and traditions are under challenge. Sometimes, the reaction leads them to rigidity in religion, and that becomes the turning point. Even the otherwise prosperous societies begin their decline when the extreme view of religion begins to proliferate. As debate gets stifled, so does innovation. Multiculturalism should have been an antidote to that rigidity. It is, in essence, a shade of acceptance that India has practised for ages. Had it flourished in the present-day world, as it was intended to, multiculturalism would have enriched societies through multiplicity of ideas.

Still, there is hope in the fact that the constant truth in the affairs of people and nations is that nothing is constant. Perceptions change periodically. Circumstances dictate covenants between nations, and opportunity erases them just as easily. Who could have imagined that there might be tranquillity of the rules-based order in the world after the scale of violence in the two world wars. Nor could those living in the 1970s think that the Cold War would end as abruptly as it did.

When the Cold War ended, there was a sense of relief that the ideological and political extremes of the East and the West would no longer divide nations. But this relief was short-lived.

Soon other apprehensions took over. Cultural differences became the new worry. Jacques Delors felt that 'future conflicts will be sparked by cultural factors rather than economics or ideology.'[4] The then Czech President Vaclav Havel offered his support to the possibility, 'Cultural conflicts are increasing and are more dangerous today than at any time in the history.'[5] David Cameron went a step further to pronounce bluntly, 'multiculturalism has failed.'[6] He may have been provoked by real grievances within Britain to go that far. But he was not wide of the mark. The fact is that the cultural divide is increasing, and not just in Britain.

There are developments that are beginning to stifle multiculturalism in other parts of the world. Over the years, Pakistan has virtually wiped out its once-substantial minority population of Hindus and Christians. China's harsh methods against the minorities are a largely untold story simply because foreigners are denied access to the cities where China is disciplining these minorities to atheism. Tibetans are long used to beatings and the attempts at brainwashing. The Uyghurs, much larger in numbers, are the latest target of the Chinese stick. Gulag-like mass camps and a spy system that is pervasive are all designed with the sole purpose of enforcing religionless uniformity.

But Pakistan and China are not the only countries enforcing repression. This intolerance of the other belief has been practised in the Gulf region ever since the oil boom started in the 1970s. Expatriates rushed in to take advantage of business opportunities and high-paying jobs. Other immigrants also flooded in to take up work as accountants, clerks, domestic helps and labourers. There was just one major rule that the Gulf states enforced—no other religion except Islam could be practised within their borders. Accept this restriction or leave; it was as simple as that. However, over the years, some accommodation has been permitted to the discreet practise of other religions. A mild sort of multiculturalism thrives there within the rigidly drawn boundaries.

Going by these examples and the record of migration through the ages, the shift of people away from the land of their birth occurs because of a variety of factors, ranging from better economic prospects abroad to persecution at home. But the continuing longing for their roots, generations after their forefathers had taken the first journey, explains their distinctive identity and the desire to preserve what they claim as theirs.

Therefore, the questions that must be asked are these: why don't people rebel against state-enforced rules that deprive them of their identity? Why do they follow the enforced line? Why should their personal beliefs and conduct be regulated by a foreign regime?

These questions were not necessary in the exuberance of post-colonialism and during the period of plenty in the western world. That liberal spirit is now in retreat.

Primitive Instinct

In contrast to the restrictive view, the term 'multicultural' refers, broadly speaking, to a society that is diverse, often as a result of immigration. It also reflects the policies of a diversity-promoting liberal society. However, there is also the other side to the argument that opposes multiculturalism. These opposing voices allege that multiculturalism in their midst has been promoted as a part of political patronage. Much of this criticism of multiculturalism in Europe is due to hostility to immigration, particularly to Muslim immigration. Therefore, the surface appearance of our modern and interconnected world may be cosmopolitan, but at its core, nationalism has begun to compose the bedrock.

It is a pity that this should be happening now when the world is interconnected like never before, when travel has eased phenomenally and when the world has changed vastly technologically. The sad fact is that despite this advance, and despite the possibility that machine and mind may merge to produce even greater technological marvels, human nature has not advanced. The primal, primitive instinct continues to dominate and determine the hostile position. Social media that transcends boundaries becomes the rabble-rouser by instantly reaching millions with incendiary news.

Migration and the subsequent struggle in the new society is one cause of this friction. The economic slide of the western societies that the migrants wanted to adopt as safe havens, in more ways than one, is another factor. But it will not be valid to pin all blame for the global fault lines on cultural factors alone. A combination of debilities, ironically almost the same set that caused much of the misery in earlier times, is at play again. This package embraces ideological, political and economic factors, besides the cultural—just as it was during the Cold War and in many folds of history before that.

In all this, where are we? Where may we be heading?

The counter-question to this anxiety is: why must we bother so much about religion? Isn't it a fact that the church- and temple-goers are declining in numbers? That may be statistically so, but it is voluntary and a matter of personal choice. On the whole, however and despite Marx's preference for the soulless condition, religion is a profound palliative against the horrors of alienation.

At the other end of the spectrum, the desire of the leader, in even the otherwise democratic states, to enforce uniformity has been viewed in this manner by Samuel P. Huntington, 'The concept of a universal civilization is a distinctive product of western civilization. In the nineteenth century the idea of the "white man's burden" helped justify the extension of Western political and economic domination over non-Western societies.'[7]

This comment by Huntington is hard to digest. His own definition of western civilization is not all-encompassing; he excludes from the term not just Russia but all countries with a religious tradition of orthodoxy. There were others who doubted the term for their own reasons, just as Kissinger did when he was the US secretary of state, 'Who do I call, if I need to call Europe?'[8]

Semantics apart, Huntington is fundamentally flawed in his assertion. The historically verifiable fact is that the concept of 'universal civilization' was not unique to the western world, nor is its origin recent. The universal civilization advocated through *Vasudhaiva Kutumbakam* was benign, voluntary and to be practised by consent. And it predated the western concept of universal civilization by many centuries.

The second part of his claim that 'in the nineteenth century the idea of the "white man's burden" helped justify the extension of Western political and economic domination over non-Western societies' is even more shocking. How can the yoke of colonialism be applauded as uplifting?

Herein lies the irony. When you take a benign view of the assertions by Cameron and Huntington, it is possible to detect a mixture of pride and frustration. Both liked the idea of multiculturalism, but they were frustrated by the form it had taken. Perhaps they were reluctant to put their respective fingers on the heart of the matter—that despite professing noble ideals, the problem lies in the fact that we are merely human. Instead of addressing and correcting the issue of migrant anger, we prefer to retreat, defeated by our inabilities. The problem also lies in implementation because our methods are flawed. But there is hope even in this temporary retreat because upheaval like this can offer the possibility of better times.

If multiculturalism could thrive in ancient times, so could it now, after the present-day extreme 'isms' have exhausted themselves. But it will be a struggle because the idea of 'secular acceptance' will also have to overcome the authoritarian in the state and the society.

13

AI OVERWHELMS I

I am the beginning, the middle, and the end of all beings.
Of all knowledge I am the knowledge of Soul.

—Bhagavad Gita (10:20)

The world is currently fumbling its way through various polarities, unable to choose between one or many masters. Multiculturalism, too, instead of providing the healing touch, lies comatose. In the midst of this confusion, the rise of artificial intelligence (AI) confounds the world with its complexity. But Kissinger, though proved wrong on many policy prescriptions, has a definite view on AI: 'Philosophically, intellectually—in every way—human society is unprepared for the rise of artificial intelligence.'[1]

It wasn't always so. The invention of the printing press in the fifteenth century was a seminal event in human history. It was the turning point that allowed the Age of Reason to gradually supersede the Age of Religion. Logic and scientific knowledge replaced faith as the principal language of human discourse, and this led to the thoughts and actions that eventually shaped the current world order. It is this system that is now in turmoil.

Some experts predict an even greater turn in human affairs will follow in about 15 years, say around 2035, when robots will be able to reach inside our brains and connect with our neocortex. These pundits add confidently that with a chip inside our brains, we would acquire superhuman qualities by combining the best of what man and machine can accomplish.

This sounds very impressive, but it is a bit frightening as well. The previous three industrial revolutions had largely benefited the world by involving processes like mechanization, mass production and automation. One can argue that they were also responsible for creating efficient war machines. This is factually correct, but the machines so created were within the control of man. The current fourth industrial revolution, however, is vastly different:

- AI technologies will merge in complex systems to permeate every aspect of human life,
- AI could misinterpret human instructions, and
- Unlike in the previous industrial revolutions, AI can turn on its creators.

As with Alfred Nobel's dynamite, the effect of AI gone rogue would be devastating. It is a pity that a distracted world has not had the time to think of its consequences. Fortunately, though, nothing of the negative sort has happened yet because we are far from realizing the full potential of AI. But we are steadily getting there as dramatic breakthroughs come about in image and speech recognition, autonomous robotics and gaming.

It is then that unbridled AI could run amok. Experts like Elon Musk, Bill Gates and Steve Wozniak have raised concerns about the dangers of wayward AI. Musk, for instance, warns: 'If AI has a goal and humanity just happens to be in the way, it will destroy humanity as a matter, of course, without even thinking about it…'[2]

Stephen Hawking, too, had cautioned that the rise of powerful AI will be either the best or the worst thing ever to happen to humanity. It could lead to the eradication of disease and poverty, and the conquest of climate change. But it could also bring us autonomous weapons and economic disruption.

AI systems themselves are also vulnerable to disruption because AI is not a single size that fits all. Simply put, there are three broad branches.

There is the narrow AI, which concerns relatively elementary functions like translation services and autonomous vehicles. Then there is the general AI, with systems that can learn from experience with human-like breadth and surpass human performance on all tasks. The third type of AI is about its application in defence technology. This third part could prove to be the most troublesome, as it might dehumanize killing. The big worry being the absence of checks so far to ensure that AI-guided decisions stay within bounds during war.

What if AI systems gain a degree of autonomy in the theatre of war? Will they fight by the rules of war? What about the future Osama bin Ladens with their twisted use of AI? The fear is that AI may then achieve results far different from what was intended at their creation.

This should certainly be a matter of concern, but the possible negatives of AI need not worry us beyond reasonable limits. It is unlikely that human decision-making will take a second position in the age of AI. Whatever be the level of its perfection on technical parameters, the artificial world will not be able to tell us what is relevant, or set for us the limits of what is morally permissible in war.

Instead, it will respond to questions in the manner that 'Alexa' does. That, at least, is the hope and the present intent of technologists. But it has also been the case that men are blind to the obvious, sometimes even blind to the fact that they are blind. So, the question they ask assumes criticality. Will an authoritarian leader ask the same type of question as a democrat does?

This is what fuels the anxiety about AI, especially its capacity to replace flawed and error-prone human judgment. It is true that humans make mistakes, and many problems persist throughout the world because of bad decisions taken by men in power. But humans also do a remarkable job of generating questions, expectations, hypotheses and theories that direct their awareness and attention towards what is relevant, useful and novel. It is these generative and creative qualities that cannot be replicated by a machine.

So far, most AI systems are of 'narrow' applications—designed to tackle a specific issue. While the product that emerges may be superior to human performance in one domain, it is not superior in other domains. However, a long-held goal in developing AI is that it should learn and adapt to a broad range of challenges.

Therefore, the risk is that as AI becomes more sophisticated and powerful, it might become super-intelligent—superior to human performance in many domains. If this happens, it could be as transformative economically, socially and politically as the Industrial Revolution. But it could also pose catastrophic risks from accidents or serious concerns over privacy, bias, inequality, safety and security. Simply put, AI is the genie that has escaped the bottle. Handled prudently, it can lead to unprecedented boon. Rubbed the wrong way, it will be Prometheus unchained.

Privacy Paradox

In 2016, there were 3.2 billion internet users, meaning thereby, that almost half the world was net-connected. Facebook had 1.7 billion accounts. Sixty billion messages a day were processed on WhatsApp and Facebook. Five hundred million tweets were sent on Twitter. Seven hours of footage in up to 76 languages was uploaded on YouTube each second. Since then, these numbers have increased further.

Connectivity on this large a scale means that you can reach out to half the world with your message. That can be positive, if the intentions are good. On the other hand, it can magnify the negative. Complicating this complex picture is the fact that despite the large reach of social media, the vast majority remain plunged in ignorance. Therein lies the risk of miscalculation because the world of the digital age is like a taut web—you tweak a string somewhere, and the whole network vibrates. This means a flare-up in Ukraine or Syria is not only about Ukraine or Syria. It affects a much wider region.

Therefore, fear has begun to pervade our societies to an extent and in ways that was not so earlier. The big difference from a Hitler or the communist-style control over people is the scale and supine acceptability of it in our age. Protest has been smothered to an odd whimper; just compare the scale of the 1968 student protests to the blink-of-the-eye prance on Champs-Élysées by the yellow vests in 2018. The glow of 1968 was lit up by intellectual spark, and its principal protagonists were long remembered for what they had to say. The 2018 protestors were a nameless mob, their cause quickly forgotten.

The other big difference from before is the fact that despite the scope for individual expression in all its variety, there is a risk that we might look to technology as a means of disciplining one another. This omnipresence of fear, unfortunately, legitimizes the idea that citizens should be made totally transparent to the state and often to each other. It can be argued that the desire to control and manipulate societies is not new; what is new is the enormity of it.

In this mix, the addictive appeal of fake news offers the believer the satisfying sense of having special, privileged access to the truth. Today, sections of media also chip in with a helping hand and promote false prophets. But news is no longer what the news media decides it should be; it is what spreads. That is why filtering the real from the fake, especially in social media, is a big concern.

In Roman times, it was the function of the 'censor' to supervise public morals. Over time, the function of a censor has embraced a wider remit to control the spread of seditious ideas and, generally, all that the government considers harmful for society. In reality, however, censorship has blurred the distinction between what is in national interest and what the government of the day thinks is necessary for its stability in power. Consequently, the debate on censorship has become more complex than it was during the Roman times.

Governments have often used this power to prevent the flow of ideas that could be inconvenient to them. By doing this, they may achieve short-term gains, but in the end, the effort to gag is counterproductive because censorship inhibits access to knowledge and stunts innovation.

Democracies are also struggling with the complexity of the coming technological age—moral distinctions between what is public and what is private are trying vainly to come to terms with this new reality. It isn't just the democracies, tech companies are also facing a 'privacy paradox'. They're caught between using data to provide better consumer experiences and violating consumer privacy.

Therefore, the question that agitates the enquiring mind is this: have the implications of widespread use of the new technology in war and peace been sufficiently thought through?

14

THE POWER OF TERROR

But men who do evil seek not me: their soul is darkened by delusion. Their vision is veiled by the cloud of appearance; their heart has chosen the path of evil.

—Bhagavad Gita (7:15)

If AI represents human surrender to the 'chip', terrorism is the weapon of the weak. It has been so historically, to make up for weakness in the military sphere. If guerrilla warfare is the angry response of a group to military force, and a nuclear war is about threatening a country with extreme force, terrorism straddles both.

Historically, small bands of terrorists were able to cause small damage—killing a few or destroying some establishments. But 9/11 and 26/11 changed that. In both cases, entire cities were held to ransom; the death and destruction was massive. Even more damaging was its effect on people's psyche—New York and Mumbai no longer look the same. Their people are worried, they look afraid and suspicious.

It isn't just these two cities that are apprehensive, many nations across the world have become wary of terror. The countermeasures employed by them are useful in preventing attacks, but they can never entirely be foolproof. A determined terrorist will find some way of slipping through the security net. In response, the increased security employed by countries has meant a massive increase in national costs through the greater number of security personnel employed and the preventive technology in use.

Today, almost seven million people are engaged in private security duties in India to protect businesses, industry, cinema halls, hotels, etc.[1] Across the US and in Europe, a passage through an airport's security check shows how overwhelming the fear is that a terrorist might somehow slip through. Since 9/11, 1,271 government organizations and 1,931 private companies have been working full-time on programmes related to counterterrorism, homeland security and intelligence in about 10,000 locations across the US. The American spending on counterterrorism was a massive $175 billion in 2017.[2] To put it in perspective, $175 billion is approximately 2.5 times the US's 2019 budget for Health and Human Services. It is also claimed that the US spent more than $2 trillion over 20 years in Afghanistan and Pakistan in a futile effort to defeat terrorism.

According to a Brown University report, the cost of America's global war on terror stands at $8 trillion and 900,000 deaths. Of the $8 trillion, $2.3 trillion is attributed to the Afghanistan/Pakistan war zone. The death toll includes US military members, allied fighters, opposition fighters, civilians, journalists and aid workers.[3]

Besides the financial drain and loss of lives, terrorism has also introduced fissures in societies. Alien cultures have become suspect; racist sentiments are in increasing evidence; and this is alarming. Equally worrying is the fact that people's anguish has not sobered down terrorists. Instead, and unlike its previous incarnations, the new terror is well-organized and more sophisticated than before. And it can have enormous resources at its disposal. While individual terrorists and their groups can be sanctioned, bounties put on them, pursued and hunted, action against a state sponsoring them falls under the category of imponderables.

The effect on societies that have to guard against the next terror strike is bad enough, but even for societies that breed terrorists and sponsor terrorism in other states, it is suicidal existence in slow motion. Still worse is the condition of people who somehow come to be governed by terrorists. They must subject themselves to the total authority of terrorists in every sphere. Parts of Iraq and Syria under the ISIS went through that numbing experience. Afghanistan is doing so under the Taliban for a second time. Paranoia, intolerance and aggression overtake the population because, to a certain extent, totalitarianism and terrorism feed off each other.

Besides being intellectually stultifying, the longer-term and more serious challenge for the world is how to deter and comprehensively defeat terror. A rational adversary will decide to draw back on calculation of costs, benefits and risks. Even if he persists, the deterrence would have forewarned him of the high costs of aggression. However, deterrence works against a visible, defined and reasonably responsible state. But how do you counter a shadowy outfit like a terror group? How can you deter something that has no fixed address?

This, by itself, is complicated enough. But add to this the quandary that the sole superpower, the US, and a large state like India find themselves in. Both know that they have been hurt enormously, consistently and over the years by terror supported and sponsored by the ISI of Pakistan. Both countries have found enough evidence pointing to the fact that in many cases, Pakistani soldiers were a part of the terror operations against them—in Afghanistan, against the American interests, and in Kashmir, against India. Yet, they have not found an effective way to make Pakistan desist from its low-cost but highly effective proxy war.

The risk of confrontation with a nuclear power state like Pakistan is a strong deterrent for action against it because a state that rashly supports terror can be irresponsibly aggressive in its response to a challenge. India held its hand after 26/11 for this reason. And to justify its non-action, it persisted with the myth that rather than the Pakistani state, its non-state actors were responsible for the Mumbai attack.

The US was faced with a similar quandary after 9/11. Michael Waltz, an advisor to Vice President Dick Cheney, described the American dilemma thus: 'If we begin to retaliate for Pakistan's support of the Taliban, how far were we prepared to go? Could we really afford to make Pakistan an enemy? Were we prepared to…fight the Pakistani army's tanks and artillery on the way in and out? Were we prepared to shoot down its Air Force, planes the United States had supplied…?[4]

Whenever the Bush cabinet contemplated such dark scenarios, it backed away. It is this reluctance of the victim states to take on the state supporter of terror that encourages the latter to carry on. For a state like Pakistan, terror has become a force multiplier with minimal costs. A part of the blame for this Pakistani impudence must also be shared by the US, which assisted financially and armed massively the first bands of terrorists against the Soviet forces in Afghanistan. This arrangement suited Pakistan perfectly because with a pliant Taliban in control of Kabul, it had hoped to finally get the strategic depth that it had long craved as a hedge against India.

It is not as if India was not conscious of Pakistan's plans. In fact, much before it started supporting the Taliban, Pakistan had taken to shadow war. Soon after its partition from India in 1947, it started pushing into India its bands of tribal terrorists. Nehru thought about the issue, but he tied himself in contradictory mental knots. His responsibilities as a leader urged him to strike at the concentrations of Pakistani raiders even if it involved crossing the border, but as an idealist stunted by indecision, he prevaricated. In the end, he chose to do nothing.

In a case of history repeating itself, Bush had pondered over the same issue. His approach towards Pakistan-sponsored terrorism was instinctively muscular. But he was unsure about the consequences. Finally, like Nehru half a century earlier, he, too, did nothing. The result in both cases was victory for Pakistan—the gain of territory in Kashmir and the defeat of the US in Afghanistan.

The ironies don't end there. Terrorists are also known to use funds obtained illegally from the victim state to attack it. Every year, the ISI makes a profit of about ₹500 crore from the counterfeit Indian currency it prints and smuggles into India. This money is then used to spread terror in India. To this must be added the enormous amounts of money the ISI makes by pushing drugs into India.

Pakistan has been consistent in its policy of using India as a punching bag. Its terror cadres smash Indian military camps and civilian establishments at will in the confidence that India will exercise restraint. On the rare occasions that India crossed the line and retaliated, its actions were not damaging enough to become a deterrent.

Those who favour the policy of not responding to terror originating from Pakistan have crafted a smart term for it. They call it 'strategic restraint'. The explanation they put forward for this is that it prevents a major conflict and allows India to carry on with its economic growth. Basically, this argument blends appeasement with cowardice. The result of this approach is that far from appeasing Pakistan, every successful terror strike whets ISI's appetite for more. Moreover, the deleterious effects of the policy of 'strategic restraint' are many. For starters, this policy ignores the fact that every terror attack is disruptive of normal life and brings communal tensions to the surface.

There are others who argue that countries like the US and the UK have not had a repeat of a major terror attack because they were firm in their response and took effective preventive steps. They add that India lacks the ability to punish Pakistan's terror masters. By not reacting with sufficient deterrence against the ISI, it is sending out the message that it will keep suffering casualties without doing much about it.

Then there are voices that quote examples of other countries and say that India must retaliate and raise the costs for Pakistan by calibrating the escalation ladder short of war. Basically, they advocate a tit-for-tat approach, involving costs to the Pakistani army, the ISI and terror groups like the LeT and JeM. And they go on to cite the example of Sri Lanka, which has largely eliminated the terror groups inimical to it by going after them with brute force.

The issue, therefore, is whether the world has a choice. Is it possible to make terror a hugely expensive exercise for those who sponsor it? Is there a way short of war to deter such states?

Crossing the Rubicon

There have been examples in recent times of different responses to terror. The US decided to eliminate Osama bin Laden, who had been hiding in Abbottabad in Pakistan in plain sight of an elite military academy. The operation carried risks, but the successful execution of the operation was a warning for Pakistan that a Rubicon had been crossed, that America had set itself free from the chains restraining it.

India, too, was long trapped in the dilemma of how to confront Pakistan for its terror misdemeanours. Finally, in frustration, India decided to cross the red line in February 2019 after 40 of its security men were killed in a terror strike in Pulwama. Its air strike, though with contested results, on terror camps deep inside Pakistan was proof that retribution would henceforth pursue terror to its roots.

But in Afghanistan, the US followed quite the opposite course. It virtually admitted defeat to terror by agreeing to talks with the Taliban, whose principal demand was that the US must set in stone the date of withdrawal of American forces from Afghanistan! The US negotiators also turned repeatedly to Pakistan for intercession every time their talks with the Taliban seemed to stumble. Only time will tell which of the two courses is prudent—the occasional US and Indian decision to confront Pakistan with force, or the American farewell to arms in Afghanistan and its submission to the Taliban.

Neither course is definitive. A single US commando action and a lone Indian air strike will not deter Pakistan. However, it is certain that American submission to the Taliban will encourage it, as also the ISI, to carry on elsewhere with its designs.

Since states that sponsor terror are likely to be financially vulnerable, one effective way could be to squeeze funds and deny aid and loans to them. The other might be a boycott of all outside contact with them, including trade, travel and all sporting contacts. In short, by naming and shaming it, make such a state an international pariah. This may not succeed entirely, but it will put some pressure on the offending state.

However, the window for action is small, and unless the world reacts quickly and resolutely, terror will consume it. In February 2013, General Valery Gerasimov, Russia's chief of general staff, published an article, 'The Value of Science Is in the Foresight', in the journal *Military-Industrial Kurier*, where he laid out a new theory of modern warfare, one that looks more like hacking an enemy's society than attacking it head-on:

> The approach is guerrilla, and waged on all fronts with a range of actors and tools—for example, hackers, media, businessmen, leaks…fake news…conventional and asymmetric military means…The Gerasimov Doctrine… declares that non-military tactics are…the preferred way to win…Chaos is the strategy the Kremlin pursues…the objective is to achieve…permanent unrest and conflict within an enemy state.[5]

This is ominous. What if states like Russia or China opt to pursue 'shadow war' much in the manner that Pakistan has practised so successfully? To take another example, what if a state like China,

Pakistan or North Korea chooses to release a Covid-19-like virus in the enemy state? The consequence would be chaos and mayhem. And what if, in pursuance of the 'Gerasimov Doctrine', China and/or Pakistan spread fake news, encourage communal divide and use asymmetric military means on a massive scale, in addition to what they may already be doing in India?

The motivations of terror groups and their state sponsors may or may not be in synch all the time, but essentially terrorism uses violence to:

- Create a sense of fear,
- Destabilize the social order, and
- Create a new reality where a liberal, secular world based on mutual respect has no place.

Quite often, liberal societies tend to downplay the threat when these symptoms of disruption first start to appear. Surprisingly, an authoritarian state can be even more casual about the approaching danger because its system of feedback is based on fear where the truth hurts.

The use, or rather the misuse, of social media by terrorists to recruit, radicalize and mobilize followers is another complex modern-day issue. The issue may not have reached worrying proportions yet in India, but it is concerned about the noxious influence of ISIS over social media, particularly among some youth in Kerala. In general, the affected world acknowledges the problem but does very little to solve it. Time, however, is not on the side of the world affected by terror. The Center for Strategic and International Studies's Transnational Threats Project discovered that the number of Salafi-jihadist fighters has increased by 270 per cent since 2001. In 2018, there were 67 terror groups operating around the world, a 180 per cent increase since 2001. By its estimate, the number of terrorists could be as high as 280,000, the highest in 40 years.[6]

Obviously then, terrorism will remain a grave fact of life

for many parts of the world. The big issue for democracies is whether counterterrorism should be treated as a military or a law enforcement issue. In the former case, terrorism should be interpreted as an act of war.

The US approach in Afghanistan was military. It had relied on a combination of targeted drone strikes, special forces raids and training small, elite units of local forces to kill the core leadership of terrorists. But here again, the ISI took advantage. Many of these strikes suited the ISI because the US was eliminating the terrorists it also wanted killed. When one set of leaders was killed, another group favoured by ISI emerged to quickly take its place. Alas, there was never a clear picture of what the US wanted.

By installing the Taliban in power in Kabul, the US has rewound the terror clock back to 2001. In admitting defeat, the US has also encouraged other violent Islamist groups around the world. The greatest jubilation at American humiliation was led by former Pakistani PM Imran Khan. He described the American withdrawal from Afghanistan as Afghans breaking free from the 'chains of slavery'.[7] However, Pakistan's celebrations may not last long. Its nightmare will begin when the Taliban's ambitions and its Pashtun nationalism merge.

The final word on the subject must be given to a former ISI chief. Appearing in a talk show in 2014, Hamid Gul famously predicted, '"When history is written… it will be stated that the ISI defeated the Soviet Union in Afghanistan with the help of America… Then there will be another sentence," Gen Gul had added after a brief pause, "The ISI, with the help of America, defeated America."'[8]

15

ON A CHESSBOARD

Listen and I shall reveal to thee some manifestations of my divine glory. Only the greatest, Arjuna, for there is no end to my infinite greatness.

—Bhagavad Gita (10:19)

From terror to actual war can just be a matter of mistimed provocation. This is not always the case, but invariably terror provokes and war enters the realm of possibility. To begin with, and from as far back as its origin goes, terror required tactical response, whereas wars were in the realm of generals and required serious, sustained measures. That's why strategy is so intrinsically linked to generals.

The natural question then is: how did the term 'strategy' evolve? Some trace it to the ancient Greek usage—*strategike epistme* (generals' knowledge) or *strategon sophia* (generals' wisdom). The Greeks also used another term that is wider in its embrace, *taktike techne*—this related to the conduct of war and included in its scope tactics, rhetoric and diplomacy. Interestingly, nearly all of the ancient wisdom, from Greek to Indian to the Chinese, emphasized the inclusive nature of a good strategy.

That comprehensiveness is of essence because strategy is about identifying objectives and finding the resources and methods to achieve these objectives. Once this is done, strategy comes into play as a dynamic concept in a conflict situation or where there is the possibility of a conflict. And it is more effectively used in conjunction with another state.

Napoleon described strategy as the art of using time and space in a military and diplomatic manner. His genius did not lie in original thinking or some new idea on strategy. It lay in the interpretation of it and in the boldness of execution. His aim was the decisive battle that could crush the enemy because an enemy with a broken army could not resist political demands.

This is where Indira Gandhi faltered. After the Bangladesh war of 1971, she had before her a defeated Pakistan Army and its demoralized political leadership. She could have got their acceptance to any and most severe political demands that she might have made. India had conquered nearly 9,000 sq. km of Pakistani territory, and it had 93,000 Pakistani soldiers as its prisoners of war (POWs). It could have dictated its terms to a humiliated Pakistani delegation at Shimla. Yet, Mrs Gandhi missed the chance at the Shimla talks with Zulfikar Ali Bhutto in 1972. She chose trust and idealism as India's strategy, and decided one more time to give the elusive goodness in Pakistan another try.

Bhutto, on the other hand, had no ace up his sleeve except deception and the ability to charm and talk his way through, with an appeal to India's good sense as the elder of the two nations.

In the strategy sessions before the talks at Shimla, India had burdened itself down with the negative lessons from history. It did not wish to repeat the 'Versailles syndrome' by imposing harsh conditions on Pakistan that would force it to take revenge in the future. It decided to adopt generosity as a strategy in the confident hope that both countries would then flourish in long-lasting peace. Consequently, it agreed to vacate the conquered territory and release all POWs.

Pakistan's strategy, all along, was to draw on the emotional strings and extract as many concessions as it could from the Indian side. It had no intention of living up to any part of the agreement. In fact, had the roles been reversed and if Pakistan was the victor, it would have followed a diametrically different strategy—one that would have rubbed the Indian nose in ground.

By and large, Pakistan has been following that path in its dealings with others. Rubbing the American nose in ground was Pakistan's pursuit in Afghanistan. Or to put it differently, America's longest war ever was a strategic mistake from the beginning. Strategic experts the world over knew that the US was chasing shadows when it decided to bomb out the Taliban in and from Afghanistan post 9/11. The Taliban quickly melted away in thousands and so did their ISI handlers (ironically, the ISI men were flown out of Afghanistan by the US Air Force) in their hundreds. But they regrouped in Pakistan to bide time and fight Americans another day.

Over 20 years of the stealth war that followed, Pakistan's army, through its Taliban proxies, succeeded in its strategy, and Americans left Afghanistan in comprehensive humiliation. Ironically, President Biden's statement announcing the 'American retreat' was captioned 'The way forward.'

Another big mistake made by the US was to consider the end of the bipolar world as the end of constraints on its freedom to act. In this exuberance of being the sole arbiter of the world, America overextended itself, dissipating its focus and losing its strategic direction.

There is enough evidence to support the view that post-Cold War military actions by the US punctured the liberal international order. It was this order that the US diplomats had nurtured throughout the second half of the twentieth century. A series of bad strategic choices followed, beginning with the war in Iraq. This war, questionable as it was, set the alarm bells ringing in West Europe. Frustrated by American callousness, its western allies began to distance themselves from Washington. At the same time, America's adversaries—Russia and China—saw in this an easy opportunity to acquire new partners.

But the US continued with its misadventures, sometimes on flimsy and occasionally on whimsical grounds. Its attack on Yugoslavia, leading to its break-up, is sotto voce ascribed to the then US Secretary of State Madeleine Albright's fascination with the young Kosovan leader, Hashim Thaci.[1] It was also on subjective grounds that America's completely unnecessary second Gulf war was launched. Bush felt slighted that the Saddam Hussein regime had placed a tile mosaic with his father's picture on it at the entrance of a luxury hotel in Baghdad so that every visitor would stamp on it before entering the hotel. A sound strategy needs to find a sweet spot between ignoring and provoking. Bush should have ignored the provocation instead of rushing into a war.

Common Misperception

The failures of strategy are not always war-related. This is a common misperception. In practice, strategy has a wider embrace.

Take, for example, the case of Brexit. Britain was a rich nation that had been doing well on most counts. It was stable and peaceful without any sign of a shadow on its political and economic horizon. Its association with the EU was a profitable enterprise on all sides. The right strategy for Britain should have been to carry on along the course that had proved itself through the years. Yet, in one misdirected rush of blood, it set fire to the arrangements that had served it well. What is worse, it did so without putting in place an alternate strategy of replacing them. One referendum had put it all in jeopardy.

As against this, there are examples of countries taking a long-term view of their strategic options. It is a different matter that they may make the wrong choice, but at least they took care to think about a policy in advance.

For example, when Germany surrendered on 7 May 1945, that same day, PM Churchill ordered an appraisal of the 'long-term policy required to safeguard the strategic interests of the British

Empire in India and the Indian Ocean.'[2] The Post-Hostilities Planning Staff of the War Cabinet was assigned the task.

A fortnight later, the top-secret appraisal report prepared by the Planning Staff was placed before him. The central point of this report was that Britain must retain its military connection with the subcontinent so as to ward off the Soviet Union's threat to the area.

In every later recommendation of the British chiefs of staff, from then on until India's independence, the emphasis was on the need to retain the British military connection with the subcontinent, irrespective of the political and constitutional changes there. Equally, they stressed the special importance of the northwest of India in this context.

This must have been a major factor in the British decision to divide India and later in Britain's partiality towards Pakistan. But this did not yield it the results that the Planning Staff's report had hoped for. This was partly due to Britain's diminished post-war status and to some extent owing to Pakistan's proclivity of keeping many strategic balls in the air without irrevocably committing itself to any. The big drawback in the strategy chalked out by the British Planning Staff was in its inability to anticipate change. The global dynamics had moved towards a bipolar system, where Britain was a mere adjunct and where the nineteenth century's Great Game was long over.

This example is also proof that a strategy built on a single foundation—northwest India in this case—is bound to falter.

A sound strategy is founded on a composite whole, the sum total of many parts. You neglect one, or remove it, the whole strategy falls apart like a house of cards. That's how Kautilya had envisaged it in the *Arthashastra*. In that magnum opus, he had given due weight to all elements that help shape a stable state—agriculture, commerce, armed forces, intelligence network, diplomacy, and soft and hard power. Measured on this Kautilyan scale, most countries today will not get a very high rating.

Strategic Autonomy

There was a time when India was admired for its soft power. Intellectuals from around the world whispered in awe about it.

Mark Twain described it rapturously, 'India is the cradle of the human race, the birthplace of human speech, the mother of history, the grandmother of legend, and the great-grandmother of tradition. Our most valuable and most instructive materials in the history of man are treasured up in India only.'

A writer's world is made of literary flourishes, and Twain was not an exception. His praise of India was gratifying, but there are rough edges in the real world. It cannot be sustained on legends.

Legends are exactly what the US found when it ordered a review of India's strategic culture in 2006. The passage of time had not done much to change the basic character of India's policy, though India did try to introduce a new nuance in its policy. After the Cold War, and in the absence of the two blocs, India started looking for a new label—a label that would assert its independence and impart a sense of importance.

What it more or less latched on to was not a perfect fit, but it sufficed in the limited objectives it had set for itself. There is still nothing official to it. No one goes about holding a placard to announce this new strategic mantra, as was the case when India called itself non-aligned. But the word 'strategic autonomy' began to be talked about as a badge of honour; as if just by repeating it, India would have erected an impregnable wall around itself.

Howsoever much the Indian strategic community may like the sound of the term, whether India is truly 'strategically autonomous' is debatable. After all, it has, in recent years, signed defence agreements with the US that make it strategically dependent on it. Moreover, how can it be strategically independent if it is dependent on most defence equipment from foreign sources?

Still, the idea of 'strategic independence' seems to be catching on. There are others as well who seem to be enamoured by the sound of the term.

'Europe can no longer rely on the United States for its security,' French President Macron said in a speech to French diplomats, in August 2018, at what he called a 'crisis moment' for European politics and global multilateralism. 'It is up to us to guarantee European security.' He went on to warn of an 'awakening of nationalists and extremes' in Europe and despaired at US President Trump's 'aggressive isolationism'.[3]

If the fear of being abandoned by the US influences the European debate, it is the concern about entrapment by the US that drives India's thinking. But there are questions that haunt this pursuit of autonomy.

Can either of them be strategically autonomous in the emerging power play around them? Can they survive its overwhelming swirl and avoid being subsumed by it? On the other hand, this churn might point to a third way. These two contradictory standpoints may lead to greater convergence between Europe and India, or at least between some major countries of Europe and India. After all, such a meeting of interests has happened before, and strategic considerations have brought together seemingly dissimilar or antagonistic sides.

This misplaced hope was a factor when the US began to woo China in the early 1970s. For a considerable amount of time during the Cold War and even thereafter, the US policy towards China was based on a belief in convergence—that closer political and economic relationship would make China liberal, pluralistic and democratic. Despite hiccups like the downing of an American spy plane in 2001, the US kept faith that China would eventually join the world order as a responsible stakeholder. If there is one person who can be held responsible for this continuity in American policy, it is Kissinger. Starting with the late 1960s, Kissinger has held China and its leadership in awe, benefitted later from commercial contacts with China, and has whispered the message of faith in China's greatness to successive US presidents over the years. Each one of them listened to and largely followed the advice given by Kissinger that America will gain by convergence with China.

Today, the American strategic community says almost unanimously that the convergence is dead. In contrast, China has followed a consistent strategy of marking time till it achieved strategic parity with the US. It is this goal that Warren Cohen talks about in his assessment of China's strategy:

> (T)he Chinese classics stressed the value of violent solutions to security conflicts and of offensive over defensive strategies. They also called for flexibility, for using non-coercive means when confronting a more powerful enemy—but only as an expedient, until China could be sure of prevailing. Negotiations were a device for delaying action until the moment was auspicious. The goal would remain annihilation of the enemy.[4]

If this Chinese resolve sounds ominous, let us take comfort in the fact that interpretations vary about the course of history. Some argue that every civilization has its special way of formulating strategy. They insist that the outside world has only a limited influence in the matter. Contrarily, it is also argued that history is a patchwork quilt, and it is the intermingling of cultures and civilizations that enriches it.

One could add to these influences the make-up of a people. Each country and its people are special—some are martial races, while others are pacifist by tradition and upbringing. Then there is the role of the leader, which determines greatly the course that a country might take. Had Yeltsin and Gorbachev been born in a different era, the course of history in the Soviet Union may have taken a different turn.

Geography, too, plays an important part in influencing the tranquillity or otherwise of a country. The fertile lands around

Tigris and Euphrates have, for centuries, tempted conquerors, just as the riches of India once did, or as the oil wealth has interested MNCs and other commercial adventurers into the Gulf.

On a different note, some countries are stoic by nature. A case in point is the ancient stillness of Indian calm, which regards the turbulence around it calmly to say, 'this too shall pass.' Perhaps it is this sense that made another American review come to the following judgment about India's strategic culture, 'The collective reference points of Indian strategic culture are timeless. The thought process is a-historical, and generally resists being event-driven or trapped by deadlines, which tend to be regarded as ephemeral.'[5]

Rodney Jones was cruelly blunt in his claim that the effect of an Indian policy is seldom sudden or overwhelming. Its official goals may be framed as five-year plans, but if they are not accomplished within that time frame, they are reset as future targets without any great disappointment. This has been so from the beginning of time, and history records that the 'this too shall pass' attitude had lost Indian kings many wars. No wonder then that Jones should be scathing in his assessment of India's strategic culture. India's omniscient-patrician type of strategic culture is a complex mosaic of sacred myths and legends and memories of ancient states and civilizations, with the subcontinent as a geographical frame of reference, and with a modern overlay of nationalism supporting a vision of Indian greatness and expectations that India be treated with unmitigated respect.[5]

Here, the contrast between India's ephemeral approach and China's goal to annihilate the enemy is striking. The difference seems even more remarkable when considering the fact that these two large neighbours boast ancient civilizations and profound strategic thinkers from their rich past.

Leader Matters

Let's go beyond India's case and revert to the question we started with. Is it the mix of historical tradition, people's DNA, economic strength and military muscle that determines a country's strategic culture?

If the examples given above are proof, then, undoubtedly, these are crucial and continuing elements in the way a nation makes its choices. But there is also the fact that choices are influenced by the state of play existing at that particular point. That's why the term 'geostrategy' seeks to weave together the dynamic field of geopolitics with the slow-changing constraints of history and geography. However, there are other factors as well that are critical to the choices a country makes.

That's why the leader matters. His decisions are not limited to what history tells him; his mental make-up is a critical factor. Given the same national clay, a dictatorial Hitler and an idealistic Nehru would have arrived at vastly different decisions. To give another example: would Clinton or Obama have taken America in the reckless direction that Trump has done? Take also the more recent case of war in Ukraine. Had it not been for Biden, smarting after the humiliation in Afghanistan, and were it not for machoistically nationalist Putin, would this war have happened? A calmer set of leaders may have found a way to paper over their differences.

To look at the issue a little differently, are leaders driven to a particular strategy by the force of circumstance because the world is a turbulent and dangerous place? In the world wars, leaders were concerned with actual fighting. After the Second World War, the great powers were caught in a decades-long tussle for positional advantage. During the Cold War, grand strategy was still concerned with mobilizing all resources. But the objectives became fuzzier with time.

All this while, China was biding its time. After Xi took over as president in 2013, a new, more aggressive strategy began to unfold. BRI was its brand vehicle, and creeping revisionism in the South China Sea, besides that in Ladakh, became the calling card of its bolder strategic intent. With it, both China and its new leader announced their arrival at the top of the world's strategic stage.

It is in moments like this that people regard geopolitics as a puffed-up word, one of those polysyllables that actually mean something very basic. Still, it is a handy label to stick on to the manoeuvrings of big powers.

The world's history in recent decades illustrates this well. In the 1930s, economic crisis and rising nationalism had shaken the confidence of many in democracy. Some saw fascism and communism as attractive alternatives. That crisis of confidence was accompanied by a breakdown of the strategic order. Some commentators warn that under Covid-19, a crisis similar in nature and of that magnitude is upon us.

They add darkly that with China and Russia in revisionist mode, the strategic assumptions of the last seven decades may no longer remain valid. To complicate matters further, the US seems to be tiring of its role as the world's 'go-to' power for all reasons and in all seasons. In this time of flux, finding new ideas about the world order is the key challenge of our age.

The objective should be to somehow mesh the disruptive politics of leaders like Xi and Putin with a diplomat's steady strategic approach. As against this, the world is confronted with the reality of President Biden's obstinate decisions on Afghanistan and Ukraine. Is there, then, a formula for wise strategy that the leaders could look to?

Anticipating the need, Roman historian Sallust had given this simple mantra of good strategy: '*Concordia res parvae crescunt, discordia maximae dilabuntur* (Small states grow with concord; discord causes great ones to dissolve).'

16

DRUMS OF WAR

If thy thought is that vision is greater than action, why dost thou enjoin upon me the terrible action of war?

—Bhagavad Gita (3:1)

Of all the spheres of human activity, warfare confounds the most because war is exempt from the rules of murder. Death and destruction also wash away the straight lines that define quiet debate.

If this is so evident a truth, why do wars happen? Is it because war is the ultimate macho test? Do human imperfections lead to war despite knowing that if peace imposes restraints on the worst of rulers, war removes them? Or, is it because the leaders of men deliberately keep the fuse short? Misunderstandings, conflict and war follow as a matter of course.

Some academics have tried to explain war in ideological terms. A view popular in the 1990s celebrated democracy as the age of peace. In practice, however, it was mostly an aspirational notion because the 1990s sowed the seeds of wars in the Gulf and West Asia. Moreover, excessive faith in democracy as the preventive for war is misplaced because, like reason, it is a weak reed on which to base our hopes for peace.

As a matter of fact, states which have adversarial relations with each other do not put the opposing state to the 'democracy test' before launching a war. Primal instincts that motivated countries to sword in an earlier age still guide their finger towards the trigger.

That burst of anger is the privilege of a leader or a general. However, no great thinker suggests the resort to sword because war involves breakdown, including moral breakdown. Sun Tzu had once advised, 'To subdue the enemy without fighting is the acme of skill.' This is a sound principle and, from time to time, it finds an echo in what other wise men like Kennedy maintained, 'Peace need not be impracticable, and war need not be inevitable... If we cannot end now our differences, at least we can help make the world safe for diversity.'[1]

This is the crux—the safety of peace and the satisfaction of morality, if forced into war, have been a recurrent theme of the right thinking from the very beginning. Still, if the call to arms becomes inevitable, and a war follows, then nations must observe rules. As the Prussian military strategist Carl von Clausewitz wrote, 'The moral elements are among the most important in war...They constitute the spirit that permeates war as a whole...'[2]

Sadly, a lot has changed since Clausewitz wrote *On War*. More importantly, the decision to launch or stop a war is no longer the exclusive preserve of the leader. There are many other factors that influence this decision.

For instance, the decision to launch a war and be shocked by its gore may not be the case in future wars as it once was when the two armies stood face to face in the open ground, awaiting the command to attack. In those few minutes, before giving the command to attack, the leader still had the possibility to reconsider. Now, a leader who ponders excessively is dubbed indecisive. There are new factors that also influence his decision.

As before, leaders and generals still control the trigger. But technology, mass media and social media can also act as instigators on a scale unfamiliar earlier. The nationalistic fervour in TV debates can drive nations to the edge as can the 'likes' and the 'retweets' of Twitter.

Despite these many ways of going to war, can war still be avoided? If there is an indication that the other side is preparing to shoot, can preventive steps succeed? Oscar Wilde seemed to think it was possible, 'Always forgive your enemies; nothing annoys them so much.'

Alas, Wilde's was a writer's fancy.

Weakness Invites Aggression

In the more practical everyday world, war is often a contest of wills settled through extreme violence. It is state-sanctioned brutality, the outcome of which is death, destruction and suffering. Because it is state-sanctioned, no amount of forgiveness, that Wilde puts so much of his faith in, can avoid the inevitable. A premeditated war is undertaken with a purpose, for example, the one that China and India had fought in 1962.

Both sides had anticipated it, yet India was ill prepared for it despite many warnings that the war could break out any time. There is a well-quoted letter of 1950 that the then Home Minister Sardar Patel wrote to PM Nehru about the Chinese intentions:

> Chinese irredentism and communist imperialism are different from the expansionism or imperialism of the western powers. The former has a cloak of ideology which makes it ten times more dangerous. In the guise of ideological expansion lie concealed racial, national or historical claims. The danger from the north and north-east, therefore, becomes both communist and imperialist. While our western and north-western threat to security is still as prominent as before, a new threat has developed from the north and north-east. Thus, for the first time, after centuries, India's defence has to concentrate itself on two fronts simultaneously.[3]

Sadly, Patel's warning remained just that—a notice of grim tidings. A war-capable China seized the opportunity, and its invasion of

1962 caught India totally off guard. It was routed on all fronts but saved total humiliation by China's declaration of ceasefire. Even years after the war ended, the defeat rancours. Sadly, that has not been India's only loss.

In 1962, India lost 38,000 sq. km of its territory in Aksai Chin to China. Earlier, in 1947–48, it had lost 72,970 sq. km in the Northern Areas and 13,297 sq. km in other parts of J&K to Pakistan. The total area lost to China and Pakistan amounts to 124,267 sq. km out of India's land area of 3.287 million sq. km. This is an enormous slice off the country's territory.

But this loss also contains a message. If capability is the key to war, communicating your message in time and effectively is essential to take the world along.

Pakistan articulates its case on Kashmir aggressively and with great confidence; India, in contrast, is diffident. As a result, the world nods to Pakistan, convinced that its protestations have a point, even though tradition and law speak for India.

Similarly, China stakes its territorial claim on what it says were centuries-old territorial limits, whereas history for the Indian negotiators seems to start with the case that Henry McMahon presented at Shimla (then Simla) in 1914. Is it any surprise then that the Indian claim should appear the weaker of the two? When, and as is often the case, Chinese soldiers intrude across the Line of Actual Control (LAC) into Indian Territory, the standard Indian response is to fudge the issue by maintaining that the boundary issue is yet to be settled. If that is so, aren't we already conceding that we don't really know the limits of our claim?

Ironically, China used British records, and the gaps in them, selectively to create a case where they did not actually have one, ignoring what did not suit them. India chose to follow the British confusions and didn't draw upon the local and Tibetan traditions, which would have buttressed its case and led to a more effective border policy in practice.

If a country does not marshal its facts well and is unable to present its case convincingly, half the battle is lost. For instance, did the history of India's relations with Tibet start with the first British expedition in the late nineteenth century?

It is along this line of doubt that Kissinger begins the prologue to his book *On China*:

> In October 1962, China's revolutionary leader Mao Zedong summoned his top military and political commanders to meet with him in Beijing. Two thousand miles to the west, in the forbidding and sparsely populated terrain of Himalayas, Chinese and Indian troops were locked in a standoff over the two countries' disputed borders. The dispute arose over different versions of history: India claimed the frontier demarcated during British rule, China the limits of imperial China.[4]

Kissinger writes further that Mao told his commanders that China had fought one-and-a-half wars in the past with India, the half war being particularly gory where Tamerlane's soldiers put a hundred thousand Indians to sword. This time, he asked the commanders to be 'restrained and principled'. Then Kissinger adds admiringly, '...the offensive proceeded much as he (Mao) described: China executed a sudden, devastating blow on the Indian positions and then retreated to the previous line of control, even going so far as to return the captured Indian heavy weaponry.'[5]

China had achieved its twin objectives—first, of crushing India to a defeat that it would not forget for a long time, and second, to keep only the territory that it had claimed was its.

Having done that, China found it prudent to return the rest of the vast chunk it had conquered. While it earned international applaud for this act, the fact is that it was not an act of generosity on China's part. Unlike Nehru and his idealism, Mao was not fired by the desire to claim the high moral ground. China withdrew because it would have found it a logistics nightmare to keep occupying the captured territory so far from its supply bases in a rough terrain. Moreover, it would also have had to contend with a restive population.

As against this clarity of Chinese objectives, a frequent lament in India is about the opaqueness with which the China policy is handled. It is not as if people want to be consulted in the formulation or the implementation of it, but they resent being kept in the dark about where we stand in relation to China. For instance, has China sliced off a further portion of territory after 1962? If Doklam was such a success for us, why did the PM have to rush to Wuhan? It is easy to explain this, as indeed every other action of the government, through a faithful section of the media, but the truth has a habit of popping out uncomfortably sooner or later. Moreover, in this age of multiple sources of information, the other side grabs the opportunity to inform with the slant it wishes.

New Frictions, Old Grudges

So far we have viewed this issue from the standpoint of a victor. But let's also briefly consider the issue from a loser's perspective. India went into a long sulk after 1962. Militarily humiliated, and despite claims of having bettered China in some later skirmishes, the nation stands psychologically wounded and unsure as to how it would effectively match up to China when there is a next time.

A few years later, in 1971, Pakistan suffered a bigger humiliation, and it was dismembered. It, too, went into a sulk, but instead of wallowing in self-pity and cramping itself with a sense of inferiority, it bounced back to rearm effectively and change tactics. Its revenge against India has taken multiple forms—from pushing drugs and counterfeit currency into India to conducting a proxy war against it. Despite the strategic misadventure by Pakistan in Kargil, its army remains confident and eager. It is now straining at the leash for the next one.

War can also leave deep psychological wounds on a society. The US as a nation was traumatized after its retreat in defeat from Vietnam in 1973. A few years later, in 1989, the Soviet Union, the other superpower, had to suffer the humiliation of being forced out of Afghanistan.

While the loser in a war curses his cruel stars, the victor gloats. Consequently, it is normal for victors to consign history to the trash can, and for victims to take it seriously. But a lesson that applies both to the victor and the vanquished is this: war does not determine who is right, it determines who is left. If that is so, and if both suffer, why do countries pick up the sword? One explanation could be what Christopher Clark says in his book *The Sleepwalkers* about the origins of the First World War, 'The protagonists were sleepwalkers, watchful but unseeing, haunted by dreams, yet blind to the reality of the horror they were about to bring into the world.'[6]

Add to this the fact that if you keep accumulating gunpowder, someone at some point could put a match to it. The global military spending in 2020 presents a sobering picture in this respect. Some of the major military spenders that year were the US ($778 billion), China ($252 billion. estimate), India ($72.9 billion), Russia ($61.7 billion), Britain ($59.2 billion), Saudi Arabia ($57.5 billion, est.), Germany ($52.8 billion), France ($52.7 billion), Japan ($49.1 billion) and South Korea ($45.7 billion).

That the US should be miles ahead of everyone else in this chart of top spenders is understandable, so is China's extravagant leap forward. But what is really interesting is the continental shift in defence spending; of the top 10 spenders, five are Asian. The three former colonial powers, i.e. France, Britain and Germany, are not in the top spenders' part of this major league. Moreover, the big defence spending by the five Asian countries is not just reflective of their increased money power, it is an ominous sign that the next really big war may start in Asia.

It is also likely that in the coming years, warfare may be conducted through means other than armaments. The world may witness more hybrid wars and threats to trade, communications and people's privacy through cyberattacks. However, these recent challenges do not exclude the possibility of war through conventional means because besides these new frictions, old grudges still simmer. Even the colonial injustices continue to rankle.

To cite some cases, between 1857 and 1867, the British are suspected of killing up to one million Indian civilians to teach the rest of the population a lesson for the Indian Rebellion of 1857. The death toll was no less in Algeria. After the civil war of 1830–45, French brutality, famine and disease killed 1.5 million Algerians, nearly half of its population then. In Congo, over 10 million people were killed by the Belgian forces between 1890 and 1910. If we go further back in time to the sixteenth century, the disease brought by Spanish explorers wiped out nearly the entire population of the native Aztecs in present-day Mexico. It declined from 25 million to approximately one million.

These hurts of the past are unlikely to result in wars of revenge against the former colonial masters. But these slights of history could help decide which side a country might choose to align with in the next world war.

Fortunately, and despite the war in Ukraine, the world is not poised at the brink again, at least not just yet. But two distinct trends seem to be emerging. The first is the declining will of the democratic world, led by the US, to maintain the dominant position it has held in the international system since 1945. In contrast, there is the activism of the two revisionist powers: Russia and China.

Both wish to act as overlords of their regions, but Russia sugar-coats its intentions. It wants security around its periphery by having a veto authority over the economic, diplomatic and security decisions of those nations. China, in contrast, wants to surround itself with states that should act as tributaries to it.

Both feel threatened by the domination of democratic powers in the international system and consider the US as the principal obstacle to their ambitions. Increasingly, China also views India acting as an adjunct to America's strategic calculus against it. Therefore, as it seeks to weaken the American-led international security order, it will consider checking India as well.

Short, Swift and Decisive

If economic capability were to be the key, then all may not remain well with China. It might be reasonable to say that China has reached its economic plateau. The favourable demographics that allowed it to become the world's factory are declining. Since China's economy is slowing and heavily in debt, its leaders might see now as the best time to use a victory in war as a diversion and, thereby, displace America's power in the region. If they calculate that war with the US carries unacceptable risks, then they might opt for a winnable confrontation with India.

Such a war might be short, swift and decisive. China would try to destroy India's ability to command and control its armed forces through missile strikes and cyberattacks. It is also likely to use its arsenal of ballistic and cruise missiles to destroy India's forward-deployed assets and military bases.

As and when China decides to launch its next big war, would Russia be involved on China's side? Will the US then be faced with a two-front war that its strategists have long speculated and worried about?

One of the nineteenth century's foremost statesmen, Otto von Bismarck had once said that in a world order of five states, it is desirable to be part of a group of three. If we reduce that number from five to three, and apply Bismarck's principle, it would mean that one should be in the group of two. So, where does that leave the US in the group with China and Russia?—in a weak position, Bismarck would have concluded.

Applying the same three-state test to a war involving India, Pakistan and China, we will do well to remember the 'two-front war' that Sardar Patel had warned Nehru about.

The possibility that a global power may have to confront more than one rival simultaneously had engaged not just Bismarck but other strategic thinkers as well. US strategic planners worked on the possibility of a 'two and one half war' through most of the 1960s.

In 1969, the Nixon administration decided to examine what had by then become both a fixation and a tricky goal. This assumed that the Soviet Union and China was one united communist bloc. It also assumed that their political and strategic interests coincided enough for them to launch simultaneous action against the US. On this basis, the planning required a large enough force to tackle the two-and-a-half front threat.

It was this military hypothesis that the Nixon administration began to examine, and the essence of Kissinger's recommendation was, 'a simultaneous Warsaw Pact attack in Europe and Chinese conventional attack in Asia is unlikely. In any event, I do not believe such a simultaneous attack could or should be met with ground forces.'[7] By accepting this recommendation, the American strategic mind started thinking of de-hyphenating Soviet Union and China, and a new diplomatic initiative was about to begin. With this, the two-and-a-half front concept gave way to 'one-and-a-half' front possibility of an attack by Warsaw forces coupled with a smaller threat elsewhere.

A lot has happened differently since then. The ideological struggle between capitalism and communism is history, and the quantitative nuclear arms race of the Cold War age is over. A new qualitative arms race is on.

Russia has been rearming and modernizing its forces, and one of its aims is to order its European neighbourhood to its strategic liking. Its war with Ukraine was in line with this pursuit. Though Russia's conventional forces could not rapidly seize Ukrainian territory, Putin's warnings about Russia's strategic and nuclear forces served to keep NATO from direct military interference in the conflict. The challenge now for Russia is in its ability to transform conventional advantages into permanent gains through the threat of a nuclear escalation that both sides fear, but by Moscow's calculation, the West might fear more.

In the East, China's conventional military can now compete with the US and its allies. Its nuclear force could be used in controlled ways to deter vertical or horizontal escalation by the US.

But the situation is not entirely hopeless for the US. Kissinger writes in *On China* that one of Mao's favourite ways to convey his thinking on the US was through the journalist Edgar Snow. He had once remarked on a helpful note, '...forces of history have divided and separated the American and Chinese peoples from virtually all communication during the past 15 years...However, I myself do not believe it will end in war and one of history's major tragedies.'[8]

This is reassuring, but times have changed and so have the circumstances. Mao is dead; now Xi's thoughts determine China's policies. And Xi has been repeatedly exhorting his troops to be ready for battle.

Alas, it isn't just Xi who is exhorting his troops. There are others in the world who anticipate war. But before they unsheathe their swords for the next major war, they should repeat slowly for themselves what Herodotus said 25 centuries ago: 'In peace, sons bury their fathers. In war, fathers bury their sons.'

17

THE SETTING

Impure wisdom has no clear vision of what is right and what is wrong, what should be done and what should not be done.

—Bhagavad Gita (18:31)

Having lived through two world wars, Albert Einstein was deeply concerned about the next one. This, he feared, might be deadlier still, 'I know not with what weapons World War III will be fought, but World War IV will be fought with sticks and stones.'[1] He could have added, if there is anyone left to fight after World War III.

Perhaps that's how it might be. But it could also turn out differently, and the unexpected may erase many of our worst assumptions. In that case, the world might continue along the largely peaceful course it followed in the late twentieth century. That, at least, was the hope of the liberals. Sadly, this bliss did not last long. A series of dramatic events followed, changing the world from the largely placid one we were getting used to. This chain of the unpleasant has not stopped yet. Every time a new cataclysmic event takes place, we shrink back in horror and hope that after it is over, the world will go back to its former languid ways.

But the evidence so far does not inspire confidence. The US did not go back to being normal after 9/11. India didn't do so after 26/11. And the world changed after the financial shock of

2008. All these created a new normal.

The two terror strikes, for instance, affected everything. People got used to maximum security—they couldn't go into a building without showing their ID proof and walking through a metal detector and couldn't get on airplanes the same way again. Something of that magnitude is going to happen after Covid-19 subsides. Social distancing and work-from-home may not become the permanent normal, but there will be a seismic shift in what we expect, what we endure and how we adapt. The world is also worried about its effect on the mental health of people, their lifestyle changes, the fate of travel and the state of economies of countries. But it hasn't had the time yet to consider what this fraught existence may mean for the system of governance in countries or for inter-state relations.

Already, this epidemic has helped autocrats grab more power. About 84 countries have declared some form of emergency since the pandemic began. But this unbridled power also poses big risks for autocrats because their delivery invariably falls short of their promises.

The pandemic is also starting to topple another assumption of the globalization era—that emerging markets have a significant role to play. The 30 largest emerging nations owed $73 trillion in 2019, an IOU[2] pile that has grown by more than one-and-a-half times over the last decade. With their extra spending, during Covid-19, on laid-off workers and an idling economy, the idea that developing nations will lead the global economy out of its malaise looks increasingly improbable. They will be lucky if their own economic sinews recover to at least the pre-Covid-19 strength. These woes, universal in nature, after the Covid-19-administered shock, will give further speed to a fragmented and an already suspicious world.

After the 2008 financial crisis, the economic pattern throughout the world was towards a gated globalization. It meant a slide towards unstated but clear national self-interest—an idea that was later put out publicly and bluntly by Trump as 'America First'. In the immediate shock of 2008, this idea involved more state intervention in the flow of money and goods, more regionalization of trade and more friction as national self-interest began to prevail over global cooperation. Over the next decade, even as trade and investment kept moving freely across borders, national walls with gates kept going up. Countries chose whom they traded with and what sort of capital they welcomed.

The question that was asked in 2008 is being asked again: is gated globalization a pause on the road to more openness or is it here to stay? There were no definitive answers then nor are there likely to be now. In fact, this time, the absolutely new conditions of human behaviour, like the enormity of American sanctions on Russia, have left pundits wondering if the conventional theories are valid any longer.

Reality Check

In that same broad vein, if one bravely sticks the neck out and ventures to look at the world 10 or 15 years hence, the sight we might see may be technologically bewildering. In some respects, the shape of the decision-making process in the world might be more mechanical as AI begins to present a restricted menu of choices to the leadership, making it a matter of choosing between the black and the white option. If the finger on the trigger were to be guided by AI, rather than by head and heart, then morality in decision-making will have been given a go-by. And so would have been morality in matters of war and peace. Then, as Voltaire wrote in *Candide*, we might find ourselves asking, 'If this is the best of all possible worlds, what can the rest be like?'

In such a world, the US will still be the predominant force. However, it will want to maintain its global power at the lowest possible cost. It will not mean isolationism, but the US might opt for a risk-reduction course:

- It will not get readily drawn into military conflicts,
- To maintain its leadership position in the world, it will try to act as an umpire resolving other countries' conflicts,
- It will have to give up its impatience in dealing with others and develop the knack for patient diplomacy or the slow compromises that diplomats nurture, and
- It will try and save its military energy for the next big war.

The likely result of this change will be that in the years to come, the US will increasingly be confronted by the limits to its power. China and Russia will test it at every turn, but it is the smaller countries that will make the US flutter like a bee without sting.

The US may put up a brave face over it, but it cannot escape the consequences of these challenges. It suffered a national trauma after the Vietnam War. Its veterans and the war wounded were directly affected, but the country's self-esteem, too, suffered a blow that took better part of a generation to heal. The retreat in defeat from Afghanistan is not a national trauma in a similar sense. Instead, it has dented the American swagger abroad. Its friends are wondering whether America any longer has the will and the capacity to engage in, and win, wars.

The problem that we might increasingly confront is not merely the superpower friction and other long-simmering inter-state conflicts. There is equally the prospect that intra-state conflicts and non-state aggression could thrust the world into turmoil. In such a milieu, where a series of wars rather than lasting peace is the dominant feature, the civilization that has given us unprecedented comforts will be under severe test.

But war is not the only factor leading to a country's decline. Some of our present-day concerns about what punctures civilizational progress were the very reasons why civilizations collapsed in the past. Thus, 'climate change', in the shape of droughts, was one of the issues that led to the decline of the Mayan and Roman empires.

The centralization of power and inequality of wealth, and sometimes shocks like overwhelming indebtedness are among the other reasons that have contributed to societal decline in the past. Collapse of a civilization could, therefore, happen because of a variety of reasons, and it could affect both great powers and small states. This has historically been the case. What is new this time, in our age, is the interconnectedness of today's global economic system. This could make a crisis spread.

This is one major reason why we are presently poised at the edge as never before. It is also true that the instruments for self-destruct are far more potent today than ever before. From biological agents to autonomous weapons and nuclear weapons—all these have multiplied the possibility of destruction that could be quick and asymmetric. A virus or a nuclear war poses existential risk for entire societies, indeed for the very extinction of our species, if the virus is particularly potent or the use of nukes is large in such a war. At the very least, it could mean the wiping out of all human progress in a nuclear cloud and a return to the 'stone age', just as Einstein had feared. Add to all this the fickle morality of our times. Unlike in the past, some of our present-day leaders are less likely to hesitate in employing weapons of mass destruction.

This is not all; some fissures brewing within countries could have an impact beyond their borders. The combined effect of subsidies, the waiving off of loans and large welfare systems are creating a new caste system in societies, and with it, fuelling resentment against people who enjoy the fruits of other peoples' labour.

When a welfare system becomes all-pervasive, those receiving payments begin to regard them as a kind of salary. Such welfare runs counter to the basic human instinct vital for an individual's self-respect. That instinct is the satisfaction of contributing something to society. Moreover, this large-scale, non-productive expenditure is being incurred at some cost to other national projects. At some point in the future, societies will have to confront this issue squarely to set limits. If this does not happen and limits of welfare expenditure are not set, then economies will begin to crumble. On the other hand, if states decide to confront the issue and put curbs on welfare schemes, the resulting protests and violence could tear societies apart.

Beyond the national boundaries, and worldwide, the big question that might come up repeatedly in the coming years will be about the stability of the international order. Here, national priorities rather than idealistic notions of goodwill will provide the clue to the resulting shape of relationships. The case of American reluctance in supplying Indian firms with the basic pharmaceutical material for Covid-19 vaccines is an example. Similarly, Russia would prefer an oil price that is closer to $100 a barrel than $50. If high oil price is the Russian goal, Beijing needs stability in oil supply and low oil prices. There are other sources of potential tension between them. China may be the largest consumer of the oil and gas produced in Russia's east, but Russia has, for long, worried about the persistent migration of Chinese workers in that region.

Democracy Takes a Back Seat

Apart from these serious material concerns, there could be other deeper and fundamental changes in the years ahead. The seventeenth-century philosopher Spinoza had predicted that democracy would, in due course, be guided by and taken over by demagogues. In the choice between freedom and chaos versus order and tyranny, Spinoza predicted that people would choose order and tyranny.

Whether it becomes an all-pervasive phenomenon affecting a large number of countries across the world remains to be seen. But, already, there are enough autocrats in some of the more important countries of the world. Under their influence, the countries they rule will witness progressively more polarized times when the differences that divide us get sharper. The catalyst for this division is the image-driven, charisma-wielding autocratic-politician who demands that you discard critical assessment of his performance in favour of unquestioning adulation. Every time the image-driven style has overwhelmed the traditional style of party politics, democracy has taken a back seat.

Clearly then, peace at home and peace abroad will not be the signature tune of the world in the years ahead. Instead, conflicts between states and tensions within would prevail.

Apart from the ideological ennui that makes people experiment periodically with political change, there are other trend lines that indicate that the world might be readying for a churn in the next decade or thereabouts because countries across the spectrum have one reason or the other to complain. Russia and Iran, for the financial sanctions that US puts on them, and China and India because they feel they are not being given their due weight in financial bodies like the World Bank, IMF, etc. Still, and despite these quibbles, there is, in theory, an entire network that should ideally make the world tick like a well-oiled machine.

Alas, this is not how it is in practice.

The UNSC should be the arbiter of the last resort for the ills of the world. But it can perform that role justly if its composition reflects the changed times. It badly needs an overhaul to represent the current power structure in the world because patterns of economic growth, technological advance or military power are not frozen in time. The rise of new great powers is inevitable, and the power landscape has changed significantly since 1945. But the high table at the UNSC does not reflect that change. As a result, its decisions do not carry the weight of the changed global might.

Once, the UN peacekeeping operations had provided some hope against violence. Today, they are not addressing the world's most-pressing wars. Iraq, Syria, Afghanistan and Yemen have seen immense human suffering, but because the big powers are involved, the UN is unwilling and unable to get a role for itself. Instead, its forces were deployed in countries that suffered only 7 per cent of total global conflict deaths in the five-year period up to 2018.

This pattern is unlikely to change, and in future, major conflicts would have to unwind themselves of their own accord. Unfortunately for the world, the UN will continue to fall short of expectations, and in the absence of a place at the global high table in the UNSC, India, Germany, South Africa, Brazil and Japan will play only a marginal role in the critical affairs of the world.

Still, and as Toynbee had hoped, India could have carved a place for itself as a moral leader of the developing world as Nehru did in the immediate post-Independence era by championing the causes dear to the emerging world, like the struggle against racism and colonialism. A little later, he was one of the principal leaders who brought about the confidence that it was possible for the weak nations of the world to maintain their dignity and remain non-aligned.

That leadership came about because Nehru dreamed a universal dream. A similar leap of imagination is unlikely in the new world because it has become far too fractious; there are too many mutinies festering in it, and the authoritarian leader fears the foreign wind.

Being Friends with God

As some of these mutinies could affect others beyond the national borders, let us turn to the crystal ball again. Will the next decade signal a more unstable world? Or, will it be a world which is largely at peace but with pockets where violent conflict is concentrated? Or, will the next few years be about the aggressive intents of China, the resurgence of Russia's power and the decline of the US's global hegemony?

These are grim tidings. Still, the chances are that the world will be around for a long time to come. But it will have become more complicated, divided between a broad American sphere of influence in Europe, and a Chinese sphere in East Asia and Africa. Regions like West Asia, Central and South Asia will be balanced precariously as they parcel out loyalties between the US, China and Russia.

Such a world would be in a continual state of flux. Moreover, the lesson of history is sobering because a major nation's rise has disrupted the position of a dominant state 16 times over the last 500 years. In 12 of these cases, the outcome was war.

Global leadership also involves costs and the ability to shoulder responsibilities on a vast scale. It helps if the package includes a strong ideological message, the type that communism promised. China may be rich and militarily strong, but it does not as yet have the administrative wherewithal or a seductive political script to convince the world that a new leader with a different message has arrived. For the time being, China itself may not want to usurp the US's position as the leader of a global order. But for us to focus on this reluctance is a mistake. Over time, Beijing wants to be powerful enough to counter Washington.

Since Russia and China are currently locked in an anti-America embrace, it leaves India in an uneasy position. This Indian discomfort is the opening that the US has long been seeking. Both these equations are a work in progress, and they may or may not result in long-term durable alliances between Russia and China on the one hand, and between the US and India on the other. But these moves portend what could be a major strategic shift in the global balance of power. It is this shift that could replay in future some of what had happened in past.

For almost 300 years prior to the nineteenth century, the colonial powers of Europe had dominated the sea lanes. This power was once articulated in the British boast 'Britannia rules the waves'.

Then, at almost the concluding phase of the Great Game, Halford Mackinder asserted in 1904 that the balance of power was shifting from domination via the sea lanes to strategic hold of the land mass. In that context, he described the Eurasian landmass as 'the World Island'. The essence of his argument was that 'who rules the World-island commands the World.'[3]

The shift that Mackinder talked of was later borne out by the fierce battle in Eurasia between Hitler's forces and those of Stalin. But there was a practical reason also for Mackinder's assertion. The colonial powers had used the sea lanes because it was convenient and the land routes were not well-developed. However, as the steam engine and car began to reduce time and distance, travel by land became an attractive alternative. Moreover, new strategic priorities also necessitated this change.

Once again, after almost a century, there is change in the offing.

This time, it will mean nearly equal weight to the sea lanes and the land route. China has accelerated this shift by a combination of its actions—setting up bases along the Indian Ocean, converting islands in the Pacific into its fortresses, besides the ambitious BRI and CPEC projects overland.

Russia, too, should have been quick to switch to this shift, because it was the original Eurasian power. But it stands reduced in size and means. Consequently, for the time being, it is content playing a supporting role to China.

India is not in the same league because of the limitations of its current power. Despite having an airbase in Tajikistan, it does not as yet have the economic and military wherewithal to become a critical factor in Eurasia. However, it has the potential to carve out a position for itself in the region because it lies in the middle of Eurasia and the Indo-Pacific. Since India, by itself, cannot match up to the resources of China, it will need the support of a greater power to achieve that critical influence.

It is true that since the 1990s, the US–India relationship has grown steadily, with every president from Bill Clinton and every

PM from Atal Bihari Vajpayee onwards viewing each other as natural allies. However, the shifting nature of the American foreign policy makes India cautious because the US is notoriously fickle in its affections. It can swing from being indulgent to complete indifference as per its calculation of what suits its interests at a particular moment. Even otherwise, consorting with America means walking on broken glass, you never know when a carelessly placed shard will hurt. Since the US is the superpower, it means that the lesser power walking with it will bleed.

As Aristotle had warned in his exploration of friendship in the *Nicomachean Ethics*, it is not possible to be friends with God. Friendship requires equality, and gods are vastly superior to mere mortals. Aristotle's logic was practical: it is difficult to be friends with a boss in the way that one is friends with one's equals. So, can India ever be an equal friend with the US? It seems unlikely as long as the US remains vastly superior to it and as long as America's approach to relationships is transactional.

Still, in contrast to the muscular yet turbulent relationship between the US and Pakistan, Indo-US relations could develop into a mature bond based on mutual needs. Even then, the US will be a demanding partner, providing episodic irritants to the prickly and self-respecting India. Moreover, in the shrinking trade environment, the US will want increasingly more from a large and expanding market like India.

Despite their differences, the US and India will not come to blows. They might bicker and trade barbs occasionally, but they are unlikely to wrestle in mud as the US and Pakistan have done regularly and so often. Still, the strength and the effectiveness of the Indo-US relationship will be tested repeatedly by China. It will be the third party in the Indo-US relationship, providing periodic agony.

Moreover, the 'strategic' relationship and other adjectives that the US and India bureaucratically conjure up periodically will not be enough to gloss over the fact that both sides allow petty disputes to dominate. Accordingly, in this relationship, the transient rather than the long-term will dominate, and the hesitations of past will remain the obstacles of future.

Mind Games

To the combined irritation of India and the US, China will increasingly play its Pakistan card against them. And Pakistan, already adept at this game, will happily play along. There may be differences between them on some issues, for example, over China's treatment of its Islamic minorities or about Pakistan's support to terrorists, but these would be minor bumps. The threads binding their relationship are so many and so strategic that China will not throw Pakistan under the bus. Even if there is a CPEC slowdown and Pakistan defaults on the payment of its debt to China, the fundamentals of their security relationship are unlikely to dilute.

There is a lesser-known defence dimension to the CPEC, which is gradually coming to public light. Increasingly, reports suggest that more than its commercial dimension, the Gwadar port would be strategically invaluable for Chinese warships and submarines to monitor and, if necessary, control the passage of energy and merchandise trade through the Indian Ocean. Up to 90 per cent of Japan's oil imports, nearly 90 per cent of South Korea's and around 80 per cent of China's are shipped from West Asia and Africa through the Indian Ocean.

China has also set up the Beidou satellite tracking facilities near Karachi and Lahore in Pakistan, which will help both countries to target their missiles with great accuracy. Some new reports add that China may also be setting up fighter aircraft manufacturing facilities in Pakistan to produce fourth and fifth generation aircraft along with their armaments.

But China's strategic assets abroad are not limited to Pakistan.

As its ambitions grow, so do its stakes. Its bases in the Indian Ocean, long called the String of Pearls, are now emerging as strategically appointed naval bases. Djibouti, the third-smallest country on the African mainland, is a modern-day Casablanca. This tiny former French Somaliland has leveraged its strategic location, at the mouth of the Red Sea and over some of the world's busiest shipping lanes running through the Suez Canal, to lease its barren, rocky land to foreign powers.

France maintains a base here, as do Americans, Italians and the Japanese. Germany and Spain maintain troops at the base hosted by the French. China inaugurated, in August 2017, its first overseas military base here. This gave Djibouti the unique and potentially parlous distinction of hosting the largest number of naval bases in the world.

Besides this confluence of bases, there is another major change coming about in world military affairs.

This concerns the shift away from the traditional dependence of armies on heavy-duty military hardware to high-tech innovations like satellite jammers, hypersonic strike technology, advanced cyber capabilities, AI, big data analytics, spectrum denial and high-energy lasers. Only a few countries led by the US, China and Russia are at the forefront of this change.

Besides these new instruments of war, sharp mind games, too, are increasingly being put to use. Pakistani, Russian and Chinese security services are practising 'reflexive control', by which you get your enemies to make mistakes. It involves analysing the opponents to understand where they get their information and why they trust it. A second part of this exercise is to insert errors and mistakes in these sources. This has huge implications for military; a piece of incorrect information can influence a general to make a mistake.

As technology advances, warfare, too, will undergo change. The current Sino-American contest differs sharply from the superpower contests of the past. If this leads to a major war, that, too, would be far different from what the world has seen up to now because:

- This would be the first time that two nuclear superpowers will actually be fighting a war,
- The war will not be limited to fighting on land, water and air. Cyberspace, AI and the digital realm will also be called into play, and
- The US–China conflict, when it happens, would include the contest for the control of the Pacific. Mao had talked about it in 1959: 'One day, it does not matter when, the United States will have to retire from the rest of the world and will have to abandon the Western Pacific.'[4]

But Mao was not an oracle of all things, nor was he right all the time. He, too, faltered. And as Warren Buffett warned in his annual letter of 2021 to shareholders, 'Never bet against America.'[5]

18

THE FINAL WEAPON

Like the fire at the end of Time which burns all in the last day,
I see thy vast mouths and terrible teeth.

—Bhagavad Gita (11:25)

One of the first to talk about an actual nuclear war was Chairman Mao. The Chinese response to the threat of a nuclear attack was articulated publicly by him in 1957 at a conference of socialist countries in Moscow:

> We shouldn't be afraid of atomic bombs and missiles. No matter what kind of war breaks out—conventional or thermonuclear—we will win. As for China, if the imperialists unleash war on us, we may lose more than three hundred million people. So what? War is war. The years will pass and we will get to work producing more babies than ever before.[1]

The Soviet leader Khrushchev found Mao's speech deeply disturbing. The other socialist leaders present there also felt that Mao had been extreme. Had someone else talked in this language, the western world, too, would have reacted with horror. But it held Mao in high esteem, with a mixture of awe and wonderment.

Since then, China itself has acquired a vast range of nuclear weapons. Still, if a war breaks out between two nuclear powers, it is not a given that nukes will be used. So far, the fear of consequences has stumped the strategic mind and restrained the finger on the nuclear button. The faith in finding a way seems to be in deterrence—that if you possess the bomb, it would somehow be the ultimate restraint, the other side will also hesitate to use its own.

However, this belief is grounded in a fragile foundation because deterrence works as long as it works. But what makes it work remains loosely defined. Is it the military strength that deters the opponent? Or, is it that the adversary never had the intention to attack? Therefore, driven by miscalculation or remorse, the nuclear age could end in a dramatic manner—a swift and complete destruction or total disarmament. Unfortunately, though, if one ending is undesirable, the other is unachievable.

For long, the nuclear haves were limited in number, and there were reasonably sound grounds for their restraint. Till China joined it in the 1960s, all members of this exclusive club were Christian. Therefore, despite communist East Europe competing fiercely with the capitalist West, the fact was that both sides of the divide in the East–West confrontation were co-religionists. They had also gone through the harrowing experience of two world wars, and made wiser by that experience, their leaders were likely to hold their hand.

The divide now is across religions—for instance, between the US and China, the US and North Korea, India and China, or India and Pakistan. Besides, the enmities between some of today's nuclear powers are intense and seemingly intractable. Though the fear of consequences continues to restrain this larger number of nuclear powers, the risk factor has increased.

To some extent, technological advances are to blame for the increase in risk factors. The miniaturized, low-yield nuclear warheads and highly accurate delivery systems have made the use of nuclear option thinkable. It has introduced an intermediate level between a conventional war and an all-out nuclear war. This 'limited' nuclear war, employing one or a few more battlefield tactical nuclear weapons would not result in apocalyptic destruction; at least, that is the assumption. But it could also work out differently.

Therefore, the possibility that one day someone might slip and use the bomb preoccupies the strategic community. It is not just the accidental rush of blood with a decision-maker that is of concern. Some of the leaders today are not stumped by the traditional argument of the destruction that its use may cause, rather they see it as an instrument, an ultimate instrument maybe, to bend the enemy to their will.

Yet, the debate about the use, or accidental use, of nuclear weapons has not kept pace with the development of weapons, their multiplicity and the improvement in the means of their delivery.

This should be a cause of concern because suspicions, misunderstandings and miscalculations have led to many wars in the twentieth century. They were all conventional wars, except in the last stages of the Second World War. But in a future war, if it happens to be nuclear, there may not be many strategists left to analyse post-event what went wrong or to count the losses.

Still, the enormity of that catastrophic possibility has not slowed the world down. It carries on, neither in defiance nor resiliently but in the confidence that their part of the world is safe. That's why everyone does not weigh, and counterweigh, the possibility and the consequences of nuclear recklessness. It is simply not on people's everyday worry radar. That, indeed, is how it should be because, by and large, the world is safe. But there are parts of the world that live dangerously.

Mao was actually confronted with a nuclear situation. In March 1969, Chinese troops had ambushed Soviet guards over a disputed border area. Soon, the two countries were fighting with heavy artillery and aircraft. The conflict escalated quickly beyond what Chinese leaders had expected, and before the end of March, Moscow was making thinly veiled nuclear threats to pressure China to back down. China was several steps behind the Soviet Union in nuclear capability then, but it had tested a thermonuclear device in Lop Nor in 1967. Since then, China has vastly improved its military capabilities and made its nuclear options far more sophisticated.

As a revisionist power, China has tightened its hold over the islands in the South China Sea to an obsessive degree, where it is ready to chase out an erring American ship or an aircraft. Besides control over the South China Sea, it has made no secret of the fact that it covets Taiwan. While neither side may desire war, the possibility of a confrontation prolonging and developing into the nuclear stage exists. Since China has dispersed many of its nuclear assets in its military concentrations, an attack by the US on China's nuclear assets could inflict large casualties on military personnel. The retaliation or a pre-emptive strike by China will then lead to consequences that nightmares are made of.

A US–China confrontation spiralling out of control is not the only nightmare. In a language that Indian Army generals have previously shied away from using, former Indian Army chief (and later the country's first chief of defence staff) General Bipin Rawat had said, 'We will call their bluff. If given the task, we will not say we cannot cross the border because they have nuclear weapons.'[2]

Desired Destruction

The situation could be just as fraught in a war of the West with Russia. During the Kosovo conflict in 1999, the US utilized modern, high-precision conventional weapons to produce highly effective results, with limited collateral damage. The Russian response was to develop a new military doctrine in 2000. By this, Russia introduced the notion of deployment of battlefield nuclear weapons to de-escalate a conflict with NATO, if the Russian forces were about to suffer defeat in a conventional conflict. This is in contrast to the strategy during the Cold War, when deterrence included the threat of inflicting unacceptable damage on an enemy. Russia's de-escalation strategy now caters for tailored damage—one which is effective and usable but limited in scope. Putin chose to use the Cold War language, in the initial stages of the war in Ukraine, to warn NATO against interfering.

Putin's message had the intended effect because between them, Russia and the US possess about 90 per cent of the world's approximately 14,000 nuclear weapons. This concentration in and around them has, for long, put European states in an awkward position. Even a nuclear attack over Russia carries the risk of nuclear cloud straying over to their soil. This dilemma continues to cramp their options.

The US and other NATO powers have pondered over and debated the fact that a war with Russia could happen and so they need to device a response that is effective enough against a nuclear threat. But a major question mark concerns their decision-making process. Unlike Russia, they would need consultations among many countries. All NATO members may not agree. But, even if they were to decide unanimously to launch a strike, would they be able to agree on the scale of retaliation quickly enough? The process of consultations among many states complicates decision-making.

Let us assume it has been decided by NATO to use the nuclear option. It will then be confronted by an equally fundamental issue of when a nuclear strike should be called into play. The European consensus, as Kissinger mentions in his book *White House Years*, is that strategic nuclear weapons should be used by the US early on in a war. The US resists this. It insists that they should be the option of last resort.

This does not mean that the US will exercise caution under all circumstances and at all times. But the decisions taken in the interests of national security are not always the best guarantee of security. Rather, they could lead to mishaps:

> (D)uring the Eisenhower Administration, the authority to use nuclear weapons was secretly delegated to relatively low-

> level American officers assigned to NATO...Once the first tactical weapon detonated on a battlefield, the escalation of the conflict would be hard to control. Communications could prove impossible amid the nuclear blasts, and a Third World War might begin without the President's knowledge or approval.[3]

This posture became more aggressive in the subsequent US administrations, and at times, it seemed the human cost was not of major consequence in these calculations. Robert McNamara was the defense secretary during the Kennedy and Johnson administrations. He was of the view that the US should have enough nuclear weapons to limit the damage of a Soviet attack by destroying its nuclear forces, '(T)he United States should always be able to kill at least a quarter of the Soviet population and eliminate at least two-thirds of its industrial capacity. That level of "assured destruction," he (McNamara) later told President Lyndon B. Johnson, "would certainly represent intolerable punishment to any industrialized nation and thus should serve as an effective deterrent."'[4]

This is serious stuff, one that massacres are made of. It also shows that, like Mao in 1957, today's leaders, too, are prepared to take massive risks. Like in the West, the Russian mind is not at rest either. Putin has already made it clear that the Russian response to such a threat is likely to be significant. In fact, Russia may itself use nuclear weapons, in line with its 'escalate to de-escalate' doctrine, to compel the termination of a conventional conflict.

The question then is: what might happen if nuclear weapons are used?

The issue was put to test at a theoretical level during Exercise Carte Blanche, a war game conducted in 1955. Three hundred and thirty-five NATO tactical weapons were used hypothetically against the invading Soviet tanks and troops, for the most part, on battlefields in Germany. McNamara outlined the results in so many words: 'It was estimated that between 1.5 and 1.7 million people would die and another 3.5 million would be wounded—more than five times the German civilian casualties in World War II—in the first two days.'[5]

Against this grim setting, one must acknowledge the even grimmer fact that today the global shop window of nuclear weapons is crammed full with variety. Every nuclear-powered country is diversifying. For example, the US Air Force has nuclear weapons mounted on cruise and ballistic missiles. Its navy is equipped with nuclear depth charges, torpedoes, cruise missiles, gravity bombs and submarine-launched ballistic missiles. The US Army has nuclear artillery shells, landmines, anti-aircraft missiles, ground-to-ground missiles and even recoilless rifles that can shoot a small nuclear projectile. The US Special Forces carry 'backpack nukes' for sabotage missions behind enemy lines.

Russia and China do not lack in this diversity. Russia is also exploring hypersonic delivery systems, while China has embarked on a modernization programme to enhance the survivability of its arsenal in case of a first strike by its enemy.

It is not the nuclear powers alone that have the nuclear material. Worldwide, at least 2,000 tons of weapons-grade nuclear material is stored in some 40 countries. It is enough to make more than 40,000 bombs of the type that was dropped on Hiroshima. Stealing some of this large material is not impossible.

Even more worrying is the symbiotic relationship that terror outfits like JeM and LeT enjoy with Pakistan's ISI. They have been used in the past by the ISI for major terror attacks against military and civilian targets. What is the guarantee that at some point of grave crisis between India and Pakistan the ISI will not decide to slip a tactical weapon into JeM's hands? This dangerous dimension is unique to South Asia, with India at a clear and constant danger of a rogue decision by Pakistan.

Even otherwise, the nuclear question should worry people in Asia. Besides the volatility of the China–India–Pakistan relationship, there is the unpredictability of North Korea and uncertainty about Israel's and Iran's intentions. There has also been speculation, for some time, as to whether Saudi Arabia has come in possession of a nuclear bomb in exchange for a large sum of money to financially needy fellow Islamic state of Pakistan. Of the big two, so far neither China nor India has used the nuclear threat as a warning to the other side. But this may not mean principled restraint would survive a major military crisis.

South Asia's Nuke Chessboard

China's no-first-use (NFU) policy is ambiguous. It claims it will not use nuclear weapons first, but the NFU policy may not apply if the targets that are necessary for nuclear deterrence are attacked. Insofar as India is concerned, China feels its vast superiority in conventional and nuclear field will continue to deter India. Because of this gap, China believes that India does not possess the capability to threaten it, and that its strategic culture is essentially defensive.

The Indian policy has verged on caution because in contrast to the world's indulgence towards China's transgressions, global powers have responded to every step of India's nuclear march, in 1974 and 1998, with punishment. India's NFU doctrine that followed in 1999 clearly stated, 'The fundamental purpose of Indian nuclear weapons is to deter the use and threat of use of nuclear weapons by any State or entity against India and its forces. India will not be the first to initiate a nuclear strike, but will respond with punitive retaliation should deterrence fail.'[6] The critical elements of this doctrine were: deterrence, no first use and punitive retaliation.

This three-step approach is an honourable intent, but India uniquely faces two nuclear-armed neighbours who are no respecters of rules. Both have been long-standing partners in proliferation. China has helped Pakistan develop nuclear capabilities and their delivery systems. On its part, Pakistan has broken every rule in the nuclear book. Given this record, how can it be said with some degree of certainty that Pakistan, or even China, will act with restraint when it comes to using the nuclear option?

Therefore, will things work according to the Indian script of NFU in the most dangerous neighbourhood of the world?

Since lasting peace between India and Pakistan, or that between India and China, does not seem to be on the cards in the near future, nuclear deterrence becomes a function of credibility. To take a measure of it, some questions need to be asked:

- Does the enemy really believe that you will follow in war what you have promised (NFU) to do during the tranquillity of peace?
- Capability is only half of the nuclear deterrence equation. The other half concerns political variables such as willpower and credibility.
- Is India, as a state, capable of taking quick decisions on issues of war?

A nuclear threat situation would require lightning fast decisions, where the command for a retaliatory strike may have to be given within minutes of the enemy launching the first strike.

The experience, so far, suggests that India's political leadership may falter in this test. Its response to the hijacking and terror attacks in the past has been far from swift. It could vacillate and eventually opt to absorb the shock even in the face of extreme provocation, like the Indian forces being attacked with a tactical nuclear weapon.

This complacent slide towards resilience has been the preferred Indian option, across its political spectrum, after major terror attacks—the Bombay blasts of 1993, the terror attack on Parliament in 2001, the terror strike of 2008, the Pathankot Air Force Station attack of 2016 and many more. The other course that

India has opted for in the past is to threaten and then do nothing. After every crushing terror attack, it announced that it would hit back at a time and place of its choosing, and then hoped the crisis would soon pass over, to be forgotten by its people. Once, it had even mobilized its troops threateningly during Operation Parakram, only to lapse into inaction.

It can be argued that India did opt for action through what it termed as a 'surgical strike' in 2016 and via the 'air strike' at Balakot in February 2019. But there are conflicting reports about the extent of punishment they inflicted and whether these actions have formed an effective deterrent. Except once, in 1971, India's response against grave provocations, be it from China or Pakistan, cannot, by any stretch of imagination, be considered as effectively punitive.

Alas, the strategic risks have not diminished for India. It still lives at the edge of a precipice. This state carries enormous downside. At some point, matters could escalate dangerously to tip it over beyond the edge of the cliff. This was the question that Bill Clinton confronted Nawaz Sharif with during the Kargil War:

> When Clinton asked him (Nawaz Sharif) if he understood how far along his military was in preparing nuclear-armed missiles for possible use in a war against India, Sharif acted as though he was genuinely surprised...Clinton decided to invoke the Cuban missile crisis...Now India and Pakistan were similarly on the edge of a precipice. If even one bomb were used...Sharif finished the sentence: '...it would be a catastrophe.'[7]

Some reports maintain that India and Pakistan were about to cross that precipice in February 2019. A report filed by the Reuters asserted, 'At one stage, India threatened to fire at least six missiles at Pakistan, and Islamabad said it would respond with its own missile strikes "three times over"...'[8]

It could be argued that this was only about non-nuclear-tipped missiles. That might be so, but how is the other side to know? The launch of even one missile by either side could have had a hugely escalatory effect because there is no known technology in the world that can determine whether the incoming missile has a non-nuclear, tactical or a nuclear warhead. In a crisis, when time is at a premium, this can lead to response miscalculation.

Additionally, if one side decides to use the nuclear option, the one attacked might find its communication network crippled via the nuclear cloud. Will it then be able to issue the retaliatory command?

Both these issues are the handicaps that may not have been factored in by states professing the NFU intent. However, both during the Kargil War and the Balakot crisis, the two sides, under persuasion by other countries, stepped back from the brink.

But sliding back from the edge may not work every time. What would then be the consequence? This exercise has been done, and the result of it is numbing: 'A war between India and Pakistan, involving a hundred atomic bombs like the kind dropped on Hiroshima, could send five million tons of dust into the atmosphere, shrink the ozone layer by as much as fifty per cent, drop worldwide temperatures to their lowest point in a thousand years, create worldwide famines, and cause more than a billion casualties.'[9]

A billion casualties, says this assessment!

Let's now turn to the Pakistani position on the use of nuclear weapons. The Pakistani briefing to the world maintains that the principal objective of Pakistan's nuclear weapons capability is to deter Indian conventional as well as nuclear aggression. In case deterrence fails, then its aim is to deny India victory in war. But the world remains unconvinced because Pakistan has not adopted the NFU policy.

A former director general of Pakistan's Strategic Plans Division, Lieutenant General Khalid Kidwai, had more candidly listed four parameters for use of nuclear weapons:

1. India attacks Pakistan and conquers a large part of its territory (space threshold);
2. India destroys a large part of Pakistan's military forces/ assets (military threshold);
3. India strangulates Pakistan economically;
4. India destabilizes Pakistan politically or through internal subversion.[10]

This gives Pakistan a large menu of flexibility, a carte blanche to react with the nuclear option as per its determination. Or, to give a practical example, Pakistan would have reached for the nuclear button, under General Kidwai's parameters, had it been subjected by India to a 1993- or the 26/11-type terror attack.

To this should be added Pakistan's declared policy of 'Full Spectrum Deterrence', which covers threat perception at the strategic, operational and tactical levels. This was in evidence during the Balakot crisis in February 2019, when the Pakistani army spokesperson repeatedly stressed that it was ready to bring into play its 'Full Spectrum Deterrence'. The danger with such a declaration is that it could become a self-fulfilling prophecy. This kind of bravado is doubly dangerous when two countries lie next to each other.

In the other possible confrontations, for instance, between the US and Russia, the US and China or the US and North Korea, the country under nuclear attack would have a few minutes warning of a missile heading its way because of the physical distance between them. Since India and Pakistan have zero distance between them, the luxury of the vital few minutes warning will not be available to them in a nuclear situation.

Add to this the fact that there are mobile platforms at play and tactical nuclear weapons, which can be deployed with army units close to the border. The use of either of these would reduce the warning time to seconds, turning this South Asian theatre into an inferno.

In May 2017, the US's director of national intelligence, Daniel Coats, released its Worldwide Threat Assessment report. Among other aspects, the report addresses Pakistan's nuclear threat: '(A)dvances in Pakistan's nuclear capabilities could risk further destabilization along the India-Pakistan border..."Pakistan's pursuit of tactical nuclear weapons potentially lowers the threshold for their use...Increasing numbers of firefights along the Line of Control...might exacerbate the risk of unintended escalation between these nuclear-armed neighbours."'[11]

This is not all. On an even graver note, it warns, 'Even a small nuclear war between India and Pakistan could trigger a nuclear winter that could send the planet into a mini ice age and starve an estimated 1 billion people.'[12]

A billion! Once again, it is about a billion people!

Shift in Strategy

Pakistan and India have survived at least five nuclear scares since 1987, giving both sides the misplaced confidence that they will survive the next one as well. This leads to a lessening of political restraints on the militaries of both countries and increases greater nuclear brinksmanship.

The attitude that somehow the next crisis, too, shall pass, misses the basic point that on all previous occasions, it was the intervention of powers like the US that brought them back from the brink. The situation is different now.

The US is a tired superpower, keen on staying away from other people's squabbles, and other powers like China may have the motivation to watch the situation unfold. Countries like Saudi Arabia and the UAE, flawed as they are, may not be effective on their own. Therefore, the course of the next Indo-Pak shooting war could be different. A former Pakistani Air Force officer maintains, 'Pakistan, relatively a small country with a deep sense of insecurity, developed nuclear weapons mainly to deter military aggression from India, and therefore nuclear weapons continue to play the central role in Pakistan's military strategy.'[13]

It could still be argued that in the event of a nuclear attack, there would only be a graduated escalation through limited strikes of tactical nuclear weapons on India's forces. But where is the guarantee that this would be so.

Contrarily, the first-strike nation, be it Pakistan or China, might launch a massive first strike. Its aim could comprehensively be to eliminate India's command and control systems, destroy its nuclear retaliatory capability, reduce the conventional offensive capability and strike at important industrial targets and some major population centres. In fact, their strategic calculus could be such that India may not get a second chance.

The possible use of sophisticated cyberattacks to cripple a country's command and control system, and disable missile launches, raises serious concern about the reliability of the second-strike option. Either of these possibilities would place India in a nightmarish state.

Over time, these dreads have been increasing. In March 2015, after Pakistan tested the Shaheen III missile, Pakistan's National (nuclear) Command Authority adviser, Khalid Kidwai, said the 2,750 km capability of Shaheen III missile is meant to reach India's strategic bases at the Andaman and Nicobar Islands. 'The purpose,' he said, 'is to deny India a second-strike capability.'[14]

Pakistan's first-use option has never been put to serious question internally. Rather, many of its political leaders have added their weight to the strategic voices in favour of using the first-strike option. With the army, the fundamentalists and the politicians as well in unanimous mode, there is a triad of powerful voices within Pakistan that could make the decision-making in a war situation readily aggressive.

In anticipation, there is recognition in India that a response to first use requires a very effective early warning system and a high degree of efficiency.

This is even more necessary when the adversary is as opaque as China or as unpredictable as Pakistan. Rather than move in a cautionary direction, Pakistan has, in recent times, lowered the threshold of nuclear use option. There is also some speculation to suggest that Pakistan's non-deployed, de-mated nuclear arsenal may be reconfigured to be deployed and ready to use. Worryingly, as a Pakistani expert Sadia Tasleem maintains, both its short-range ballistic missiles (SRBMs) and sea-based systems may involve delegated control over warheads, 'The country's ongoing arms buildup, continuing fissile material production, and investment in sea-based second-strike capabilities suggest a shift toward a complex deterrence posture…Pakistan might… move away from the non-deployment of its weapons. Its evolving sea-based capabilities, as well as its short-range ballistic missiles (SRBMs), may also necessitate a shift from centralized to delegated command and control.'[15]

This shift in strategy will further complicate the situation.

Delegated command and control of tactical weapons means that it is up to a relatively young brigadier to take the decision about lobbing a nuclear shell across the border. What then is the guarantee that the hot blood of an indoctrinated middle-aged army officer will keep flowing with equanimity in a war situation, and that his angry finger will not move impulsively towards the trigger? As two well-regarded Pakistani scholars put it:

> Even the finest diplomacy may not work in the midst of a storm strong enough to knock over the pieces on the south Asian nuclear chessboard. With an emboldened army in Pakistan sooner or later seeking once again to push India to the brink—this time determined to escalate rather than back down if things go badly—staving off nuclear warfare on the subcontinent may be a race against time.[16]

That Pakistan may not back down in the next one may also be due to its assessment that bad generalship had plagued the Indian

Army during the Kargil War, and that India's military wisdom had taken over a month to mobilize troops for Operation Parakram.

The issue then, for India, or for any other country placed in such a dire situation, is of preservation and the best way of preventing the unthinkable. For that to happen, the resolve of a democratic country must be firm and appear to be so for the adversary. Successful deterrence relies on being able to demonstrate a military threat that is credible and realistic.

The Indian language of denial and its grammar should be straightforward: if Pakistan or China aggresses, it will be defeated. Either of them will not achieve its military or political objectives under any circumstances. Should there be an escalation, the costs will be far greater than any benefit.

What this means is a pre-emptive option that sidesteps the NFU question. It may or may not involve the use of nuclear assets, but it clearly aims at striking at the enemy's offensive facilities. When and where to strike is a delicate issue under most circumstances, and it gets tougher still if the strike is against nuclear assets. The risk factor for both sides escalates enormously and immediately.

India can possibly exercise one of the two options:

- It attacks many of Pakistan's or China's missile launchers in one go, or
- It can cautiously target just a few sites.

In the first case, it might look to the other side as an all-out attack. Inevitably, and almost immediately, it would trigger an all-out response from their side.

In the second case, it would be interpreted as a sign of weakness. This would embolden them to seize the advantage from India and retaliate with great force. A small, non-nuclear demonstration of this was the large retaliatory response by the Pakistan Air Force on the morning after the 2019 Balakot air strike by India.

Therefore, the critical element in a limited strike is what happens thereafter. In the pause that comes after a strike, fateful decisions affecting thousands, perhaps more, lives can be made. In this pause, Pakistan or China will have the following to choose from:

- Unleash a devastating counterstrike,
- Give a more measured response, or
- Do nothing.

In the days after the Balakot air strike, there was the rumoured Pakistani intent to up the escalatory ladder to the nuclear option had the strikes and counterstrikes carried on. Therefore, once the shooting starts, the big imponderable is that a limited strike could start an escalating cycle of attack and counterattack graduating to a full war, including the use of the nuclear option.

Beyond the Nuclear Taboo

The alternative to a limited strike is a full-fledged, no-holds-barred, all-out attack against every single nuclear facility of the enemy. But an attack against the entire nuclear arsenal of a country is a tough target because:

- No one has full intelligence about where each and every nuclear weapon is stored in China or Pakistan,
- All of their nuclear assets are not deployed in easy-to-attack positions. Some are stored on mobile platforms, which are harder to find, track and target, and
- Some nuclear assets are in hardened shelters or deep underground in mountains that are both tricky to target and difficult to destroy.

Moreover, nuclear-tipped cruise missiles are said to be mounted on three of Pakistan's five French-built diesel-electric submarines. Whether it is so, and technically feasible, is in doubt. But this capability is the message that Pakistan has chosen to convey. Pakistani military authorities are also considering the possibility of putting nuclear-tipped cruise missiles on naval ships.

India had, in August 2016, deployed its first nuclear submarine, the INS Arihant. A second, more advanced nuclear submarine, the INS Arighat, began sea trials in November 2017, and four more boats are scheduled to join the fleet by 2025. But as a former Indian Navy chief cautions, there is a need to tone down the expectations about the reach of Arihant's missiles:

> From a submarine patrol area in mid-Bay of Bengal, Islamabad is 2,500 km, while Beijing and Shanghai are over 4,000 km. Even from the northern-most edge of the Bay of Bengal, Kunming is 1,600 km and Chengdu 2,000 km. Therefore, to target cities and nuclear forces deep inside China or Pakistan, from a 'safe haven', India needs a submarine-launched ballistic missile (SLBM) of 6,000–8,000-km range. The missile, reportedly, carried by the Arihant is the K-15, whose range falls below 1,000 km.[17]

The limitations of range apart, there is another cause for concern. Pervez Hoodbhoy, a Pakistani nuclear physicist, sketches out this worrying scenario: 'The new danger for both countries is that the problem of command and control over submarines becomes very tenuous. With land-based weapons, the warhead is separated from the delivery system. You can't do that with warheads on a submarine. When it leaves the port, it is already armed.'[18]

Whether the warheads are armed or mated is not the issue. The complicating factor here is the fact that it is extremely difficult to communicate with a submarine once it is in sea. Besides the risk of detection, there is also the fact that normal frequency waves can effectively communicate with a submarine at shallow depths only. Once it is submerged in deeper waters, only countries like the US, Russia, India and China have the capability to communicate with their submarines through very low-frequency waves. But even that has its limitations; it can send command in short spurts only, a few words at a time.

So the commander of a nuclear-armed submarine (be it that of China, Pakistan or India) in a war situation, especially a war that is not going well for his country, would be practically on his own in deep depths.

A miscalculation, excessive patriotic zeal or a heroic impulse in favour of his losing side could make him put his finger on the nuclear trigger because in a war situation, he would not have the possibility of remaining in touch with his superiors. On the other hand, quite the opposite could happen. Because of the communication difficulties, the submarine may not receive the signal that the command to launch a second strike has been issued! In that blissful state of ignorance, the captain of the nuclear-armed submarine may do nothing, burying thereby the potency of the third leg of the triad.

Besides, new technology could also blunt the potency of this option. The second-strike capability rests, in large measure, in the confidence provided by the naval leg of a nuclear triad. Thus far, it has been considered the most survivable part of the triad, since it is hidden away in the deep sea. However, the ability now of the new technology drones to detect nuclear-powered, ballistic missile-carrying submarines (SSBN) may puncture this confidence. In that case, the first-strike nation would hold all the cards.

Given the possibility of nuclear escalation, it is not at all clear if an Indian PM would easily order a cross-border retaliatory strike. But there are some indications to suggest that India could consider going in for a pre-emptive nuclear strike in case of a war: 'This would not formally change India's nuclear doctrine, which bars it from launching a first strike, but would loosen its interpretation to deem pre-emptive strikes as defensive. It would also change India's likely targets, in the event of a war, to make a nuclear exchange more winnable and, therefore, more thinkable.'[19]

Once the 'nuclear taboo' has been broken, nobody can be certain what might happen next. At Hiroshima and Nagasaki, nuclear weapons were used against a nation that did not have them. Since then, the world has not seen nuclear bombs being used in a war situation. This is fortunate, but this fact also poses a dilemma—it means that no one in the world knows how to handle the situation in the event of a war between two nuclear powers.

Second Nuclear Age

Unfortunately, there is more aggressive energy now in the world than at any other time during the last 70 years. One sign of it is the fact that in January 2022, for the third year in a row, the Bulletin of the Atomic Scientists set the Doomsday Clock at a hundred seconds to midnight. This is the closest to the most dangerous level since 1953, when the US upgraded its nuclear arsenal with the hydrogen bomb.

The countdown of the Doomsday Clock was established in 1947 by a group of experts who were working on the Manhattan Project to build the first atomic bomb. At first, the clock was set at seven minutes to midnight. The world reached its safest point in 1991, when it read 17 minutes to midnight as the Cold War ended and the Strategic Arms Reduction Treaty led to the reduction of strategic nuclear weapons deployed by the US and Russia.

Since then, the world has become more fractious, and the nuclear risk is more ominous, as the clock's present setting at just a hundred seconds to midnight indicates. However, this setting is a global measure. To that extent, it is not an accurate public warning of the level of dangers, which may vary from region to region. For instance, the risk of nuclear use in the Ukrainian war may be higher than in the frequent Israeli strikes against Syria. South Asia is another area where the state of nuclear button is a constant worry, in contrast to Africa and South America. Since the threats are variable, there is a need to convey their differing status by giving regional settings, too, for the Doomsday Clock.

To add to the global woes, the nuclear powers seem to be in a new rush towards acquiring greater nuclear capabilities. Instead of following up on Obama's hope that global nuclear disarmament could be achievable, the US, Russia, China, India and Pakistan have new nuclear plans to pursue.

However, capability is only half of the nuclear deterrence equation. The other half concerns political variables such as will power and credibility. As there is no previous precedent, it is possible that the leadership of a state under nuclear attack may show decision paralysis when faced with destruction on a vast scale.

On the other hand, an unstable leader could make moves that lead to vast destruction. Trump's erratic behaviour in the last days of his presidency had greatly alarmed the army chief and some others in the American establishment. It was feared that for domestic political purposes, Trump could order a nuclear strike on China, leading to a full-scale conflict. To avoid that nightmarish possibility, the American army chief reached out to his Chinese counterpart to warn him of it.[20] This episode reflected poorly on both—Trump, for being officially certified as wayward, and the US army chief, for indiscretion. It also brought into sharper focus the danger that a whimsical decision-maker may pose.

The threat to use the nuclear option was even more ominous when Putin first asked NATO to stay out of the Ukraine conflict, warning it of 'consequences they have never seen.'[21] He followed it up, on 27 February 2022, by announcing that he ordered 'the deterrence forces of the Russian army to a special mode of combat duty.'[22]

It could be argued that there are advanced missile defence shields to counter missiles carrying the first nuclear strike. But missile defence systems provide the illusion of safety more than safety itself. They perform less than perfectly even under ideal test conditions. An S-400 or a Terminal High Altitude Area Defense (THAAD) battery can knock down one or two incoming ballistic missiles, but stopping dozens of them is out of the question. Moreover, the effective strike range that a country gets from an S-400 battery will be only 240 km, and not 400 km. There is an additional handicap as this system's maximum altitude for anti-missile defence is 27 km, whereas the hypersonic missiles move at around 80–90 km altitude. The hypersonic missiles of the type being readied by China travel into space before dropping down at speeds that could outwit the current crop of anti-missile batteries. Then, there are reports that Israel has developed Electronic Warfare Systems (EWSs) that can paralyse the S-400.

Under the circumstances, there is no foolproof defence against a nuclear aggressor. The best guarantee to ensure a safe world is to eliminate nuclear weapons. But that is even more complicated because it is no longer a bipolar world, and nuclear arms control is no longer governed by a two-power equation. There are multiple nuclear powers now, and no equation stands by itself. Therefore, this requires the nuclear world to think afresh. But how is that fresh thinking possible if India, Israel, Pakistan and North Korea are not even officially admitted by the nuclear club as its members?

As that change coming through in the near future is only a vain hope, the next best effort should be that all nuclear powers, by common consent, adopt a NFU policy. Even this is easier said than done because NFU is, in essence, a reactive policy. By its very nature, it limits the choices available to the political leadership in case of a crisis.

Unknown to most people is also the fact that the world has entered a second nuclear age. Some experts maintain that the dividing line between the first and the second nuclear age was the Cuban Missile Crisis of 1962. But I would prefer to term the 1998 nuclear tests by India and Pakistan as the dividing line.

Till 1962, the conversation was largely about the nuclear haves. Though, by the 1970s, India and Israel had come to possess nuclear arms, the discussion on this issue, up to the late 1990s, concerned the capability or otherwise of the recognized nuclear powers. All along, Pakistan was hesitant to come out of the purdah and conduct a test to tell the world that it, too, had the bomb. India's test of 1998 was the opportunity that Pakistan had long sought. Once its nuclear genie was out in the open, its swagger changed and so did its nuclear dare. The subsequent acknowledgement of a de facto situation where the nuclear club's exclusiveness had effectively been dented should really be regarded as the time when the world entered the second nuclear age.

More than the first nuclear age, this second age is driven by uncertainties because there is no restraining influence that can command compliance. Rather, each major nuclear state has to guard its flanks—China has to watch the US, Russia and India; Russia keeps its focus on the US and China; India watches warily Pakistan and China; Israel's focus remains razor sharp on Iran; while the US keeps a sharp eye on Russia, China, Pakistan and North Korea; Pakistan rests in relative ease, comforted by India's promise of NFU.

Will the Living Envy the Dead?

Let us consider a situation when a leader has to give the go-ahead for a nuclear strike. How is he likely to issue these instructions? The US relies on the 'football' for this purpose:

> Officially known as the 'president's emergency satchel,' the so-called nuclear 'Football'—portable and hand-carried—is built around a sturdy (aluminium) frame, encased in black leather...the Football does not actually contain a big red button for launching a nuclear war...Its primary purpose is to confirm the president's identity, and it allows him to communicate with the National Military Command Center in the Pentagon, which monitors worldwide nuclear

> threats and can order an instant response. The Football also provides…a simplified menu of options—allowing him to decide, for example, whether to destroy all of America's enemies in one fell swoop or to limit himself to obliterating only Moscow or Pyongyang or Beijing.[23]

Though there is no official confirmation about its origin, it is believed that the 'football' came into use after the Cuban Missile Crisis. President Kennedy was alarmed by the possibility that a nuclear war could be set off by a decision of two individuals. It was he who ordered safety procedures to be established on nuclear warheads, and the briefcase was a part of that precautionary protocol. Kennedy had posed two simple questions then: 'What would I say to the Joint War Room to launch an immediate nuclear strike? How would the person who received my instructions verify them?'[24]

Since then, other safety features have been added to the football and its nearly 40-pound briefcase. One essential element of that is the code word printed on a card called the 'biscuit' that the President must use to order a strike. Clinton is said to have mislaid his laminated code card for several months in 2000. Earlier, in 1981, after an assassination attempt, Ronald Reagan was stripped of his clothes at the hospital. The clothes contained the biscuit, and both were found after a frantic search in the hospital's trash bag.

Despite these mishaps, the football is by far the safest system. That must be the reason why the leaders of Russia, India, China, Israel and Pakistan are seen trailed by security men carrying bulky briefcases. Yet, so far, no system known to man can restrain the sudden rush of blood in an aggressive leader. If a Musharraf can launch a misadventure like Kargil, he could also punch the code into his biscuit. Besides, the introduction of dual-use technologies, cyber capabilities and hypersonic missiles is making the task of defence ever more complicated. There is also the possibility that, one day, a state might develop the cyber capability to cripple an enemy's nuclear command and control system, or to immobilize the 'biscuit'!

On the positive side, there is no nuclear weapon state in Africa, South America and the Pacific. Nor has a new nuclear state emerged after the 2006 nuclear test by North Korea. Therefore, just around 4 per cent of the countries of the world possess nuclear arms.

Still, there is only a thin line dividing restraint and provocation. One day, a road rage of nuclear variety could break this taboo. The chance of that happening in the next decade or so cannot be ruled out because Russia, Pakistan and North Korea play the nuclear card far too often through statements and by maintaining ambiguity about their intentions. If a nuclear weapon does get used in the coming years, then the safe bet would be to say that any of the nuclear states, including those swearing by the NFU doctrine, could use it. But if one goes by the past record of a country's proliferation, its support to terror and the predominance of military in its decision-making process, then the chances are that Pakistan might be the one to use it first, with North Korea following behind as a close second.

If there is such inevitability about its use, isn't it possible that someday, somehow, the nuclear powers may unanimously decide to give it all up?

Despite the gloom surrounding the issue, the world has seen instances where states have voluntarily given up the nuclear option. South Africa is one such example. It had assembled six nuclear weapons during the apartheid regime. But before the changeover to the African National Congress-led government in the 1990s, South Africa dismantled its nuclear weapons, becoming the first state in the world to voluntarily do so.

USSR's was another example, and on a much larger scale. When it splintered into 15 republics, both Russia and the US saw the need to act together regarding the considerable nuclear stockpiles in Belarus, Ukraine and Kazakhstan. They acted in concert to remove those nuclear arms and missiles.

These instances are reassuring, but they are exceptional cases of cooperation. They have not been repeated since. Yet, these precedents give hope that if it could happen then, why not again.

Extending this logic further, there is no doubt that our past lies spread before us. It is, therefore, relatively easy to understand and interpret. There is also comfort in the fact that after the Second World War, the world has not been scorched by nuclear fire. The future, however, is cumbersome because it moves moodily in spirals rather than in a straight line. To that extent, it is an illusion and so is the answer to the question whether someone will press a nuclear button.

Were it to happen, the consequence might be as the Soviet leader Khrushchev had predicted: 'The living will envy the dead.'

19

2035

When thy mind leaves behind its dark forest of delusion, thou shall go beyond the scriptures of times past and still to come.

—Bhagavad Gita (2:52)

Every major pandemic leaves its mark on the world—blots of ink on our imaginations, smouldering pyres in crematoriums and half-buried bodies left to be consumed by sandbanks. Invariably, the story is the same from the beginning till almost near the end. As pestilence spreads, humans lose their humanity, people grow fearful of one another, families lock themselves in their houses, schools bolt their doors, hospitals fill, arts wither, and societies descend into chaos and governments, into anarchy. All through, the world is topsy-turvy.

This is a familiar script for the world, looping over and over again in more or less the same form through centuries. The end is uncertain and long in coming. At last, as the end approaches, exhausted people begin to wonder if humans will remain human. Yet, people survive and begin a new climb towards civilization.

They did so after every major pestilence and each catastrophic war—most recently, the Second World War. Bizarrely, there were some remarkable coincidences then. The formation of NATO, the emergence of the Soviet Union as a nuclear power and the proclamation of PRC by Mao, all this happened in 1949.

It was also the year George Orwell's dystopian novel *Nineteen Eighty-Four* was published, containing a nightmarish vision of a world divided geographically, politically and militarily into three rival superstates: Oceania (North America plus Britain), Eurasia (Russia and Europe) and East Asia (China).

Today's world may not be fractious in the exact manner that Orwell had thought of, but chances are that there would be three broad divisions when countries unsheathe their swords next time. There is reasonable likelihood of such a contest happening by 2035.

As if in anticipation, America is withdrawing its forces—some in entirety from their present positions abroad, in other cases, it is thinning down their presence. Whether these decisions are backed by a grand plan remains to be seen, but the world seems set for a churn.

There are multiple reasons for it—some of them grounded in historical inequities like the lazy map-making done arbitrarily by colonial powers in parts of Africa and Asia. Since this incision ignored the geographical and historical realities of the region, the results have not satisfied the countries that were carved out artificially or those that were divided. Conflicts and wars of the future may try to settle these issues, but the fear is that these efforts might mess up a messy situation further. As it is, some later western adventures in the Arab world have produced the barbarism of the ISIS.

Moreover, as the geostrategic tussle between NATO and Russia has shown, war is an ever-present possibility even in Europe. It means states will keep their focus on the 'balance of power' in their neighbourhood and attempt to increase their relative position within it. This is the theoretical wisdom.

But historical evidence points out that the hegemon, whoever it is at a particular point in history, is so driven by its ambition that it does not take into account the power of nationalism, which makes people rebel against the foreign attempts to intervene in their affairs. This was the case in Afghanistan, Yemen and Ukraine.

We must add to it the fact that the smell of blood is difficult to resist. Invariably, it pollutes sophisticated debate, consuming argument. War follows inevitably. Ironically, it was Hitler who said, 'The beginning of every war is like opening the door into a dark room. One never knows what is hidden in the darkness.' Since very few plans of battle survive contact with the enemy, it is the people who perish.

Beyond the fierce energy of conflict, there are other issues that will confront us tomorrow—migration, climate change, AI and the like. Large migrations from countries in Africa and West Asia could disrupt western governments and affect the social fabric of Italy, France, Germany and Spain. These shifts of population need not be because of political and economic compulsions alone. According to the UN's Department of Economic and Social Affairs (DESA), by 2030, water scarcity could displace 700 million people worldwide. The most vulnerable areas in this respect will be around the Nile, Ganga, Brahmaputra, Indus, Tigris, Euphrates and Colorado rivers. Three of these rivers—Ganga, Indus and Brahmaputra—flow through India.

There would be other worries as well, some of them from unexpected quarters. Hydroelectric dams are ageing throughout the world. China and India have nearly 28,000 large dams with an average age of 46 and 42 years, respectively. American dams average 65 years. Britain and Japan have the oldest dams, averaging 106 and 111 years, respectively. By 2035, most of humanity will live downstream of large dams built in the twentieth century that will be at increasing risk of failure. If a major earthquake were to strike one of these dams, the effect would be devastating.[1]

India and China are at the greatest risk of dam failures because of their vast numbers and because of the seismic zone they straddle. To illustrate this point, two examples should suffice. In 1975, the Banqiao Dam in Henan province of China burst, sending 7 miles wide and 20 feet high water waves downriver at

30 miles per hour. It killed an estimated 26,000 people, including the entire population of the town of Daowencheng. This was the deadliest structural failure of a dam in history. Yet, it was kept a secret from the outside world by China for many years. Four years later, in 1979, the disintegration of the Machchhu Dam in Gujarat during a flood killed nearly 25,000 people.[2]

We do not have to wait to find out how devastating climate change can be, and how interconnected global events are. In a chilling instance, the droughts in Russia have been connected to the rise of the Arab Spring. In 2010, Russia experienced a severe drought. Following that, it banned the export of wheat, affecting directly its importers in West Asia and North Africa. Within a year, bread prices in Tunisia and Egypt shot up. That price rise and the food shortages were critical factors that led to riots and later the revolution.

Instability in other fields, too, may be the watchword of the future. It will manifest itself in nationalism, changing demographics, competition for resources and challenges to global structures. Territorial conflicts will compel countries towards alliances. Since all this is too complex and disparate for a single power to handle, tomorrow's world may be moving towards contested regional spheres of influence, not quite Orwellian in structure but more or less similar in form.

Besides the physical contest for influence, the contest of soft powers will also come into play. Unlike in the past, the West no longer has the monopoly hold over global culture. Other civilizations and faiths are competing for a share of that space. Some of this has already come about. Today, Bollywood captures people's imagination with the same intensity as Hollywood. Yoga provides a calming influence the world over, and China is the go-to country for millions of curious tourists. The enquiry about the East is no longer about its exotic otherness; it is more about its market potential.

Therefore, on the larger global platform, there are many areas of change just as there are possibilities of conflict. But let's first take a brief look at the smorgasbord.

New Cold War with Economic Characteristics

By 2050, the populations of India and China will be around a billion and a half each, adding up to a third of the estimated global population then of 9 billion people. Among the other large populations, both America's and Pakistan's may be over 400 million; those of Indonesia, Bangladesh, Brazil and Nigeria, about 300 million each. Because China and India are so populous and are developing quickly, they will be responsible for a significant share of global change. By 2035, they will be a major geographic centre of the global economy.

There will also be vast differences in the age profile of western and non-western populations—the former will have a large number of 80–90-year-olds, and the latter a relatively young population of 20–30-year-olds.

As the military, economic and even age profile shifts in favour of non-western countries, so would their aspirations for a greater say in the affairs of the world. In 1946, when President Truman picked the first head of the World Bank, India was not yet independent and the PRC was yet to be formed. The US provided most of the capital, and American financial markets needed reassurance about the World Bank's stability, which, to them, could only be provided if the control of this institution was in American hands. Over the years, the American share of the World Bank's capital has reduced, bringing it down to 17 per cent. Today, China is the world's second-largest economy and India is one of the fastest-rising among the big economies. Yet, the US continues to choose the president of the World Bank, and it lets the Europeans choose the head of IMF.

Despite the obvious need for change, there is no guarantee that this is how the world will take shape. Further, today's world is far too closely connected for countries to consider solo forays. Whether they like it or not, countries or groups of countries may find themselves acting in concert with one or the other bloc. Because of the resulting friction, we could see the emergence of at least three power centres in the world by 2035—the US and the West being one, China and Russia providing the second, India (and other regional powers) could be the third.

With these big powers seeking their separate spheres of influence, cleavages that had divided the world into rival camps during the Cold War are developing again. Should Russia succeed in reasserting control over parts of the former Soviet Union, and Xi's China gains control over maritime commerce in the western Pacific, or Khamenei's Iran gets to dominate the oil reserves of the Persian Gulf, the current global order would be severely dented. In fact, the entire swathe stretching from Southeast Asia to the edge of Europe, with a few exceptions like India and Saudi Arabia, would be under the China–Russia sway. In other words, most of Asia, which had otherwise been pro-America for the last seven decades, would have turned its back on the US.

As for West Europe, it has lost the nerve to defend liberal civilization. It hopes that by lying low it can somehow avoid attacks on itself. But that is not going to happen. Instead, it needs to pick up the courage to rescue itself from its own manias. But with an ageing population and shrinking economy, its slide into a stagnant sulk is more likely over the next decade. In this tired state, it will no longer be able to excite the world of ideas with the effervescence of its vibrant past.

However, the big disruptor in this equation would be the fact that two of these power centres have their faith rooted in democracy and a rules-based global order, whereas China and Russia hold different views. But the contest has just started, and there will be many false starts and swerves before the winning post. That's why divining the future is risky enterprise, and even in retrospect, history often befuddles those who write about it.

For instance, despite the advocacy and the obvious need for reducing energy consumption, the projections point in the opposite direction. Instead of coming down, the global demand for oil and gas is expected to rise by 13 per cent by 2030.

On the political front as well, the prospects of inter-state amity do not seem promising. Relations between China and the US are strained in almost every field, and a cold war between them is already underway. This strategic tension between them is unlikely to reduce. What remains to be seen is the timing of the hot war. In the years ahead, smiling photos of American and Chinese leaders together will be interspersed with tensions and caustic comments. Had it just been an issue of complaints about trade imbalance, matters could have been resolved over time. Even if full satisfaction was not found, it could have at least resulted in cold peace with trade delegations gnawing at each other across conference room tables. But the issues that divide them are fundamental and many.

This pugilistic relationship will unsettle the regional nerves further. But the US policy in Asia will continue to be erratic and self-serving as it works out its issues bilaterally and sporadically. An inhibiting factor for its policymakers will be the fact that since 1945, the US has lost every major war it has fought. The list includes its invasions in Korea, Vietnam, Cambodia, Iraq and Afghanistan. Notably, each one of these was fought in Asia.

Bruised by these previous wars, it will not readily jump into the fray to fight other people's battles. If Beijing invades Taiwan or begins a war against India, the US may not quickly respond to a call to arms. It is more likely to repeat the words of Neville Chamberlain, the British PM, who described the German bid to carve up Czechoslovakia in 1938 as 'a quarrel in a far away country, between people of whom we know nothing.'[3]

If, like Chamberlain, the US opts to look the other way, it will only be reinforcing the feeling that there is no place for sentiment in geostrategy, and that when it comes to the crunch, nations defend their own interests not others. Though sometimes nations decide their interests are best served by joining alliances.

Taking this literally, the US is currently busy fashioning alliances for each occasion and its every need. AUKUS (Australia-UK-US) may have been given the garb of a security relationship, but it was, in reality, a thinly disguised commercial stab in the back to France. Its other partnership, the QUAD, has yet to create its charter. It has also not invested itself with any substance, fearing that it will be dubbed an 'Asian NATO'.

While QUAD languishes uncertainly, Biden's promise to transfer advanced technology, including submarine nuclear-propulsion to Australia under AUKUS throws into stark relief India's failure to acquire any significant high technology from the US.

But it will not be fair to apportion all the blame for it on the US. India has also been faulted for its inertia and less-than-optimal absorptive capacity. Critics maintain it should have been more proactive and cite China's example. China owes its pole position to the advanced technology it was given or it purloined from the US over a 30-year period. All that India has to show for its 'strategic partnership' is the nearly $22 billion worth of military hardware purchased from US companies.

In a rapidly changing strategic environment around it, speed is of essence. At a time like this, India needs to sharpen its international interaction. But the last few years have seen the Indian foreign policy trapped in a linguistic swamp, where the sound of words matters more than the substance of a policy. Meanwhile, its single-minded pursuit of relationship with the US seems to have become a case of promise over-performance.

This is a pity because as in India, so in many countries of Southeast Asia, people view the US with a mixture of wonderment at its achievements, with awe because of its power, and with irate indulgence at its occasionally errant behaviour. It is this last aspect that makes people complain that all too often US policymakers live only in the present. They add wistfully that the US would benefit from past analogues to current predicaments. For the moment though, China may not want to take up the US's position as the leader of a global order, but its aim is nearly as consequential. China wants complete dominance in the Indo-Pacific region. It wants to force the US out and become the region's unchallenged political, economic and military hegemon.

Even before that contest happens and the fate of the region is settled, it is becoming increasingly clear that our age is passing through a period of disruption. The existing world order is under strain. Some of it lies broken. But the new systems and the rules that could replace them are still forming. This churn is seen by China as its opportunity to take the lead in crafting a new system—from a rule-taker it wants to be the rule-maker.

But there is a major difference between the contest of big powers now and their previous contestation.

During the Cold War, the Soviet Union was not connected with the US-dominated global economy. The present-day revisionist powers are a part of it. Russia is an important player in the world energy market and a major exporter of defence equipment. China has the world's second-largest economy, with deep stakes in global trade. Since China is a crucial economic partner of the West, this interdependence will complicate its containment.

Still, the US can take comfort in the fact that it has overcome the previous challenges to its supremacy. In 1956, Khrushchev, then first secretary of the Communist Party of the Soviet Union, told the West, 'We will bury you!'[4] He proved to be utterly wrong. Then, there was speculation in the 1980s that Japan would be 'number one'. It turned out to be way off the mark. China is now being touted as the challenger most likely to succeed.

This may well happen, but its ambition could also trip China along the way. It has been pursuing the policy of ultra-high investment and rapid debt accumulation. This kept it growing fast after the 2008 financial crisis, but it also made China vulnerable to a sharp deceleration. Consequently, China is unlikely to replicate the success of the other East Asian high-growth economies because the distortions in its economy are large, and the global environment is increasingly turning hostile to it.

Russia is in no better position economically, and the effects of enormous sanctions on it can be crippling and long-term. But even if they weaken internally from economic stress, Russia and China will still have influence of an imperial dimension far beyond their borders. A related consequence of this and their internal fragility could be the reflex reaction to divert people's attention away from domestic woes. It is in the nature of these highly centralized regimes to then turn aggressive beyond their borders because nationalism can serve as a unifying element in times of societal stress.

It is against this background that we are living what can best be described as a kind of new cold war with economic characteristics. It is, of course, different from the last one in key respects—it is less rigid; it takes place in a world that is far more interdependent; and it creates far more grey space in terms of alignments and spheres of influence. It is, therefore, possible that in the near term:

- Terrorism will be a continuing problem, but great-power competition will remain the bigger threat to global security and economy.
- There is going to be hedging, deterrence and some cooperation with China, all happening at the same time.
- Russia is in demographic and economic decline. Still, it retains enormous resources that it can employ as a spoiler in everything, from nuclear-arms control and cyber conflict to West Asia. It can tilt the balance in a future major war.
- The US–China–Russia relationship could worsen further. Their militaries are busy preparing for a face-off, creating a dangerous dynamic of deterrence and counter-deterrence.

- The US, Japan and Europe together represent the largest part of the global economy. They still have the capacity of shaping Chinese behaviour in a rules-based international order.
- As for India, it now has a posture towards China, but there are questions about its strategy. At some point, India will have to choose. It must then jump off the railing and land on a side—be that on the American turf or on the Chinese soil.
- Insofar as China is concerned, President Xi made its intention ominously clear in the beginning of 2019, '(T)he armed forces must…take on responsibilities for preparing and waging war.'[5] All along, China would be on track to restore its historic role as the Middle Kingdom, bringing the world to a pass that Napoleon had warned about, 'China is a sleeping giant. Let her sleep, for when she wakes, she will move the world.'

No End to Global Woes

Beyond the limited circle of strategists, the world was ticking along well till the beginning of a new decade in January 2020. There was anticipation of plentiful prosperity on the back of the most technologically comfortable world in history. Cushioned in this smugness, we forgot that the unexpected is often unanticipated.

Even the most vivid imagination could not have thought that a disease such as Covid-19 would be so all-encompassing, so comprehensively global and so completely devastating in its effect.

In a short span, the Covid-19 crisis has brought into the open some contradictory forces. It made human interactions transactional, and each transaction, standalone, but there were examples also of sharing and sacrifice. After this crisis, the world will take stock of the fallen, both the people and the ideas that did not make it through the crisis. Over time, it may alter some parts of global behaviour, with the impact varying from country to country.

Alas, Covid-19 is not going to be the end of global misfortunes. It is more than likely that the next decade will keep the world on a nervous edge for other reasons too. Let's go beyond the current wrath of nature and turn our thoughts towards 2035, by when the world may have achieved its best and even the worst ever.

This combination of force and technology will be the general state of the world in 2035, much like a dry forest in deep summer, awaiting a spark. The world had lived through a similarly dark and depraved period in the 1930s, with multiple strains of discord. Therefore, with the benefit of that hindsight, one could dare and predict:

- The decline of dollar as the global currency is certain. The aspirations of yuan and euro are one factor. Increasingly, however, digital currency will replace paper as the preferred exchange.
- As growth splutters, the economic pie around the world will shrink. National boundaries will stunt global trade.
- Clash of civilizations will keep tensions simmering in many European countries, but it is unlikely to boil over to conflict with the Arab world. Instead, many clashes may take place within Europe.
- After the failure, or near failure, of communism, capitalism and liberalism, the world's new mantra of 'ism' will be authoritarianism and nationalism. The big wars of the future are more likely to have roots in 'clash of egos' rather than in 'clash of civilizations'.
- The future conflicts will also be fought over bread-and-butter issues like climate change, transnational rivers, freedom of seas, trade and epidemics.
- China will fight one or possibly two major wars before

2035. The first of these could involve either Taiwan or India. If the result of the first war favours China, the second could soon follow. A prolonged conflict may see other countries joining in.

- A major US–China war may take place before 2035.

20

THE BIG WAR

There are three gates to this hell...the gate of lust, the gate of wrath, and the gate of greed.

—Bhagavad Gita (16:21)

The challenge of the coming age will be the next big war, only the timing of it remains uncertain. But why are we assuming there will be a war, that too a big war? Wasn't there 'long peace' after the Second World War? Alas, it was not so, and this claim is flawed on many counts. First, it assumes that if the West was conflict-free, all was well with the world. One has to ask people in Vietnam, Iraq, Afghanistan and Syria if they agree with this assessment. Second, peace even in the western world was not the result of a liberal order but a consequence of precarious balance of power between the Soviet Union and the US during the Cold War. More than anything else, this peace was the result of a society that was content. This contentment may not continue to last.

Another notion popular in the 1990s celebrated democracy as the age of peace. But, in practice, it was largely an aspirational notion. The US, the greatest democracy of our times, has been responsible for initiating most of the wars in recent decades.

What we are witnessing now is a new episode of the old truism, that of conflict between a rising challenger and a declining hegemon. This is just as true of the animal kingdom in a jungle as it is in the affairs of men and states. As an ascendant power, China chafes at the rules of the existing order. This, again, is typical in an evolving contest, and it invariably happens when a rising power gains ground on an established power. Consequently, their tensions multiply, leading eventually to conflict. As Thucydides wrote, 'The growth of the power of Athens, and the alarm which this inspired in Sparta, made war inevitable.'

But the assumption that there will be just one huge, big-bang war is flawed. In fact, there might be variations of this theme with smaller, localized flare-ups before the big one. But in tracing that path, we are venturing into uncharted territory. Experts give great attention to the prediction of extraordinary, black-swan events such as the next financial crises or another earthquake. But a prediction about war has been of relatively little interest. For once, however, a team of international financial investors led by Christopher Joye has developed a model for predicting future conflicts and the possibilities of wars. By their model, '(T)he probability of a low-intensity military conflict over the next decade between the US and China is…at around 46%…between the US and Russia…at 30%; between China and Russia, 44%; between China and Japan, 46%; and between China and India, 55%.'[1]

This is about a 'conflict' taking place. A 'war', on the other hand, seems a less likely prospect, but the possibility exists:

> …China and India have a 22% likelihood of engaging in a war in the next 10 years. The likelihood of outright war between China and the US is 12%; between China and Taiwan, 11%; and between China and Japan, 10%. Any such war would have potentially cataclysmic consequences. The risk of outright war between the US and Russia is, interestingly, much lower, at 2%.'[2]

Joye's model is categorical in asserting that the risk of an India–China conflict or war is the greatest in the world. We should add to this the ever-present possibility of a war with Pakistan.

Since India no longer faces just unidirectional threats, it has to take a 360-degree view and prepare accordingly. Making the challenge dire is the fact that it is not a mere two-front war that India faces, but more likely a 'single continuous war' along two fronts. This war, when it happens, might stretch from one extremity of the Indo-Pak boundary to the other end of the Indo-China border. In that case, India will have to contend with a 'collaborative war' that involves interoperability between China and Pakistan across the entire military spectrum. Such a war will be fought both in the deep seas and on the high Himalayas.

Moreover, India may not have the luxury of time to catch up with China. Just to give one example, India is still at the 4G stage. China has advanced well into 5G, and it is now helping Pakistan progress towards that. How can India, with its 4G technology, counter their more advanced EWS? It needs to urgently adopt new military techniques and add to its armoury. This means:

- It needs to upgrade military technology with the latest in AI, drones and electronic warfare.
- It needs to move away from its traditionally defensive approach because it is physically impossible for it to guard every inch of the over 6,800-km stretch of borders it shares with China and Pakistan.
- It must invest in grey zone operations in the enemy areas.
- It must adopt a whole of government approach in countering threats to its security.
- Increasingly, India will have to find responses to the 'cognitive war' tactics of its enemies. Add to this the possibility of 'No contact' warfare and the use of 'unmanned platforms' in war.
- There is no reason to expect that, in any future war with China and/or Pakistan, India will understand their nuclear Rubicon or that the Indian armed forces will not

inadvertently cross one or more.

- India must lessen its economic dependence on China in critical sectors.
- The US has become an increasingly critical partner for India. But this dependence raises serious questions as to whether it actually enhances India's strategic imperatives or if it opens up new vulnerabilities.
- India's effort should be to create issue-based coalitions. It will have to work with other countries who feel threatened by the overwhelming preponderance of the two great powers and who fear their marginalization in a world of contention and strife.

To add to its list of hurdles, the strategic setting around India does not present a comforting picture. Despite the affinities of culture, ethnicity and history, the modern processes of nation-building have created sharply etched national identities in South Asia. In a thus divided subcontinent, the commonalities have progressively lessened.

Against this setting, should India compete with China for dominance of Asia or should it stay focused on its own rise till it is strong enough to compete with it globally? Advisedly, an emerging power should stay focused on building its capacities while cultivating good ties with immediate neighbours, deep engagement with extended neighbours and balancing between great powers.

Chinese Dream

A major reason why America won the Cold War against the Soviet Union was that the causes it championed enjoyed broad support of people of the world. A US-sponsored resolution against the Soviet interests would invariably win close to two-thirds support of the UN members. Accordingly, in the East–West confrontation, the dice was loaded in America's favour. President Reagan captured well the American sentiments when he described the Soviet Union as the 'evil empire'.[3]

In contrast, the US still needs to credibly caricature China as a villain. Moreover, most countries want to remain neutral in the geopolitical contest between the US and China. As a result, the US finds itself in an uncomfortable position, where its advantages against China do not appear overwhelming. And by positioning China as its greatest strategic competitor, the US has prematurely ensured an almost equal status to China.

Sadly, the American apprehension of losing its hegemony is combined with its fear of China. While there has been a growing sense of catastrophe in the West, what China seeks is a two-step approach. It does not want subordination to the US, but it expects a central role in global leadership. Even if Beijing cannot establish an exclusive Sino-centric world, it will be a relentless and ruthless competitor in its efforts to maximize its wealth, power and influence relative to the US.

But China's goal of 'displacing' the US as the world's leading state is flawed in its ambition and objective. 'Displace' does not necessarily mean 'replace'. Becoming the sole superpower means accepting responsibilities. It is true that the US was often rash and arrogant in its dealings with other nations, but it did not covet their territory, which China does.

This is not their only difference in approach to dealing with the world. From ancient times, Chinese writers have maintained that negotiations are a device for delaying action until the moment is auspicious. The goal must remain annihilation of the enemy, and the best way to respond to a threat is to eliminate it by force. China sees the world as subservient. It uses the language of subjugation—others should admit their mistakes. And in realization of its objectives, it discards casually the promises it had made solemnly.

In 1951, China signed a treaty with the Dalai Lama's government that 'guaranteed' Tibet's government and respect for its culture and way of life. That guarantee lasted just eight years. Later, in 1984, China promised in a joint declaration with the UK, 'one country, two systems' to Hong Kong. But China has gone back on it to restrict political and media freedoms in the former British colony. In 2021, China decided to end Hong Kong's 'one country, two systems'. With that, it broke the commitment that China's 'socialist system and policies shall not be practised in the Hong Kong Special Administrative Region' and that 'the previous capitalist system and way of life shall remain unchanged for 50 years.'[4]

It is not just with Tibet and Hong Kong that China has been double-faced. It has been deceitful with India too. When China decided to enter and occupy areas across the LAC, it broke the protocols worked out in the 1980s and violated the Border Peace and Tranquility Agreement of 1993.

Asian Hegemon

It is China's record of deception that keeps Taiwan on edge. But why should Taiwan be on guard? After all, the economic relations between China and Taiwan have steadily increased. In 2018, more than 100,000 Taiwanese businesses were operating in the mainland, and nearly 40 per cent of Taiwan's exports went to China.[5]

This is sizeable, yet the volume of trade and investments is by itself not enough to propitiate China. It wants the fulfilment of its one-China ambition. There are two possible ways in which it might pursue that objective. It could launch a sudden invasion, taking the US and much of the world by surprise. In its present procrastinative state, the US policy of strategic ambiguity leaves unanswered what it might do in the event of an invasion by China on Taiwan. Let us assume that after mulling endlessly over the issue, it eventually rouses itself to action.

By the time it does so, China would have got the first mover advantage. Despite losses of men and material, its forces would have taken control of some part of the island. This would mean that by then an American intervention will be in the form of an invading force against the Chinese army already ensconced in Taiwan. In the frantic battle that follows, American forces will be faced with an onslaught of Chinese weapons.

As the war escalates, the US might respond with stealth fighters and stealthy submarines. Since both sides will battle for air and sea superiority, they might simultaneously try to blind one another with cyber operations, electronic warfare and space attacks. Eventually, and that is if the US prevails in this high-tech battle, the US army would have to put boots on ground in great numbers. This is the trickier part because the logistics of maintaining a supply chain going at short notice, and from far away, could be a major issue. There is no guarantee that the US will be able to quickly overwhelm the Chinese army, and the Americans do not relish counting body bags.

But it might happen differently because China may not want to start a war over Taiwan, at least not immediately. It is conscious that invading Taiwan may not mean easy victory. On the contrary, its forces might face severe and prolonged resistance. China will also be conscious of the fact that a war over Taiwan is likely to draw in the US, Japan and Australia. That will be a formidable challenge for China because despite its recently acquired military swagger, it knows that they are no pushovers.

Therefore, however much Xi is urged by the PLA to sort out early the Taiwan problem, he knows that an invasion would immediately trigger an all-out Taiwanese response. More than half of any Chinese invasion fleet could be sunk by concentrations of shore-based Harpoon cruise missiles supported by a host of Taiwanese air- and sea-launched land attack and anti-ship cruise missiles. China will suffer huge losses in war and spend years trying to pacify Taiwan, militarily and politically. Clearly then, the forcible seizure of Taiwan would impede, not advance China's goal of regional hegemony.

Taiwan, therefore, is not the key that unlocks China's regional ambitions as the hegemon in Asia. Instead, an invasion of Taiwan could hamper and delay it.

Rather than suffer a bloody nose, and the consequent loss of reputation, China is unlikely to start a war over Taiwan unless it is sure it can win. It would then want this war to be a swift operation, leaving America with the least possible time to react. Otherwise, and if the US and other countries get involved, the war will have far more serious dimensions than China may have catered for. Given the uncertainties involved, it is unlikely to launch a Taiwan operation immediately. America's Indo-Pacific Command optimistically gives a six-year timeline for such an attack: 'The Taiwanese assess perhaps a three-year time frame before an attack, while US Indo-Pacific Command in Honolulu considers a military assault in six years to be possible.'[6]

So, even as Taiwan remains the prize it covets, China might first opt for a swift victory elsewhere. It need not look far for such a war, one that firmly establishes it as the Asian hegemon. And unlike its multiple contacts with Taiwan, China and India can best be described as distant neighbours. It is a pity that as two great contiguous civilizations, they should know so little about each other. Their contacts, in the previous centuries, were infrequent and speckled mainly with some spiritual and limited commercial exchanges. In modern times, when China came to know more about India, it was not impressed. China's appraisal of post-independent India remains ungenerous, even adversarial for reasons like these:

- India is a 'soft state', unlike China's muscular identity.
- Its presumed role as a counterbalance to China is exaggerated.
- India's growth capabilities lack sustained vigour.
- Its recent diplomacy has made it even less compatible

with Chinese interests.

- China–India relations will need to be so managed that India's ambitions do not pose a threat to Chinese objectives.

To add to these negatives, India's military relations with China remain delicately poised. The border issue has defied solution for the last 70 years. Their competing ambitions have periodically introduced a sore point. Both aspire for the peak position on a mountain called Asia, but China is in no mood to share that space with India. Rather, China loses no opportunity to pull India down, irritating it further.

On its part, if ever India had a strategy of dealing with China, it was one of stalling for time and hoping for the best. China played along but on its terms. India was aware of this steady accretion at its cost, but it preferred to squeeze shut its eyes, expecting thereby that no one in or outside India would discover the loss. The introduction of satellites with immensely effective cameras capable of recording every little change on ground punctured that glum assumption.

India still blustered and denied any loss of territory, but photographic evidence suggested otherwise. Meanwhile, an increasingly confident China kept preparing for a decisive blow. Its aim is twofold—to settle the boundary issue once and for all, on its terms, and second, to deliver a massive military humiliation of the type it delivered in 1962 so that the message of Chinese strength echoes across the world.

According to most experts, there is a serious and growing asymmetrical relationship between China and India. If effective diplomacy is the art of optimizing resources to one's benefit, then India has miles to go before it can come anywhere close to what China has achieved already. It leads India in all respects—from military to economic; from efficacy of governance to social discipline; from assertive self-confidence to amoral pursuit of goals. India faces negative asymmetries on all these issues.

Ideally speaking, both China and India will benefit from cooperation rather than a confrontational relationship. Just one example illustrates the point. It is the expectation of some economists that the middle-class markets in China and India, in 2030, will account for annual expenditures of $14.1 trillion and $12.3 trillion, respectively. The free flow of a part of this large trade between them will benefit not just their people but the wider Asian region as well. However, that seems unlikely as long as their troops remain locked in confrontation at the LAC.

Till then, China would like to undermine India, relegate it to a regional identity, keep it economically underslung and, most of all, keep it engaged by all other means short of war. But it will also be prepared for the next war.

A Revisionist Power

The fabric weaving India and China together has been fraying faster from the time Xi took power. On four occasions since 2012, China has indulged in salami-slicing along the largely un-demarcated India–China border. Some experts feel if the situation continues to deteriorate, it could lead to war. They place India at a disadvantage both in a conventional war and during an escalation to nuclear war. However, this is an unduly pessimistic view. A war with China may be poised more evenly than many think. But if the situation turns really grim for India, it, as a nuclear power, has that final card to play.

So far, China's territorial faits accomplis have been imposing gains at the expense of India without getting into a war. They are limited land grabs on the assumption that India will not risk a larger fight. But the growing friction between India and China could trigger either a major conflict involving potentially destructive escalation or a manageable 'new normal' with some small-scale conflicts.

Both these possibilities are in the negative category because even a small conflict can quickly escalate into a full-fledged war. Given their stark strategic asymmetries, India has to play a much more cautious and much less risky hand. Yet, India has some cards up its sleeve:

- In a war, China will not be an automatic winner nor is India a pushover.
- China might engage in pugnacious behaviour, but it also has its own stakes to protect. By antagonizing India beyond a point, it risks instigating reactions from India that affect China's interests.
- A conflict with a large country like India will have consequences even in its relations with other countries.

Any willingness on India's part to respond forcefully to China would be welcomed in the US, where successive administrations have sought to integrate India into America's Indo-Pacific strategy. This does not mean the US will promptly jump into the fray. A president like Biden is more likely to mull over the issue till it is late. India will do well to note what a former American Defense Secretary Robert Gates wrote about him, '(Biden) has been wrong on nearly every major foreign policy and national security issue over the past four decades.'[7] Moreover, there are practical issues to contend with. The logistics of moving American troops and equipment to the Himalayan mountains, and acclimatizing the troops to those heights, would be a time-consuming affair. On the other hand, the idea of pre-positioning them, in anticipation, would be political dynamite in India.

Therefore, when this war breaks out, India could well be reminded that the US has 47 treaty allies, and it is not one of them. It is more likely to be given moral encouragement through strong diplomacy, and it may even be transferred defence equipment as per its needs, but American military force is unlikely to be readily deployed to fight shoulder to shoulder with the Indian Army against China.

This scepticism has grown following America's humiliating withdrawal from Afghanistan. People, even the normally non-involved person next door, ask if the US can cast Afghans to the Taliban wolves, where is the guarantee that it will join the next battle in the region? Worse still are the allegations that the US pushed Ukraine into an unnecessary war with Russia, where it watched from the sidelines.[8]

The war will cripple Ukraine and damage Russia. But it will also send scarring ripples across the world, including wheat shortages, food inflation and rising oil prices. Moreover, the barrage of Western sanctions against Russia is unprecedented in its scope and severity against a permanent member of the UNSC. These economic measures, wielded savagely, aim to cut Russia off from the world's financial arteries. They are powerful, but they also signal that the West is unwilling to meet a nuclear adversary on the battlefield.

It is against the background of multiple doubts that new questions are being asked about the US's strategic intentions. US's miscalculations in its recent wars, and a string of presidents ranging from pacifist Obama to unpredictable but war-risk-averse Trump to vacillating Biden, have not helped either. It is also being said that the US did not just retreat from Afghanistan but also from a principle and its values. After its disgrace there, Biden declared from the podium of the United Nations General Assembly (UNGA) that henceforth diplomacy will replace war in America's global engagements. He may have said so to paper over his Afghan blunder, but he forgets that ideological contests between countries are zero-sum in nature. If your rival is evil, compromise becomes appeasement. This is particularly the case when diplomacy aims to manage competition through compromise, conciliation and the search for common ground.

The Lonely Gun

Even if war is not inevitable in international affairs, preparation for war is necessary to avoid it. If India appears ill-prepared for war, the awareness of its purpose will be marked by a big doubt. Given this background, and the US's current vacillation in readily joining other peoples' war, India may find itself wielding a lonely gun in its next big confrontation. That major flare-up could start with Pakistan and may draw in China, or it could be the other way round. Unlike a single-front war, many unknowns lurk here:

- Pakistan and China are building capabilities that give them the benefit of surprise to impose their will.
- With cyber weapons and long-range conventional strike capabilities, they have the option of controlling escalation.
- Pakistan is more likely to choose nuclear escalation if it perceives that India can significantly degrade its conventional operations.
- In a war with Pakistan, India may not anticipate correctly Pakistan's nuclear 'red lines'. It could also happen the other way round, where Pakistan makes the misjudgment,
- Pakistan could employ chemical weapons and/or tactical weapons against the Indian Army in a future war. But the Indian Army may not be fully prepared to absorb their shock use.
- India needs capabilities that can blunt this aggression. It also needs to device credible options for threatening retaliation and escalation to deter the adversary and its escalatory options.

Just as Pakistan assumes that China will be at its side, Xi can confidently factor in that Pakistan will be its military aide in a battle with India. As for Russia, it may be China's current brother, but it has been India's friend over decades. In war, it might steer clear of taking sides. Therefore, it may pass on a few critical items to India and intelligence information to China. Whatever the ultimate alliances and partnerships, the consequences of an Indo-China war will be bad enough, but with Pakistan joining in, it will be the stuff of nightmares for India.

Pakistani generals are aggressive by training and impulsive by nature. The fact that they are not constrained by a political leadership, which could raise a restraining finger, makes it likely that they would be quick to nuclear rage. The question that follows is: will they use tactical nuclear weapons first or will they decide to drop the nuclear bomb? Regardless of what they choose, once a nuclear weapon has been used, its devastation could either stun the three sides to a pause or it may lead to the larger war, with Russia and the US joining in.

Will that signal the beginning of a much larger conflagration that will also draw in Japan, Australia, some European countries and Taiwan to fight on India's side? It could also mean others like Iran, North Korea and Turkey lining up to be with the China–Pakistan combine. Hopefully, this scary scenario will not happen because it is incendiary combinations like this that can lead to an inferno, a step short of the feared apocalypse. It is either that or the rest could decide to play it safe and watch India fight a two-front war, while they counsel restraint.

Mercifully for the world, and despite the war in Ukraine, other regions do not present an alarming picture on a global scale. There are certainly hotspots, like Israel's frictions with Iran and Hamas, Russia's hot border with Ukraine, or North Korea's prickly relations with South Korea and Japan. But these are likely to be on a relatively smaller scale.

It is the South and East Asian region that is the potential powder keg of the world. In every such event, be it China's invasion of Taiwan or a war with India, both Taiwan and India will have to factor in the record of America's fickle loyalties.

In an extreme crisis, when they need it, they will do well to recall Cambodian Prince Sisowath Sirik Matak's letter to the

American ambassador as Americans withdrew hastily from his country:

> I never believed for a moment that you would have this sentiment of abandoning a people which has chosen liberty. You have refused us your protection and we can do nothing about it. You leave, and my wish is that you and your country will find happiness under the sky…I have only committed the mistake of believing in you, the Americans.[9]

Whichever path the world chooses in the difficult decade ahead, it should keep reminding itself that history is the consequence of its choices. The responsibility then is also its.

Under these grim tidings, let us recall the words of Stephen Hawking, 'We are all time travellers journeying together into the future. But let us work together to make that future a place we want to visit.'[10]

Hopefully, far into the future, the world will remain at peace with itself, a place that we would want to visit.

ACKNOWLEDGEMENTS

The first tribute must go to you, dear reader. It is your support that took me beyond book number 1. This is specially so in the age of social media, television and impatient attention span. Fortunately, and despite these distractions, there are many who, like Groucho Marx, say to themselves, 'I find television very educating. Every time somebody turns on the set, I go into the other room and read a book.'

Among the first readers of this book have been those whose judgment I value. I was fortunate to have served with Shri Yashwant Sinha when he was the External Affairs minister. There were many occasions when I accompanied him during his visits to the Central Asian countries. They were, for me, good windows to observe how well he combined administrative wisdom with political astuteness. I am grateful for his generous comments about the book.

I have, so far, not had the opportunity to meet Shri Jairam Ramesh. But I have read with profit his deeply researched books. In fact, our correspondence started almost simultaneously as I finished reading *Intertwined Lives*, and he had coincidentally read *Durand's Curse*. He has now been gracious with a heart-warming endorsement.

Multitalented ambassador Nirupama Rao is grace personified. In the long years that we have been colleagues and close friends, I have always been gifted with her affection and sincerity. For me, Nirupama's endorsement of the book is both an encouragement and a sign of good augury.

It is my good luck that the Foreign Service brought me in close contact with some gifted professionals. Ambassador Bhaswati Mukherjee has been a constant well-wisher and a dear friend. She read and gave valuable suggestions on a portion of the book. Equally well-received were the carefully chosen comments by Ambassador T.C.A. Raghavan. Both Bhaswati and T.C.A. are established and well-regarded writers themselves. I am grateful to them for taking some time off to go through a part of the book.

Sometimes providence also arranges things in your favour. A chance encounter at a common speaking engagement brought me together with Vice Admiral Satish Soni (retd). His knowledge of the undersea aspects of warfare helped bring clarity to my understanding of the issue.

But a book remains in the realm of ideas if it cannot find a publisher. I have been lucky on that score. I acknowledge with appreciation Kapish Mehra's ready welcome to my manuscripts. Moreover, Team Rupa, headed by Yamini Chowdhury, senior commissioning editor, was a delight to work with. Yamini has been a constant source of strength for me, always careful with her words and encouraging when she felt the need.

Finally, dear reader, I turn to you once more. I am torn between two somewhat conflicting emotions—the hope that it turns out to be a bestseller and the desire that this book becomes a classic on the subject. As I struggle to make a choice, I am reminded of Mark Twain's warning, ‘“Classic.” A book which people praise and don't read.’ Thus warned, I end with the modest hope that you have enjoyed what you read in my book.

ENDNOTES

Chapter 1: Healing Wells

1 Baldwin, James. *The Price of the Ticket: Collected Nonfiction: 1948–1985,* Beacon Press, 2021, p. 322.
2 'Leon Trotsky 1879–1940: Russian revolutionary', Oxford Reference, https://tinyurl.com/2p9c5bnz. Accessed on 28 March 2022.
3 Khalid, Asma. 'How Biden is trying to clean up his comments about Russia and Ukraine', *NPR*, 20 January 2022, https://tinyurl.com/3xj2yzza. Accessed on 22 March 2022.
4 'Letter from Marx to Arnold Ruge in Dresden', marxists.org, https://tinyurl.com/cy4x7d3d. Accessed on 28 March 2022.
5 Cox, John. 'Racism and colonialism: overlooked features of the "Great War"', John Cox Center for HGHR Studies, Dept of Global Studies, 12 November 2018, https://bit.ly/3s0WZ5v. Accessed on 31 January 2022.
6 Huntington, Samuel P. *The Clash of Civilizations and the Remaking of World Order,* Simon & Schuster, 2007.

Chapter 2: All under Heaven

1 'Xi Jinping calls for self-reliance amid change "unseen in 100 years"', *Business Standard*, 1 January 2019, https://tinyurl.com/mhjarjsf. Accessed on 28 March 2022.
2 Ranade, Jayadeva. 'Xi Jinping is striving to achieve the "China Dream"', *Sunday Guardian Live*, 28 March 2022, 'https://tinyurl.com/yck9x5wu. Accessed on 22 March 2022.
3 Ratner, Paul. 'In 1973, an MIT computer predicted when civilization will end', *Big Think*, 23 August 2018, https://bit.ly/3rw0EcF. Accessed on 7 February 2022.

4 'Stratfor has 11 chilling predictions for what the world will look like a decade from now', *Business Insider India*, 25 December 2015, https://tinyurl.com/yweetwp5. Accessed on 7 February 2022.
5 Ibid.
6 Ibid.
7 Keynes, John Maynard. 'Economic Possibilities for our Grandchildren (1930)', https://tinyurl.com/ykfxn79z. Accessed on 28 March 2022.

Chapter 3: China: The Challenger

1 Kissinger, Henry. *White House Years*, Simon & Schuster, 2011.
2 Ibid.
3 Bosco, Joseph. 'The One China Policy: What Would Nixon Do?' *The Diplomat*, 5 January 2017, https://tinyurl.com/knk5z3vu. Accessed on 23 March 2022.
4 Becker, Jasper. 'On China by Henry Kissinger – review', *The Guardian*, 21 May 2011, https://tinyurl.com/bd47jftw. Accessed on 14 March 2022.
5 Congressional Research Service, 'China's Economic Rise: History, Trends, Challenges, and Implications for the United States', Updated 25 June 2019.
6 Graceffo, Antonio. 'Could China's Massive Public Debt Torpedo the Global Economy?' War on the Rocks, 2 December 2021, https://bit.ly/3LknQlY. Accessed on 10 February 2022.
7 Becker, Jasper. 'On China by Henry Kissinger – review', *The Guardian*, 21 May 2011, https://tinyurl.com/bd47jftw. Accessed on 14 March 2022.
8 Pillsbury, Michael. *The Hundred-Year Marathon: China's Secret Strategy to Replace America as the Global Superpower*, Henry Holt & Company, 2014.
9 Gracie, Carrie. 'Collision course? Rise of China a stress for the US', *BBC*, 26 September 2015, https://bbc.in/3Jc1lh8. Accessed on 10 February 2022.
10 Allison, Graham. 'Opportunity for Diplomacy: No Russian Attack Before Feb. 20', *Russia Matters*, 4 February 2022, https://bit.ly/35uKuYP. Accessed on 4 March 2022.
11 Cohen, Warren I. 'China's Strategic Culture', *The Atlantic*, March 1997, https://bit.ly/3gyZ3fZ. Accessed on 10 February 2022.
12 'China Military Spending/Defense Budget 1989–2022', MacroTrends, https://bit.ly/3vBUie8. Accessed on 4 March 2022.
13 Kristof, Nicholas D. 'The Rise of China', *Foreign Affairs*, Nov/Dec 1993,

https://fam.ag/3oCOlZY. Accessed on 10 February 2022.
14 Gertz, Bill. 'Pentagon: China's navy is now world's largest with 460 warships by 2030', *The Washington Times*, 8 November 2021, https://bit.ly/35OyKzX. Accessed on 4 March 2022.
15 Jain, Akshita. 'Xi Jinping says those who bully China will "get their heads bashed" on Communist Party's 100th anniversary', *Independent*, 1 July 2021, https://tinyurl.com/49b5wrx3. Accessed on 23 March 2022.
16 Menon, Shivshankar. 'What China's Rise Means for the World', *The Wire*, 2 January 2016, https://tinyurl.com/2p9ck35u. Accessed on 23 March 2022.
17 McCarthy, Niall. 'China Is Closing the Gap with the U.S. in R&D Expenditure', *Forbes*, 20 January 2020, https://bit.ly/3Lq2L9A. Accessed on 10 February 2022.
18 Kania, Elsa. 'China's Artificial Intelligence Revolution', *The Diplomat*, 27 July 2017, https://tinyurl.com/46dkd68y. Accessed on 29 March 2022.
19 Gehrke, Joel. 'FBI director: Chinese spies "a whole-of-society" threat to US', *Washington Examiner*, 13 February 2018, https://tinyurl.com/2wketepy. Accessed on 10 February 2022.
20 Ambassador George F. Kennan wrote to the Secretary of State with a lengthy analysis of Soviet policy in an attempt to explain their uncooperative behaviour. This message would later become famous as the 'Long Telegram'.
21 'The Longer Telegram: Toward a new American China Strategy', Atlantic Council, https://bit.ly/3HK16d4. Accessed on 10 February 2022.
22 Allison, Graham. 'The chairman of everything: why Chinese president Xi Jinping will change history', *The New Statesman*, 4 December 2017, updated 9 September 2021, https://tinyurl.com/yckxsjrk. Accessed on 31 March 2022.
23 Carter, Ash. 'Reflections on American Grand Strategy in Asia', Belfer Center for Science and International Affairs, October 2018, https://bit.ly/3HK2egO. Accessed on 10 February 2022.
24 Iyer, K. 'A warm Indian welcome to a neighbour', *China Daily*, 16 September 2014, https://bit.ly/3uKKZZ7. Accessed on 10 February 2022.

Chapter 4: Russia: Racing Along

1 Hodge, Carl Cavanagh, and Cathal J. Nolan. *U.S. Presidents and Foreign Policy: From 1789 to the Present,* ABC-CLIO, 2007, p. 400.

2 United States Congress House Committee on Un-American Activities, *The Communist Conspiracy: Communism outside the United States*, 1956, https://tinyurl.com/2p8jz8fh. Accessed on 29 March 2022.

3 Goldgeier, Jim. 'Promises Made, Promises Broken? What Yeltsin Was Told About NATO in 1993 and Why It Matters', War on the Rocks, 22 November 2019, https://bit.ly/3oH4TQP. Accessed on 14 February 2022.

4 Allison, Graham. 'China and Russia: A Strategic Alliance in the Making', *The National Interest,* 14 December 2018, https://tinyurl.com/yckvm2ux. Accessed on 29 March 2022.

5 Chatzky, Andrew. 'Have Sanctions on Russia Changed Putin's Calculus?' Council on Foreign Relations, 2 May 2019, https://tinyurl.com/muvjj4c6. Accessed on 31 March 2022.

6 The White House Office of the Press Secretary, 'Remarks by President Obama at G20 Press Conference', 16 November 2014, https://bit.ly/3JuU3p3. Accessed on 14 February 2022.

7 Wintour, Patrick, and Ben Doherty. 'Vladimir Putin leaves G20 after leaders line up to browbeat him over Ukraine', *The Guardian*, 16 November 2014, https://bit.ly/3GOgmV1. Accessed on 14 February 2022.

8 Muraviev, Alexey. 'Factoring in Russian military power in the Indo-Asia–Pacific strategic calculus', *The Strategist*, 15 February 2018, https://tinyurl.com/yekfj58a. Accessed on 29 March 2022.

9 Foer, Franklin. 'Putin's Puppet', *Slate,* 4 July 2016, https://bit.ly/3GNI2sT. Accessed on 14 February 2022.

10 'Zbigniew K. Brzezinski: A Life of Service and Strategy', Center for Strategic & International Studies (CSIS), https://bit.ly/3JkCms2. Accessed on 14 February 2022.

11 Bochkov, Danil. 'Russia is not sulking. She is composing herself', CGTN, 24 December 2021, https://tinyurl.com/32bx5dyx. Accessed on 29 March 2022.

Chapter 5: America First

1 Guilbaut, Serge. *How New York Stole the Idea of Modern Art*, University of Chicago Press, 2020, p. 60.

2 Schiavenza, Matt. 'China Economy Surpasses US in Purchasing Power, But Americans Don't Need to Worry', *International Business Times,* 10 August 2014, https://tinyurl.com/ycxn9hya. Accessed on 30 March 2022.

3 Patton, Mike. 'U.S. Role in Global Economy Declines Nearly 50%', *Forbes*, 29 February 2016, https://tinyurl.com/ynz3k3dp. Accessed on 30 March 2022.
4 Meacham, Jon. 'Obama's Shades of Gray', *TIME*, 7 May 2014, https://bit.ly/3HNWIJX. Accessed on 16 February 2022.
5 Epstein, Richard A. 'Presidential Indecision', Hoover Institution, 8 September 2014, https://hvr.co/3BpJuAz. Accessed on 16 February 2022.
6 Brzezinski, Zbigniew K. *The Choice: Global Domination or Global Leadership*, Basic Books, 2004.
7 Setterfield, Ray. 'The General, The Schoolgirl, And The Famous One-Word Despatch', On This Day, https://bit.ly/3BsuORo. Accessed on 17 February 2022.
8 Farrow, Ronan. *War on Peace: The End of Diplomacy and the Decline of American Influence*, W.W. Norton & Company, London, 2018.
9 'Supporting the National Defence Strategy, A Profile of Relevant RAND Research', RAND Corporation, https://tinyurl.com/4bhuhp79. Accessed on 31 March 2022.
10 'Providing for the Common Defense: The Assessment and Recommendations of the National Defense Strategy Commission', Unites States Institute of Peace (USIP), https://tinyurl.com/2p97a77y. Accessed on 31 March 2022.
11 Horsley, Scott. 'A Churchill "Quote" That U.S. Politicians Will Never Surrender', *NPR*, 28 October 2013, https://n.pr/3JzHhpb. Accessed on 17 February 2022.
12 Schwarz, Benjamin, and Christopher Layne. 'A New Grand Strategy', *The Atlantic*, January 2002, https://bit.ly/3gOoUk9. Accessed on 17 February 2022.
13 Kennan, George F. 'A Fateful Error', *The New York Times*, 5 February 1997, https://nyti.ms/33wDbyU. Accessed on 17 February 2022.
14 Zhang, Wei-Bin. *America the Great and Its Self-Destruction: Viewing the Superpower through the Lenses of Ancient Confucianism and Chaos Theory*, Algora Publishing, 2021, p. 170.

Chapter 6: India's Long Wait

1 Marx, Karl. *Karl Marx: Selected Writings*, Oxford University Press, 2000.
2 Kissinger, Henry. *White House Years*, Simon & Schuster, 2011.
3 Yew, Lee Kuan. *From Third World to First: The Singapore Story: 1965–2000*, HarperCollins, 2000.

4 Ibid.

5 'Exports of goods and services (% of GDP)', The World Bank, https://bit.ly/35NpYT9. Accessed on 4 March 2022.

6 'Exports of goods and services (% of GDP)—Korea, Rep.' The World Bank, https://tinyurl.com/2p9f4mc8. Accessed on 30 March 2022.

7 'China: Exports, percent of GDP', The Global Economy.com, https://bit.ly/3sFEPYx. Accessed on 4 March 2022.

8 Kant, Amitabh. 'Export Or Perish: Why India must achieve a quantum jump in exports to drive growth', *The Times of India*, 19 July 2018, https://bit.ly/3pzNidO. Accessed on 4 March 2022.

9 'Share of India's exports in global exports from 2015 to 2019', Statista, https://bit.ly/376ayKp. Accessed on 4 March 2022.

10 Sankhe, Shirish, Ireena Vittal and et al. 'India's urban awakening: Building inclusive cities, sustaining economic growth', McKinsey Global Institute, 1 April 2010, https://mck.co/3GX0QWA. Accessed on 17 February 2022.

11 Ibid.

12 Jayapalan, N. *Indian Political Thinkers: Modern Indian Political Thought*, Atlantic Publishers, 2000, p. 268.

13 Hopkirk, Peter. *The Great Game*: *On Secret Service in High Asia*, Oxford University Press, 1990.

14 Mohanty, Aayush, and Avni Sharma. 'A Shift in India's Grand Strategy on Security?' The Fletcher Forum of World Affairs, https://bit.ly/3uXjOdE. Accessed on 17 February 2022.

15 Yew, Lee Kuan. *From Third World to First: The Singapore Story: 1965–2000*, HarperCollins, 2000.

16 Perkovich, George. *India's Nuclear Bomb: The Impact on Global Proliferation*, University of California Press, 2001.

17 Ramesh, Jairam. *Intertwined Lives*: *P.N. Haksar & Indira Gandhi*, Simon & Schuster India, 2018.

18 Datta-Ray, Sunanda K. 'Between history and propaganda', *Business Standard*, 12 July 2021, https://bit.ly/3GU2xUT. Accessed on 17 February 2022.

19 CIA, 'Sino-Indian Border Dispute, Section 1: 1950-59, DD/I Staff Study, CIA/Rss, Reference Title Polo X V I', Bibliogov, 2013.

20 Ibid.

21 Mehta, Ashok K. 'Kailash card used, Depsang in limbo', *The Pioneer*, 24 February 2021, https://bit.ly/3MmH9eT. Accessed on 4 March 2022.

22 Andrew, Christopher, and Vasili Mitrokhin. *The Mitrokhin Archive II: The KGB in the World*, Allen Lane, London, 2005.

23 Taneja, Kabir. 'By striking terrorists in Pakistan, India has changed the ground rules in South Asia', Observer Research Foundation, 6 March 2019, https://bit.ly/3sDunkr. Accessed on 4 March 2022.

Chapter 7: Pakistan: The Puppeteer

1 Gall, Carlotta. *The Wrong Enemy: America in Afghanistan 2001–2014*, Penguin, 2014.
2 Coll, Steve. *Directorate S: The C.I.A. and America's Secret Wars in Afghanistan and Pakistan, 2001–2016*, Penguin UK, 2018.
3 Gall, Carlotta. *The Wrong Enemy: America in Afghanistan 2001–2014*, Penguin, 2014.
4 Ibid.
5 Coll, Steve. *Directorate S: The C.I.A. and America's Secret Wars in Afghanistan and Pakistan, 2001–2016*, Penguin UK, 2018.
6 'Bush faults Pakistan on extremism', *Dawn*, 10 November 2010, https://tinyurl.com/246yvddh. Accessed on 24 March 2022.
7 Ahmed, Javed. 'Pakistan's Secret War Machine', *The National Interest*, 7 May 2018, https://bit.ly/3H0fnkH. Accessed on 18 February 2022.
8 Coll, Steve. *Directorate S: The C.I.A. and America's Secret Wars in Afghanistan and Pakistan, 2001–2016*, Penguin UK, 2018.
9 Powers, Thomas. 'The War Without End', *The New York Review*, 19 April 2018, https://bit.ly/34QPkiL. Accessed on 18 February 2022.
10 Ibid.
11 Partlow, Joshua. *A Kingdom of Their Own: The Family Karzai and the Afghan Disaster*, reprint edition, Vintage, 2017.
12 Press Trust of India. 'Pak poses mortal threat to world: Hillary', *NDTV*, 23 April 2009, https://bit.ly/3561fc4. Accessed on 18 February 2022.
13 Hoodbhoy, Pervez. 'Why Bangladesh overtook Pakistan', *Deccan Chronicle*, 10 February 2019, https://bit.ly/3CgzBWC. Accessed on 4 March 2022.
14 'US embassy cables: Saudi influence in Pakistan', *The Guardian*, 20 November 2007, https://bit.ly/3BCW0Nl. Accessed on 18 February 2022.
15 Arpi, Claude. 'Mr Straw, do you know who created the Kashmir mess?' *Rediff.com*, 28 May 2002, https://bit.ly/3MjxFBd. Accessed on 4 March 2022.
16 Haidar, Suhasini. 'Through a backchannel, steps forward', *The Hindu*, 12 April 2021, https://bit.ly/3MmITEX. Accessed on 4 March 2022.

17 'Annual Threat Assessment of the US Intelligence Community', Office of the Director of National Intelligence, 9 April 2021, https://bit.ly/3gSYmy4. Accessed on 18 February 2022.
18 Smith, David O. '9/11 in Islamabad: The First 72 Hours', War on the Rocks, 10 September 2021, https://bit.ly/3I0gOAF. Accessed on 18 February 2022.

Chapter 8: Afghanistan: The Return of the Taliban

1 Coughlin, Con. 'Lessons from Winston Churchill: Withdrawal from Afghanistan', The History Reader, 7 January 2014, https://bit.ly/3sV0VFt. Accessed on 21 February 2022.
2 Tare, Kiran. 'Why the Taliban named a military unit after "Panipat"', *India Today*, 16 February 2022, https://bit.ly/3vDl5XI. Accessed on 4 March 2022.
3 'Afghanistan GDP', Y Charts, https://bit.ly/3sHVOK2. Accessed on 4 March 2022.
4 'Per capita GDP at current prices - US dollars', UN Data, https://bit.ly/3pABMPz. Accessed on 4 March 2022.

Chapter 9: West Is Resting

1 'Winston Churchill's Landmark Speech at the University of Zurich 1946', University of Zurich, https://bit.ly/3BJ9hUO. Accessed on 22 February 2022.
2 Malraux, Andre. *Felled Oaks*: *Conversation with De Gaulle*, Holt, Rinehart and Winston, New York, 1972.
3 'Statistics on migration to Europe', European Commission, https://bit.ly/35KF77x. Accessed on 4 March 2022.
4 'Piraeus Port Wins the Fourth Place in Container Handling in 2020', Ferry Shipping News, 11 March 2021, https://bit.ly/35uj9pE. Accessed on 4 March 2022.
5 Hillman, Jonathan E. 'China's Belt and Road Initiative: Five Years Later', Center for Strategic & International Studies (CSIS), 25 January 2018, https://tinyurl.com/5cxxam5b. Accessed on 31 March 2022.
6 'European Union: Gross domestic product (GDP) from 2016 to 2026', Statista, https://bit.ly/3sHHsJG. Accessed on 4 March 2022.
7 Carpenter, Ted Galen. 'Many predicted Nato expansion would lead to war. Those warnings were ignored', *The Guardian*, 28 February 2022,

https://bit.ly/3HKVYV4. Accessed on 4 March 2022.
8 'EU "can no longer rely on US," says France's Macron', *Deutsche Welle*, 27 August 2018, https://bit.ly/3twixHY. Accessed on 4 March 2022.
9 Walt, Vivienne. 'How Nationalists Are Joining Together to Tear Europe Apart', *TIME*, 11 April 2019, https://bit.ly/36lS3B2. Accessed on 22 February 2022.
10 Ratcliffe, Susan. *Oxford Dictionary of Quotations by Subject*, OUP, Oxford, 2010, p. 158.

Chapter 10: East Stirs

1 Mukherjee, Sanjoy. 'Learning and Openness', *Swarajya*, 31 December 2015, https://bit.ly/3IIT6cI. Accessed on 4 March 2022.
2 Johnson, Keith, and Robbie Gramer. 'How the Bottom Fell Out of the U.S.-Saudi Alliance', *Foreign Policy*, 23 April 2020, https://tinyurl.com/46jxzwr5. Accessed on 30 March 2022.
3 'Foreign Relations of the United States, 1969–1976, Volume XXV, Arab-Israeli Crisis and War, 1973', Office of the Historian, Department of State, United States of America, https://bit.ly/3t1yllT. Accessed on 24 February 2022.
4 'India Exports to Japan', *Trading Economics*, https://bit.ly/35OIPwN. Accessed on 4 March 2022.
5 National Security Strategy of the United States of America, December 2017, https://tinyurl.com/2p8at7xs. Accessed on 3 April 2022.
6 Mackinder, H.J. *Democratic Ideals and Reality: A Study in the Politics of Reconstruction*, Forgotten Books, 2018.
7 Coll, Steve, and Adam Entous. 'The Secret History of the U.S. Diplomatic Failure in Afghanistan', *The New Yorker*, 10 December 2021, https://bit.ly/3vhYwYb. Accessed on 24 February 2022.

Chapter 11: The Age of Many Worlds

1 'First Inaugural Address of Richard Milhous Nixon', The Avalon Project, Yale Law School, Lilian Goldman Law Library, https://tinyurl.com/3vmbzaau. Accessed on 24 March 2022.
2 Durant, Will. *The Case for India*, Gyan Publishing House, 2017.

Chapter 12: Let Hundred Flowers Bloom

1 Wood, James. 'Wounder and Wounded', *The New Yorker*, 23 November 2008, https://bit.ly/35lU8MW. Accessed on 25 February 2022.
2 Ahmed, Khaled. 'Integration vs The Ummah', *The Indian Express*, 3 November 2018, https://bit.ly/3LWZHlL. Accessed on 25 February 2022.
3 'State multiculturalism has failed, says David Cameron', *BBC*, 5 February 2011, https://bbc.in/3ImnRnp. Accessed on 25 February 2022.
4 Huntington, Samuel P. *The Clash of Civilizations and the Remaking of World Order*, Simon & Schuster, New York, 2011.
5 Ibid.
6 'State multiculturalism has failed, says David Cameron', *BBC*, 5 February 2011, https://tinyurl.com/yukypjdn. Accessed on 31 March 2022.
7 Huntington, Samuel P. *The Clash of Civilizations and the Remaking of World Order*, Simon & Schuster, New York, 2011.
8 Brunnstrom, David. 'EU says it has solved the Kissinger question', Reuters, 20 November 2009, https://tinyurl.com/2acu6evv. Accessed on 31 March 2022.

Chapter 13: AI Overwhelms I

1 Kissinger, Henry A. 'How the Enlightenment Ends', *The Atlantic*, June 2018, https://bit.ly/3Hjs0ao. Accessed on 25 February 2022.
2 Browne, Ryan. 'Elon Musk warns A.I. could create an "immortal dictator from which we can never escape"', CNBC, 6 April 2018, https://cnb.cx/3IM9clO. Accessed on 4 March 2022.

Chapter 14: The Power of Terror

1 Baishya, Dipayan. 'The private security guard is symptomatic of what ails India', *The Times of India*, 23 March 2019, https://bit.ly/3pB0rnd. Accessed on 4 March 2022.
2 Priest, Dana, and William M. Arkin. 'A hidden world, growing beyond control', *The Washington Post*, 19 July 2010, https://wapo.st/3HGltqw. Accessed on 4 March 2022.
3 Providence, R.I. 'Costs of the 20-year war on terror: $8 trillion and 900,000 deaths', News from Brown, https://bit.ly/3sAQYhH. Accessed on 28 February 2022.
4 Waltz, Michael G. *Warrior Diplomat: A Green Beret's Battles from*

Washington to Afghanistan, Potomac Books, 2014.

5 Mckew, Molly K. 'The Gerasimov Doctrine', *Politico Magazine*, September/October 2017, https://politi.co/3C1SgFh. Accessed on 28 February 2022.

6 'Transnational Threats Project', The Center for Strategic & International Studies (CSIS), https://bit.ly/3pmEZly. Accessed on 28 February 2022.

7 PTI, 'Afghans have broken "shackles of slavery": Pakistan PM Imran Khan', *The Hindu*, 16 August 2021, https://bit.ly/3thBn5s. Accessed on 28 February 2022.

8 Talukdar, Sreemoy. 'Afghanistan: Time for India to shed political conservatism and talk directly with the Taliban', *Firstpost*, 3 June 2021, https://bit.ly/3hpZg5u. Accessed on 28 February 2022.

Chapter 15: On a Chessboard

1 Chossudovsky, Michel. 'Secretary of State's Love Affair with Kosovo Liberation Army', Scoop, 10 April 2012, https://bit.ly/35NJ8YI. Accessed on 3 March 2022.

2 Kasli, Shelley. 'Echoes of British Colonial India in Plans to Partition Syria', *Geopolitical Monitor*, 21 March 2016, https://tinyurl.com/2p8k6n4y. Accessed on 1 April 2022.

3 Chrisafis, Angelique. 'Europe can no longer rely on US for security, says Emmanuel Macron', *The Guardian*, 27 August 2018, https://bit.ly/3hBCQyg. Accessed on 3 March 2022.

4 Cohen, Warren I. 'China's Strategic Culture', *The Atlantic*, March 1997, https://bit.ly/35KD4Am. Accessed on 3 March 2022.

5 Jones, Rodney W. 'India's Strategic Culture', Federation of American Scientists, 31 October 2006, https://tinyurl.com/5n7ns68c. Accessed on 21 March 2022.

6 Ibid.

Chapter 16: Drums of War

1 'Commencement Address At American University, Washington, D.C., June 10, 1963', JFK Library, https://bit.ly/3vRdch6. Accessed on 9 March 2022.

2 Clausewitz, Carl von. *On War*, Princeton University Press, 2008, p. 184.

3 'Sardar Patel's Letter to Prime Minister Jawaharlal Nehru dated

November 7, 1950 warning India about dangers from China', Friends of Tibet, https://bit.ly/3Myc2wZ. Accessed on 9 March 2022.

4 Kissinger, Henry. *On China*, Allen Lane, New York, 2011.

5 Ibid.

6 Clark, Christopher. *The Sleepwalkers: How Europe Went to War in 1914*, Penguin, 2012.

7 Kissinger, Henry. *White House Years*, Simon & Schuster, 2011.

8 Snow, Edgar. 'Interview with Mao', *The New Republic*, 27 February 1965, https://bit.ly/3vRfg8U. Accessed on 9 March 2022.

Chapter 17: The Setting

1 Lockie, Alex. 'Putin gave an ominous warning about World War III and nuclear competition with the US', *Business Insider*, 7 June 2018, https://bit.ly/3J2V7AI. Accessed on 11 March 2022.

2 Phonetic acronym of the words 'I owe you', and, in financial terms, means a document acknowledging the existence of a debt.

3 Scott, Margaret, and Westenley Alcenat. 'Revisiting the Pivot: The Influence of Heartland Theory in Great Power Politics', Macalester College, 9 May 2008, https://bit.ly/3tRsvnl. Accessed on 11 March 2022.

4 Escobar, Pepe. 'Chinese scholar offers insight into Beijing's strategic mindset', *Asia Times*, 5 January 2019, https://tinyurl.com/3wdvu3xu. Accessed on 1 April 2022.

5 Li, Yun. 'Warren Buffett says "never bet against America" in letter trumpeting Berkshire's U.S.-based assets', *CNBC*, 1 March 2021, https://tinyurl.com/5p7mnm6s. Accessed on 1 April 2022.

Chapter 18: The Final Weapon

1 Talbot, Steve. *Khrushchev Remembers*, Little, Brown and Company, New York, 1974.

2 Pandit, Rajat. 'Will call Pakistan's nuke bluff if tasked to cross border: Army chief', *The Times of India*, 12 January 2018, https://bit.ly/3I412nM. Accessed on 11 March 2022.

3 Schlosser, Eric. 'The growing dangers of the new nuclear-arms race', *The New Yorker*, 24 May 2018, https://bit.ly/3MRWODo. Accessed on 11 March 2022.

4 Ibid.

5 Ibid.

6 Draft Report of National Security Advisory Board on Indian Nuclear Doctrine, 17 August 1999, https://bit.ly/3vY5S3y. Accessed on 11 March 2022.
7 Talbot, Strobe. *Engaging India: Diplomacy, Democracy and the Bomb*, Brookings Institution Press, 2004.
8 Miglani, Sanjeev, and Drazen Jorgic. 'India, Pakistan threatened to unleash missiles at each other: sources', *Reuters*, 17 March 2019, https://reut.rs/3KD6MGu. Accessed on 11 March 2022.
9 Schlosser, Eric. 'The growing dangers of the new nuclear-arms race', *The New Yorker*, 24 May 2018, https://bit.ly/3MRWODo. Accessed on 11 March 2022.
10 Haider, Ejaz. 'Lessons from the Brink', *Dawn*, 10 March 2019, https://bit.ly/3CyPhEE. Accessed on 11 March 2022.
11 Conn, Ariel. 'The U.S. Worldwide Threat Assessment Includes Warnings of Cyber Attacks, Nuclear Weapons, Climate Change, etc.', The Future of Life Institute, 18 May 2017, https://tinyurl.com/5489xy9t. Accessed on 7 April 2022.
12 Ibid.
13 Sultan, Adil. 'Pakistan's emerging nuclear posture: Impact of drivers and technology on nuclear doctrine', *Strategic Studies*, Vol. 31, No. 4, 2011, pp. 147–67.
14 Tasleem, Sadia. 'Pakistan's Nuclear Use Doctrine', Carnegie Endowment for International Peace, 30 June 2016, https://bit.ly/3sYmQwK. Accessed on 11 March 2022.
15 Ibid.
16 Hoodbhoy, Pervez, and Zia Mian. 'Managing Pakistan's Bomb: Learning on the Job', *Bulletin of the Atomic Scientists*, 17 August 2018, https://bit.ly/3hWELxs. Accessed on 11 March 2022.
17 Prakash, Arun. 'The Significance of Arihant', *The Indian Express*, 7 November 2018, https://bit.ly/3tQVqrV. Accessed on 11 March 2022.
18 Hundley, Tom. 'India and Pakistan are quietly making nuclear war more likely', Vox, 4 April 2018, https://bit.ly/3JaI0xu. Accessed on 11 March 2022.
19 Fisher, Max. 'India, Long at Odds With Pakistan, May Be Rethinking Nuclear First Strikes', *The New York Times*, 31 March 2017, https://nyti.ms/35HdRY9. Accessed on 11 March 2022.
20 Zompa, Tenzin. 'Top US General called China over fears Trump could order military strike, new book says', *ThePrint*, 15 September 2021, https://bit.ly/3tNc3EW. Accessed on 11 March 2022.
21 Roth, Andrew, Shaun Walker et al. 'Putin signals escalation as he puts

Russia's nuclear force on high alert', *The Guardian*, 28 February 2022, https://tinyurl.com/8459u42j. Accessed on 24 March 2022.

22. Ibid.

23 Dobbs, Michael. 'The Real Story of the "Football" That Follows the President Everywhere', *Smithsonian*, October 2014, https://bit.ly/369DBvO. Accessed on 11 March 2022.

24 'Nuclear Briefcases', Atomic Heritage Foundation, 12 June 2018, https://bit.ly/3MEjRkX. Accessed on 11 March 2022.

Chapter 19: 2035

1 Pearce, Fred. 'Water Warning: The Looming Threat of the World's Aging Dams', *Yale Environment 360*, 3 February 2021, https://bit.ly/3N6CQEO. Accessed on 21 March 2022.

2 Ibid.

3 'Chamberlain addresses the nation on peace negotiations', BBC Archive, https://tinyurl.com/3z8xue93. Accessed on 24 March 2022.

4 Guzeva, Alexendra. '"We will bury you": What Nikita Khrushchev actually meant', Russia Beyond, 13 January 2022, https://tinyurl.com/2p9et2m8. Accessed on 1 April 2022.

5 'Xi Jinping calls on army to be battle-ready', *The Economic Times*, 5 January 2019, https://bit.ly/3ioYEgQ. Accessed on 21 March 2022.

Chapter 20: The Big War

1 Joye, Christopher. 'Predicting global conflicts', Australian Strategic Policy Institute, 13 October 2021, https://bit.ly/3ioTuBF. Accessed on 22 March 2022.

2 Ibid.

3 'RONALD REAGAN, "EVIL EMPIRE SPEECH" (8 MARCH 1983)', Voices of Democracy, The U.S. Oratory Project, https://tinyurl.com/y9xa8m3a. Accessed on 1 April 2022.

4 'LCQ6: The capitalist system and way of life in Hong Kong after 2047', The Government of Hong Kong Special Administrative Region, Press Releases, https://tinyurl.com/zhxbs9fn. Accessed on 24 March 2022.

5 Singh, Teshu. 'India-Taiwan Relations: Burgeoning Economic Engagements', *Indian Foreign Affairs Journal*, Vol. 14, No. 3, 2019, https://www.jstor.org/stable/48636728.

6 Jennings, Peter. 'Stronger deterrence will avoid war over Taiwan',

Australian Strategic Policy Institute, 18 October 2021, https://tinyurl.com/2f6ezvas. Accessed on 22 March 2022.

7 Bump, Philip. 'Robert Gates Thinks Joe Biden Hasn't Stopped Being Wrong for 40 Years', *The Atlantic*, 8 January 2014, https://bit.ly/3tr7DVc. Accessed on 22 March 2022.

8 'Putin Says the U.S. Wants to Push Russia into War', *The New York Times*, 30 March 2022, https://nyti.ms/3qurWz3. Accessed on 3 April 2022.

9 Thompson, Larry Clinton. *Refugee Workers in the Indochina Exodus, 1975–1982*, McFarland, 2010.

10 'Professor Stephen Hawking's message sent into space', Pureland Foundation, 19 June 2018, https://bit.ly/3L0Nyeg. Accessed on 22 March 2022.

BIBLIOGRAPHY

For a comprehensive list of links to articles/journals/research papers/archival material that the author has consulted in the course of writing this book, please scan the QR Code given below.

INDEX